Two week loan

Please return on or before the last
date stamped below.
Charges are made for late return.

LF 114/0895   UNIVERSITY OF WALES, CARDIFF, PO BOX 430, CARDIFF CF1 3XT

CRIMINALIZING THE DRINK-DRIVER

To my parents and family

Criminalizing the Drink-Driver

ROY LIGHT
University of the West of England

Dartmouth

Aldershot . Brookfield USA . Hong Kong . Singapore . Sydney

Published by
Dartmouth Publishing Company Limited
Gower House
Croft Road
Aldershot
Hants GU11 3HR
England

Dartmouth Publishing Company
Old Post Road
Brookfield
Vermont 05036
USA

British Library Cataloguing in Publication Data
Light, Roy
    Criminalizing the Drink-Driver
    I. Title
    364.1

Library of Congress Cataloging-in-Publication Data
Light, Roy
    Criminalizing the drink-driver / Roy Light.
        p.   cm.
    Includes bibliographical references and index.
    ISBN 1-85521-456-3 : $59.95 (est.)
    1. Drunk driving--Great Britain. I. Title.
KD2618.L54   1994
345.41'0273--dc20
[344.105273]

93-37294
CIP

ISBN 1 85521 456 3

Printed and Bound in Great Britain by
Athenaeum Press Ltd, Newcastle upon Tyne.

Contents

List of tables

Acknowledgements

Many people have assisted me during the preparation of this book. I would like to thank the University of the West of England for the sabbatical leave which enabled me to carry out the research and the staff at the Institute of Criminology, University of Cambridge, where I was based; particularly, Professor A.E.Bottoms for his expert supervision, guidance and support. Valuable comments on the work were received from Professor K.J.M.Smith, Brunel University, Professor J.P.Martin, University of Manchester and J.R.Spencer, Selwyn College, Cambridge. Thanks are also due to many other individuals and organisations for their advice and assistance. Last, but not least, I would like to acknowledge the continuing support of my parents and family.

Roy Light
July 1993

Introduction

The consumption of alcohol and the operation of motor transport are commonplace throughout the Western world, enjoying a high level of social approbation. Yet both have high morbidity rates - 4,568 people were killed and over 311,000 injured in road accidents in Britain in 1991 (see Appendix 1 Table 4) and 'estimates of the deaths attributable to alcohol consumption in England and Wales vary from 5000 to 40,000' (Royal College of Physicians 1991:30). Additionally, alcohol when combined with driving has been implicated as a factor in many road casualties. More particularly, in Britain, it has been estimated that 1,400 road accident deaths in one year (drivers, passengers, cyclists, pedestrians and motor cyclists) were associated with drinking (Department of Transport 1985), with one study finding that one in three (two in three at night) driver fatalities had been drinking alcohol (Department of the Environment 1976). While establishing causality is obviously problematic, one recent study attributed wholly or partly to alcohol 23 per cent of a sample of road accident deaths (Foster et al. 1988); another claimed that 'impairment by alcohol when driving is the single largest factor leading to accidents on the road' (Sabey 1988); and the cost of drink-related traffic fatalities in Britain for 1987 has been put at approximately £200 million (Maynard 1989). Drink-driving also has a significant impact on the criminal justice system. For example, in England and Wales in 1991 some 562,000 roadside screening breath tests were carried out; 103,800 drivers were convicted of a drink-drive offence; and 4,300 prison sentences were passed on convicted drink-drivers (see Appendix 1 Tables 5,9,10).

1

Attempts by the criminal law to control the drink-driver are often assumed to be a relatively recent enterprise, but they have a long history. In 1806 an Act was passed which made it an offence to be 'incapable of driving' by reason of 'intoxication', and today, nearly 200 years later, the criminal law continues to occupy a primary position in the range of drink-driving countermeasures. Yet, drink-drive offences generally have not been perceived as serious; are, in view of the number of deaths and injuries with which they are associated, treated relatively lightly by the courts; and appear to carry little social stigma.

Further, motoring crime generally and drink-driving in particular have attracted scant criminological and academic legal interest. However, there is a huge national and international literature on alcohol and road safety located in other disciplines, including both the natural and social sciences. The former engaged, for example, in developing scientific testing apparatus and investigating the effects of alcohol on driving ability; the latter examining matters such as social attitudes to drink-driving and the efficacy of the legal response to the offence.

Before the passing of the Road Safety Act in 1967 no significant legal or criminological study of drink-driving had been carried out in England and Wales. What material there was could be found in one of the handful of studies carried out on motoring crime - for example, Willett (1964) which investigated the 'serious motoring offender'. The Road Safety Act 1967 generated much academic debate and wide public interest around road safety matters, particularly drink-driving. A large number of books, articles and case notes appeared on practical aspects of the Act; while criminological investigation of drink-driving remained limited to more general studies. For example, Hood (1972) examined the sentencing of motoring offenders and Willett (1973) investigated 'drivers after sentence' (Willett 1973). Later studies have addressed the impact of legal policy on drink-driving - mainly in the context of deterrence theory. Foremost among these is the work of the American sociologist H.L.Ross (1973, 1975a, 1977, 1979, 1987, 1988), and more recently David Riley of the Home Office Research and Planing Unit (1985, 1991); while the Transport and Road Research Laboratory has conducted work on the effectiveness of the legislation as well as investigating the profile of the drink-driver (e.g. Clayton 1986; Clayton et al. 1984; Sabey 1978, 1990).

In the United States drink-driving has received more academic attention than in England and Wales, but there are still few major works (see, for example, Gusfield 1981; Ross 1984; Laurence et al. 1988; Jacobs 1988a, 1989); and this is true of Scandinavia also, which in the public mind is traditionally associated with a progressive approach to drink-driving (see Andenaes 1988). Recently, some interesting studies have begun to emerge from Australia, particularly those dealing with random breath testing (Homel 1988), and from several other jurisdictions (see Noordzij & Roszbach 1987) but the subject remains under-researched. There is a relative dearth of criminological/legal discourse on drink-driving and no comprehensive analysis of its development in England and Wales. What historical perspective there is tends to be sketched into the exposition of a particular contemporary debate or the investigation of 2a specific aspect of drink-driving; or appears in a more general discussion of alcohol policy or motor transport - here as in the US it remains true that 'drunk driving has hardly made a mark on the criminological agenda' (Jacobs 1989). Having said that, some writers have provided an outline or overview of sections of the the legal response to drink-driving in England and Wales (e.g. Havard 1960,1985; Ross 1984) but these have been brief and have lacked comprehensive analysis; others have attempted more detailed studies of particular time spans (Baggott 1990; Tether & Godfrey 1990) but although they make informative reading they too have lacked depth and breadth of analysis; forming parts of wider investigations into the politics of alcohol or alcohol policy. Ross (1973) and others have provided thorough contemporary accounts of particular stages in the development of the legal response to drink-driving in England and Wales. This book aims to fill the gap in the literature by providing a definitive account of the development of legal policy and the drink-driver in England and Wales and to offer a historical perspective within which to locate current debates, and inform future policy making.

Legal policy and the drink-driver

Legal policy in relation to the drink-driver encompasses several branches of law, including revenue and licensing law, civil law policy (the law of tort and compensation schemes), the law relating to insurance and, of course, the criminal law.

Since the beginnings of motorised road transport the criminal law has been utilised as a principal method of regulating drivers. However, perhaps partly due to the acceptance of traffic casualties as 'accidents', and to the fact that 'Road traffic law prohibits, in the interests of road safety, much behaviour which would otherwise not be regarded as wrong' (Department of Transport/Home Office 1988), motoring crime has always been seen as somehow different from other crimes. From the earliest days of motor transport there was a feeling among motorists, who were generally well-off and influential, that they were being persecuted by the police, while other 'real crime' was going unchecked. These early motorists saw themselves as law-abiding and respectable members of the community; they were not used to being on the receiving end of the criminal justice system. Many motoring offenders continue to see themselves as 'law abiding law breakers' and may well find themselves on the wrong side of the law only in motoring situations (or at least only *apprehended* in such situations). This has had important implications for the development of legal policy and the drink-driver.

The last 30 years have witnessed a massive growth in road traffic law, including the law relating to the use of alcohol by road users. This book examines the influences which have shaped this growth, including policing issues, political pressures, the role of interest and pressure groups and the part played by scientific and medical developments. Statistical data is provided to identify patterns in the commission of drink-drive offences, the road casualties associated with alcohol and the criminal law response to the offences. A central theme is the apparent reluctance of the legal system to 'criminalize' the drink-driver.

3

Developments in the criminal law provisions are used to provide a chronological framework for the book, which for the purposes of exposition can be divided into six chapters. Chapter 1 (to 1929) traces the origins of the road safety debate and the emergence of legislation designed to deal with the *drunken* driver (developed from earlier legislation aimed against public drunkenness generally). Chapter 2 (1930-1960) sees the introduction and evolution of the first efforts to legislate for the *drinking*, or 'incapable' driver as the 1930 Act phrased it and Chapter 3 (1961-1966) charts the introduction of the term 'impaired driver' and, albeit in discretionary terms, scientific evidence in the form of blood-alcohol concentrations.

The major shift in legal policy, which came with the introduction of a fixed blood-alcohol limit, the 'breathalyser' and compulsory blood-alcohol testing, under the Road Safety Act 1967, is examined in Chapter 4 (1967-1975). The Act proved effective, but only in the short term and this led to a period of 'rethinking the drink-driver' which forms the basis of Chapter 5 (1976-1982); which opens with the publication of the Blennerhassett Committee report in 1976 and culminates in 1982 with the coming into force of the new drink-drive law contained in the Transport Act 1981. Chapter 6 (1983-1992) examines the operation of the 'new drink-drive laws' which introduced evidential breath testing and sought to close the legal loopholes which had developed under the old law; and reviews subsequent developments in legal policy. The historical analysis is followed, in Chapter 7, by an evaluation of recent development in legal policy and a consideration of the major themes in contemporary debates. The final chapter presents a re-examination of practical and theoretical perspectives on legal policy and the drink-driver. It is suggested that there has been a failure to fully maximise the possible gains from the legal response, which flows from several sources - neglecting to look beyond simple deterrence; the unintended consequences of attempts to change public attitudes to drink-driving; the incomplete and confused literature on drink-driving; and the fact that to 'criminalize' the drink-driver would widen considerably the net of the criminal justice system. It is argued that legal policy will be unable to move beyond its present stage of development until these issues are confronted.

Alcohol/transport policy

Legal policy seeks to control drink-driving in order to reduce road casualties. Alcohol and transport policies are obviously of fundamental importance to this enterprise as they define the environment in which the drink-driver operates.

Alcohol policy

The use of alcohol as a mood altering drug has a long history (Williams and Brake 1980), and from the earliest accounts we can read of both its benefits and its dangers (e.g. Mandelbaum 1967; Royal College of Psychiatrists 1986). This is perhaps common to most drugs, but the dangers associated with alcohol in the modern Western world are made particularly acute by its widespread social acceptability. Generally, it is regarded not as a powerful drug, but as a morally neutral substance in common daily use - occupying a central position in most social settings as 'our favourite drug' (Royal College of Psychiatrists 1986). Yet this everyday substance, freely available and openly consumed by some 90 per cent of the population (Hunt 1982), is increasingly recognised as posing one of the biggest public health issues facing late twentieth century Britain, 'overshadowing even that of tobacco and dwarfing the problems of illicit drug abuse' (Royal College of Psychiatrists 1986). Further, it has been recognised that in order to understand and do something about the harm caused by alcohol it is not enough simply to look at those who abuse the substance, for whatever reason. Research studies have suggested that when *per capita* consumption of alcohol rises, so too do all levels of alcohol-related harm (including that caused by the drink-driver);[1] although this co-relation is not always present and difficult methodological problems exist in the studies (Davies & Walsh 1983). Nevertheless, any exploration of alcohol-related harm cannot ignore the implications of consumption theory.

A public health perspective sees alcohol problems and harm as not just related to what the relatively small groups of 'problem drinkers' or 'alcohol abusers' are doing, but to the levels of consumption in the population generally. Thus if overall consumption is reduced, a drop in alcohol-related harm should follow (Smart 1987; Hauge 1988). Harrison (1987) notes that convictions for drink-driving offences have moved broadly in tandem with *per capita* consumption levels, and for Tether & Godfrey (1990:139) it is 'not surprising that drinking and driving emerged as an area of policy concern when consumption levels began to increase markedly in the 1960s'. But, as we shall see, the equation is not that simple, other factors are involved, particularly in the case of drink-driving. For example, the number of vehicles on the road, and the behaviour of drivers and law enforcement agencies.

What governs levels of consumption? It appears that the two most important factors are price and availability. An interesting illustration of the effect of availability on consumption occurred in Sweden in 1963. A labour dispute at the state-owned company with the legal monopoly of the retail distribution of alcohol in Sweden led to a sharp restriction in the supply of alcoholic drinks. During the period of the dispute (27 February - 26 April 1963) there was a drop in the frequency of drunken driving, followed by 'a marked increase in drunken driving when the supply of alcoholic drink was resumed' (Andreasson & Bonnichsen 1966:284). Price and availability can be controlled by fiscal and licensing changes (Royal College of Physicians 1991). Increases in taxation and restrictions on availability (not any form of 'prohibition'), by measures such as the de-licensing of supermarkets and less liberal licensing hours, should be followed by a drop in *per capita* consumption and alcohol-related harm. But this approach has not found favour with a government subject to strong pressure from a powerful drink trades lobby (the drink industry is a major employer in the United Kingdom and its exports contribute substantially to the balance of payment); committed to a free market economy and more flexible licensing laws (the price of alcoholic drinks have, in real terms, and in relation to average income, been allowed to fall over the years, while availability has increased); and

5

in receipt of high levels of revenue from taxes on alcohol.[2] In any event the general adoption of an increased price/reduced availability strategy could well throw up other problems. For example, an increase in illegal production and distribution. And the limits to such a strategy have yet to be properly thought out and fully articulated (Harrison 1987).

Organisations such as the Temperance League, the British Medical Association (BMA) and more recently Action on Alcohol Abuse (until 1990) and Alcohol Concern have campaigned enthusiastically on alcohol-related issues; and the last two decades have seen the emergence of a rapidly expanding health education and community care response to alcohol-related problems. During the 1980s these bodies came together to develop a coordinated response to alcohol issues, and helped to increase public awareness of and concern over all aspects of alcohol-related harm, including drink-driving. The influence of these bodies, and the strategies which they developed, have played an important part in the evolution of legal policy and the drink-driver.

Evolution of motor transport

The eighteenth century saw the development of the steam engine, which was to power the industrial revolution, the ships and railways of the nineteenth century and the first self-propelled road vehicles. Although there had been earlier attempts, a French army engineer named Cugnot is generally credited with designing the first successful self-propelled road vehicle. His steam carriage, designed for hauling field artillery, was constructed in 1769. Able to carry four passengers at speeds of between two and six mph, it needed to stop every 15 minutes to boil water. It is credited with the first motorised road accident, when it went out of control, with Cugnot driving, and knocked down a wall.

By the early nineteenth century, steam carriages were being built in many parts of the world, but it was in England that they enjoyed their greatest early success. Ironically, this was facilitated by the improved road network developed by men such as Telford and Macadam for the huge expansion in coaching which had followed the Napoleonic Wars; and which the steam carriages now sought to challenge. From the 1820s, steam carriages took to the roads in ever increasing numbers, providing the first motorised public transport. But they were dangerous vehicles, with 'primitive boilers, shaky steering and laughable brakes' (Stein 1966), as well as being uncomfortable and very noisy. They blew smoke and sparks about, causing fires and apprehension around the countryside; and were sometimes attacked by angry citizens, particularly in rural areas, where 'agricultural labourers considered all machinery injurious to their interests' and would, 'with a cry of "Down with all machinery", set upon the carriage and its occupants' (Young 1904).

It was, however, a lack of commercial viability that put an end to the steam carriage; for they alarmed the horse interests as well as the horses (the coach and carriage trade and wealthy stud owners) while toll-keepers worried for their road surfaces. The steam carriages were no match for the vested interests of traditional coaching (e.g. on the turnpikes they were charged tolls of ten to twenty times that of horse drawn coaches), nor could they compete with the rapidly expanding railway network. By the 1840s, despite some attempts to support them (see below), steam carriages had almost disappeared from the roads (sadly, not one of them has been preserved). Steam carriages had demonstrated the possibility of self-propelled transport, and in England a few road steamers were built for individual rather than public transport. But the 'Red Flag Act' of 1865 (see below) effectively curtailed development of self-propelled road vehicles in England, until its repeal at the turn of the century. By which time, although some steam powered road vehicles were to persist until the late 1920s (most notably the Stanley Steamer, which was produced in the US until 1927), the age of the road locomotive was ending. It was to be replaced by the motor car, born out of nineteenth century mechanical innovation, and, in particular, the development of the internal combustion engine - credit for the first practical working example of which is generally given to a Frenchman named Lenoir in 1860.

The first motor driven vehicle was produced by the German, Siegfried Marcus, who in 1865 mounted an engine on a hand cart, and then, in 1874, built what is usually called the first motor car (in fact three were made, and one is preserved in the *Technisches Museum* of Vienna). An internal combustion engine vehicle was produced by Benz in 1885, and by Daimler in 1889. This was the start of Germany's (and indeed the world's) motor industry. By the turn of the century Benz and Daimler were each exporting motor cars to many other countries. The popularisation of motor cars took place in France, where, using German engines, cars such as the Panhard et Levassor and de Dion Bouton were produced. These began to be imported into England in the 1890s, where home produced petrol engined cars soon started to appear, built by Lanchester, and under licence from Daimler. By 1900, petrol-powered cars were in the ascendancy, but still far from being universal acceptance or approval (Masterman 1910). The correspondence columns of *The Times* bulged with letters on 'the motoring problem' and 'cads on castors upsetting horses and hurling insults' (Willett 1964); a leader published in 1900 stated that: 'it is a fact that in some parts of the country the motor car is an object of hatred ... It is not surprising, because there are a number of drivers who are a curse to the neighbourhood in which they drive ... drivers who seem, when they mount their cars, to put from them altogether the instincts of gentlemen' (quoted in Willett 1964:67). As Spencer (1983:71) notes:

> Unlike traction-engines and steam-rollers, motor-cars did not set fire to roadside property; but with their tendency to backfire they were quite as adept at scaring horses, and with their much greater speed, were infinitely more capable in bad hands of running down pedestrians, cyclists and animals, colliding with other vehicles, wrecking street furniture, and raping shop fronts.

The attitude of these early motorists towards those unfortunate enough to be pedestrians is graphically demonstrated by Spencer using contemporary literature: 'Loafers are a great nuisance to motorists, and no sympathy can be felt for them, even though they may suffer martyrdom to the cause of loafing, and then public sentiment and indignation are aroused and prejudice against motorists fostered' (*The Autocar*, 25 February 1905). Further, as Spencer points out, the primitive mechanics of these early motor cars meant that 'they were clearly capable of doing serious damage even when driven with all possible care'. Not surprisingly, these early motor cars provoked considerable hostility and opposition. In a Parliamentary debate in 1903 a Mr Wason spoke of 'those stinking engines of iniquity from which harmless men, women and children have to fly for their lives at the bidding of one of these slaughterers' (quoted in Willett 1964:68). A society was set up to ban motor cars, 'People pelted them with stones and, after the invention of pneumatic tyres for cars, strewed tacks on the road in front of them. Enraged farmers sometimes fired shotguns at them, and as late as 8 November 1912 correspondents to *The Times* were advocating a resurrection of the law of deodand against motor-vehicles which caused death' (Spencer 1983:73).

However, by the outbreak of war opposition had started to wane and, in any event, was proving to be ineffective in the face of the rising tide of support that motoring was beginning to attract. The battle between the pro- and anti-motorist lobbies continued to be waged, but the motor car was winning. In particular, as Plowden (1971) has shown, the aristocracy had taken to the motor car in a big way, as had other influential figures. So that by 1909 with the likes of King Edward VII (who had become patron of the RAC in 1903), the Lord Chancellor, the Lord Chief Justice, both Law Officers, both Archbishops, five members of the Government, the Leader of the Opposition, several judges and certain chief constables being active motorists and members of the AA or RAC the future of the motor car was secured; and opposition was largely futile, 'because most of the moneyed and intelligent classes of this country are either motorists or well disposed towards motoring' (*The Autocar*, 18 March 1905 quoted in Spencer 1983). By the end of the Great War 'the bulk of prejudice against the motor car which had so inflamed so many in the pre-war years (had disappeared). Henceforth, as the demand for small cars increased, motorists ceased to be "fur clad murderers", "goggled assassins", or even "shrieking stink pots"'(Keir & Morgan 1955:59). As motoring increased in popularity and became more respectable, so too did the need to protect motorists and others against the risk of damage and injury from these high speed projectiles controlled by fallible human beings. Lee (1959:178) graphically describes the first double-decker buses to appear in his village:

Those solid-tyred, open-topped, passenger chariots were the leviathans of the roads at that time - staggering siege-towers which often ran wild ... Our Uncle Sid, one of the elite of the drivers, became a famous sight in the district. It was a thing of pride and some alarm to watch him go thundering by, perched up high in his reeking cabin, his face sweating beer and effort, while he wrenched and wrestled at the steering wheel to hold the great bus on its course. Each trip through the town destroyed roof-tiles and gutters and shook the gas mantles out of the lamps, but he always took pains to avoid women and children and scarcely ever mounted the pavements.

8

Runaway roarer, freighted with human souls, stampeder of policemen and horses - it was Uncle Sid with his mighty hands who mastered its mad career.

The twentieth century witnessed a rapidly escalating number of motor vehicles on British roads: motor cars from 8,465 in 1904 to 132,015 by the outbreak of war; by which time there was a total of 388,860 motor vehicles on the roads of Britain (see Appendix 1 Table 1). As Briggs (1960:44) has put it: 'The invention of the internal combustion engine has had an enormous effect on the shaping of the twentieth century, transforming metropolis, cities and countryside, changing the balance between them, altering social habits' (see also Barker 1987; Foreman-Peck 1987).

In 1909 373 people are recorded as having died in road accidents involving mechanically propelled vehicles and 585 in accidents involving horse drawn vehicles. By the outbreak of war, while deaths from horse drawn vehicle accidents remained much the same at 584, the number killed by motorised transport increased to 1,329 (see Appendix 1 Table 2). In the 100 years since motor vehicles first appeared they have claimed an estimated 15-20 million lives throughout the world and maimed hundreds of millions more. Since the earliest days of dangerous vehicles and untrained drivers society seems to have become conditioned to accept these casualties as 'accidents'; but as the numbers of vehicles increased the need to control them and the damage which they caused became ever more acute. Road deaths in Britain peaked in 1941 at 9,169 and outside of wartime at 7,985 with 392,000 injured in 1966. Since 1966 the figures have fallen. Injuries in 1991 stood at 311,000; while deaths declined more significantly to 4,568 (see Appendix 1 Table 4) - despite a virtual doubling of the number of licensed vehicles on British roads over the same period (although miles driven per vehicle have also fallen over the last 20 years).

The first decades of the twentieth century saw the rapid development of the motor car which in the thirties and forties, an era of great technical advance, was transformed from the plaything of the rich into practical transport for millions (by 1950 there were some 4.4 million vehicles with current licences in Britain - see Appendix 1 Table 3). During the fifties and sixties car ownership continued to expand and the car became the symbol of prosperity; so that by 1970 the number of licensed vehicles in Britain had risen to 15 million. But by the seventies and eighties the impact of oil crises, safety and environmental considerations and worsening traffic conditions at last began to call into question the Western world's virtual surrender of the environment to the motor vehicle, of which by 1991 there were some 24.5 million licensed in Britain.

Transport policy

The roads are full to choking point. The countryside is being torn up to make room for more. The air is thick with poisonous fumes. Our public transport is overcrowded, underfunded and insalubrious: few use it who can afford a seat in a traffic jam. For motorists and non-motorists alike, the simplest journeys are fraught with frustration and danger. Travel doesn't have to be like this. (*The Observer*, 15 April 1990)

Ultimately, nothing will influence road safety more than the country's general transport policy and priorities. For example, a shift away from private towards public systems of transportation and from roads to railways has huge potential for reducing the dangers of travelling around the country (Plowden & Hillman 1984). A major reappraisal of transport policy in England and Wales was contained in the White Paper, *Transport Policy*, published in 1966 (Ministry of Transport 1966), which expressed the need for the 'nation to face up to the implications of the motor age'. The White Paper accepted the expansion of motor traffic and expressed the view that 'whatever is done over the next two decades to improve our railways, roads will continue to have the dominant role in the movement of passengers and goods'. It included proposals for a road building and upgrading programme and, recognising that 'as traffic increases, so do the risks of death or injury', proposed to deal with road safety 'on three fronts - safer roads, safer vehicles, safer drivers and pedestrians' (para.46).

From the late 1960s, government transport policy gave priority to road rather than rail, and private rather than public transport (Mogridge 1990). The increased risks associated with this approach were to be met by the coordinated development of a programme of road, vehicle and driver/pedestrian safety measures. The White Paper promised the publication of 'its forward programme for attacking the problem' and in July of the following year another White Paper, *Road Safety - A Fresh Approach* (Ministry of Transport 1967) was published. This again addressed the issue of road safety under the three heads of roads, vehicles and people. Under the last of these, the strategy for drink-driving was to reinforce the new 'breathalyser' law (which was to come into force in October 1967) with a public education campaign.[3] This threefold approach is basically unchanged today (e.g. Department of Transport 1987; 1989a).

Notes

1. See, for example, the figures produced by the Royal College of Psychiatrists (1968:109). The argument seems to derive largely from the empirical work carried out by Lederman (1956).

2. The alcoholic drinks industry employs almost 100,000 people, contributes about £7 billion to the exchequer, around £2 billion to the gross domestic product and some £500 million to the balance of trade (Martin 1990). See further Maynard & Jones 1987; Maynard & Tether 1990; Godfrey & Robinson 1990.

3. Although road and vehicle issues may be of relevance. For example, the siting of drinking establishments on highways and the installation of breath testing devices in vehicle ignition systems.

1 The drunken driver (to 1929)

The first 'road traffic' Act was passed some 200 years ago in 1788 (28 Geo.3c.57). 'An Act for limiting the Number of Persons to be carried on the Outside of Stage Coaches or Other Carriages', it intended to avoid the 'great Mischiefs ... and bad Accidents' which were causing concern among coach passengers. The driver, or owner, of the coach was liable to a fine for each illegally carried person. The fine was to be shared equally between the local surveyor of the highway and the informer (an early 'Crime Stoppers' scheme). A further Act in 1790 (28 Geo.3c.36) made the driver liable to a fine if he endangered passengers by 'furious driving', negligence, or misconduct, with the fines going for the repair of the highway. A third Act passed in 1806 (46 Geo.3c.136), provided it would be an offence if any coach driver 'shall become incapable of driving ... or properly attending to the concerns thereof by reason of Intoxication or otherwise, whereby the Safety of Passengers may be endangered' (s.7).

These enactments were repealed by an Act of 1810 (50 Geo.3c.48), which re-enacted many of the provisions of the earlier statutes, in particular, s.11 dealt with intoxicated driving. Then came an Act in 1820 (1 Geo.4c.4) which extended the protection against wanton, negligent, and presumably intoxicated (not specifically mentioned in this enactment) coach drivers from passengers to any persons. These Acts were replaced by the Stage Carriages Act 1832 (2&3 Will.c.120), s.48 of which imposed a penalty of five pounds on carriage drivers or guards who endangered people or property through intoxication, negligence, etc. In 1847 the Town Police Clauses Act (10&11 Vict.c.89) imposed a similar

11

penalty on those 'intoxicated while driving' (s.61), with the power to impose two months imprisonment in default added. Both sections are still in force, but have fallen into disuse. Also remaining in force are the London Hackney Carriage Acts of 1831 (1&2 Will.c.22) which imposed a fine of five pounds on the proprietor or driver, and 1843 (6&7 Vict.c.86) which allowed a claim for compensation to be made against the proprietor, in both cases for damage or injury caused by intoxicated, wanton or reckless driving.

Enter the machine

The nineteenth century belonged to the railway and its impact on all aspects of society was enormous. But as early as 1831 a Parliamentary Select Committee, 'Steam Carriages, Turnpike Tolls' (Ford & Ford 1972:198) reported on 'the present state and future prospects of land carriage by wheeled vehicles propelled by steam or gas upon common roads'. The rest of the century saw dozens of Parliamentary papers on locomotives, tolls, turnpikes, roads and bridges (as well as attempts to turn road vehicles into railways, as trams) (Ford & Ford 1969a:51-2).

The report of the 1831 Committee was favourably disposed to the new 'horseless carriages', and its recommendations were supportive of them. Parliament, however, viewed them differently. They were seen 'not as a blessing, but as a threat to life, limb, and tranquillity, as well as to the financial interests of farmers and horse breeders' (Willett 1964:65). The second half of the nineteenth century saw the introduction of legislation aimed at bringing motorised transport under strict control, which was to stifle its development until the end of the century - by which time it was no longer possible to ignore the developments which had taken place in countries governed by less repressive legislation. The first of these early regulatory enactments was the Locomotives Act 1861 - which contained regulations on tolls, construction and use, and speed limits (10 mph in the country and five mph in urban areas). This was followed by the Locomotives Act 1865 which contained further construction and use regulations, lowered the speed limit to four mph in the country and two in town (s.4) and laid down that 'while any Locomotive is in Motion, (a person) shall precede such Locomotive on foot by not less than Sixty Yards, and shall carry a Red Flag constantly displayed, and shall warn the Riders and Drivers of Horses of the Approach of such locomotives' (s.3).

Further construction and use regulations were introduced by The Highways and Locomotives (Amendment) Act 1878 which also provided for the licensing of locomotors. Chiefly as a result of these drastic devices, contrived to regulate the use of motorised vehicles, by the end of the 1870s the highways and byways of England had changed very little, aside from the occasional novelty of the sight of a man with a red flag being slowly followed by a lumbering steam locomotive. However, the peace of the British roads, and the dominance of the horse upon them, were soon to end. First came the bicycle, which in the 1880s enjoyed its heyday as a source of leisure activity, and then, the mid 1890s saw the appearance of the first motor cars.

The motor car was given the 'freedom of the road' with the passing of the Locomotives on Highways Act 1896, the 'Motorist's Magna Carta' (still celebrated by the annual London to Brighton run), which provided that various provisions, including those contained in the Acts of 1861, 1865 and 1878, were no longer to apply to 'light locomotives'; which were defined by s.1(1) as propelled by mechanical power and under three tons unladen weight. The days of red flags and men walking in front of motor vehicles were over and the maximum speed for light locomotors was raised to 14 mph (s.4). The 1896 Act committed the twentieth century to one of its most significant developments.

Motorists continued to struggle for increased freedom to operate their machines and were particularly keen to be able to do so at higher speeds. But this was matched by increasing concern at the escalating rate of road accident casualties; so that demands were also being heard for legislation aimed at stricter control of motor vehicles. The legislation which emerged was the Motor Car Act 1903 which, despite being denigrated by some as a second motorists' charter, made a comprehensive effort to legislate against the potential danger of the motor vehicle. It introduced, *inter alia*, the offences of reckless and negligent driving and failing to stop after an accident; the registration of vehicles; and the licensing of drivers (along with the power of the court to endorse, suspend and disqualify from holding licences). The Act also increased the speed limit to 20 mph, but gave local authorities the power to impose a maximum limit of ten mph in any specified area.

Drink-driving

The 1903 Act and the 'road traffic Acts' passed in the second half of the nineteenth century were silent on the question of drink-driving - and, although as early as 1907 an editorial in the *Lancet* was expressing concern at 'the appalling risks that may arise from the intoxication of an engine driver or chauffeur' (Anon 1907), it was not until the Criminal Justice Act 1925 that the first specific legislative provisions relating to alcohol and motorised transport appeared.

A number of Parliamentary Papers had been published on drunkenness, intemperance and liquor licensing in the nineteenth century (Ford & Ford 1969b:102-3); while legislation aimed against drunkenness had been promulgated at least as early as 1606 (A.Q. Jacobi.C.5) and against intoxicated driving in an Act of 1806 (see above). In 1872, there appeared as a minor part of an Act 'passed for the purpose of regulating the licensing and general management of public houses, beerhouses, and other establishments of a like nature' (*JPN* 36:553, 31 October 1872) a provision which made it an offence for any person to be:

> drunk while in charge on any highway or other public place of any carriage, horse, cattle or steam engine ... (and further provided that any such person) ... may be apprehended, and shall be liable to a penalty not exceeding forty shillings, or in the discretion of the court to imprisonment with or without

hard labour for any term not exceeding one month. (s.12 Intoxicating Liquor (Licensing) Act 1872)

This provision, unlike that contained in the 1832 Act, made it an offence simply to be drunk in charge of a carriage on the highway; there was no need to prove that damage or injury had been caused or that the safety of others had been endangered. The Act provided for a lesser penalty than did the previous legislation, but due to its simpler form, and the fact that it conferred a power of arrest, the 1872 Act became the usual charge in cases involving drunken drivers. During the passage of the Bill the tone of the arguments reflected a concern for the harm caused by those who were drunk in certain circumstances, including driving, but also demonstrated the view that drunkenness was not really something which should be punished, at least not severely. Thus one Member considered s.12 to be 'the most tyrannical ever inserted in an Act of Parliament - that any man who was driving, and was said to be in the slightest degree drunk, was liable to be put in prison for a month'(*Parl.Debs.*(Commons) 252:1699).

By 1910 the petrol engine had revolutionized road transport and car ownership in Britain had widened considerably - cars numbered 53,196 and total vehicles 143,877 (see Appendix 1 Table 1). The law had not kept pace with these developments. The 1903 Act was in urgent need of reform and it, together with the provisions relating to drunk-driving, started to come under increasing criticism. A note in the *Law Times* (128:244) in 1910 pointed to the inadequacy of the penalty available under the 1872 Act: 'the sum, then, of two pounds is considered sufficient to mark an offence which may cost the lives of several persons, or at any rate, cause serious danger or annoyance'. It went on to compare this with similar sized penalties being given out by magistrates for minor speeding offences and suggested that 'surely there should be a greater severity awaiting those who first get drunk and then drive to the common peril' (ibid.). Concern over the incidence of drunken driving was expressed in many quarters. The police, called upon to deal with the results of drunken driving, were so concerned about an outbreak of drunkenness among taxi-cab drivers in London that Scotland Yard in 1911 proposed medical inspections of taxi-drivers to check physical conditions such as eyesight and also for a satisfactory standard of sobriety. A proposal which led the *Law Times* (131:225) to say:

> A mechanical vehicle is wonderfully safe and reliable in the hands of a sober driver, but is peculiarly dangerous when in those of an inebriate. In all these cases a spirit of moderation is requisite, and for equity's sake it is not right to impose ever severer conditions on one type of vehicle and to exercise no restraint on other types. If a medical examination is really necessary either for health or sobriety, let it be applied to all and every class of driver of vehicles.

By the early years of the twentieth century the regulation of motor transport was a major issue, with many Parliamentary Papers being produced (Ford & Ford 1957). Of particular importance was the Royal Commission on Motor Cars,

14

which reported in 1906. This was a substantial work, the report (vol.1) and minutes of evidence (vol.2) running to 846 pages. Various recommendations were made in relation to such matters as speed limits, dangerous driving and road improvements. The report also recommended 'a special penalty for being drunk when in charge of a car'(vol.1:136). Several witnesses had given evidence in the strongest terms on the need for a separate offence of drink-driving - as 'it is a terrible thing to think of a man being drunk in charge of a car' (vol.2: para.11470).

The years leading up to the war saw a huge increase in the number of motor vehicles (388,860 in 1914) and fatal road accidents and injuries (59,846 accidents in 1914) (see Appendix 1 Tables 1, 2). The situation was particularly acute in London, prompting the establishment of a Parliamentary Select Committee 'To enquire into the circumstances which have led to the large and increasing number of fatal accidents in the Metropolis, due to motor omnibuses and other forms of power driven vehicles, and to make recommendations as to the measures to be taken to secure greater safety in the streets' (1913 (278) viii). The report described the increase in motor traffic as 'stupendous', with the associated problems becoming 'month by month more intractable'. It suggested various models for improved traffic administration and also recommended measures designed to improve safety (special speed limits, closer control exercised by the police, etc.), but no mention was made of drink-driving. The *Law Times* (135:433-4) observed that the report 'has aroused considerable comment in the lay Press' and described the Motor Car Act 1903 as being 'insufficient to afford complete safety to the public using the highways', so that 'it is quite clear that the active attention of the Legislature' is needed.

Other Parliamentary Papers followed (Ford & Ford 1969), and the Departmental Committee on Taxation and Regulation of Road Vehicles in Great Britain and Northern Ireland was established with wide terms of reference, including traffic safety - but its reports were silent on drink-driving. By the 1920s calls for the reform of road traffic legislation were very strong, both from the motorists' side, which felt that the Motor Car Act was hampering development of road transport, especially the 20 mph speed limit; and by those alarmed at the increasing toll of road accidents. The number of fatal road accidents had almost doubled between 1914 and 1925 from 2,220 to 3,971 (see Appendix 1 Table 2). As the *Law Times* (153:294) put it in 1922 'no one can doubt that the time has arrived for a general reconsideration of the law in relation to the regulation of mechanically-propelled road vehicles'. And perhaps a little less impartially in 1923 (156:172): 'by all means let condign punishment fall on the road-hog, and especially if his sobriety is impugned, and by all means let his licence be suspended for a substantial period'.

Criminal Justice Act 1925

A Criminal Justice Bill came before Parliament in 1923 (it failed to pass into law because of a General Election in the autumn of that year) and again in 1924 (another General Election halted its progress). The Bill reappeared and was passed into law in 1925. The recommendations of the Royal Commission in 1906 relating to drunken driving were a welcome inclusion in the Bill. For as Willett (1964:71-1) has put it:

> Hitherto drunken drivers had been charged under the Licensing Act, 1872, which provided for 'drunks' of all kinds, from those in charge of steam engines to those in charge of firearms. The maximum penalties were only one month's imprisonment or a fine of forty shillings, but the Act was disliked by motorists since it empowered anyone to apprehend suspects.

The Bill had its Second Reading late at night and an attempt was made to rush it through. Several members objected to this and in the debate which followed the drink-drive provisions came under heavy attack. It was suggested by one member that they, together with the provisions on dangerous driving, should be held over to the Minister of Transport who was preparing a Road Traffic Bill (*Parl.Debs.*(Commons) 183:1599-660); and this was supported by another member who felt that the provisions should be in a statute dealing with road traffic rather than in a criminal statute. A similar debate, long and heated, at the Report Stage, led to the dangerous driving provisions being dropped; with a new Act being promised in the near future (ibid.,188:801-30) - it arrived five years later.

The drink-drive provisions were enacted and the Criminal Justice Act 1925 (in force 1 June 1926) provided that: 'Any person who is drunk while in charge on any highway or other public place of any mechanically propelled vehicle shall, on summary conviction, be liable in respect of each offence to imprisonment for a period not exceeding four months or to a fine not exceeding fifty pounds, or to both such imprisonment and fine' (s.40(1)).[1] The Act also introduced compulsory disqualification from holding a licence to drive for a minimum of 12 months from the date of conviction and the requirement that such disqualification be endorsed on the offender's licence and notified to the council by whom the licence was granted (s.40(2)). This measure was added when the Bill passed through Committee in the House of Lords. Moving to insert the provision Earl Russell suggested that this was 'the most appropriate punishment for a drunken driver. He is a person whom you want to remove from the streets, and I am sorry to say that magistrates are somewhat too tender with him' (*Parl.Debs.*(Lords) 62:1443). This view found support elsewhere and was termed 'a useful addition' by the *Law Times* (157:236), which went on to say that 'To a certain class of drivers fines are no deterrent and some Benches have a reluctance to inflict imprisonment. The compulsory disqualification of drunken drivers for a considerable period is a move in the right direction'.

The courts already had powers to remove a driver's licence, but this was the first time it had been compulsory for them to do so. Concern was expressed in Parliament about interfering with the discretionary powers of those exercising judicial functions, but Lord Russell argued that 'this matter of drunken drivers has become so prevalent and is so great a public danger that I think it would be a useful thing to try ... whatever view the magistrates might take' (*Parl.Debs.*(Lords) 62:1443). The Lord Chancellor informed the House that the amendment was not supported by either the Home Office or the police as it was not in the public interest because 'an automatic penalty if severe, may prevent conviction' (ibid.:1449). The debate was fairly evenly divided and the House included the amendment - by 40 votes to 37 with a proviso that an application could be made for review after three months or by leave of the court after a shorter period. The Commons after a similar debate also accepted the amendment, but with the proviso redrafted to give to the court before which the offender was convicted the power to remove the suspension 'having regard to the character of the person convicted and his conduct subsequent to conviction, the nature of the offence, and the other circumstances of the case' *(Parl.Debs.* (Commons) 189:2236-44).

'Drunk'

The requirement under s.40(1) that a person needed to be 'drunk' in order to commit the offence gave rise to obvious difficulties of definition and proof. What exactly did drunkenness mean? How could it be established? These problems had already arisen in relation to other offences which involved drunkenness and had led to the practice of calling medical evidence in support of prosecutions. This practice had also been adopted in driving cases brought under the 1872 Act. It was a cause of great and continuing difficulty to the courts, which on the one hand were concerned to protect the public 'against the selfish person who renders himself temporarily insane with alcohol and then drives about the highway in a powerful locomotive', and on the other to 'fulfil their primary function of doing justice, without regard to extraneous considerations' *(JPN* 88:282-4).

But the law lacked a clear and authoritative definition of what drunk in charge of a motor car meant; although there were many attempts by commentators to provide one. The *Law Times* (158:304) reported in October 1924 that Sir Robert Wallace, Chairman of the London Sessions, had stated that 'it simply meant that, through drinking, a person had so destroyed his balance that he could not drive with safety.' Sir Robert's definition commanded wide support and it was thought 'strange that Parliament has not yet seen fit to enact a provision in those terms, avoiding the use of the controversial word 'drunk' altogether' *(JPN* 92:114). In fact, an amendment had been moved to the Criminal Justice Bill to remove the word 'drunk' and replace it with 'in a state of intoxication whereby his capacity to act is impaired', but after a quite lengthy debate the amendment was defeated *(Parl.Debs.*(Commons) 188:801-8). In January 1925, the question was considered by Sir James Purves-Stewart, Senior Physician at Westminster Hospital,[2] who submitted as a definition: 'A drunken person is one who has taken alcohol in sufficient quantity to poison his central nervous system, producing in his ordinary processes of reaction to his surroundings a temporary disorder which causes him to be a nuisance or danger to himself or others'. While these formulations may have gone some way towards a definition of drunkenness, they did little to assist with the further problem of how such a condition in an accused person was to be established.

There was a need to develop acceptable tests for drunkenness. Sir James had emphasised that 'the important point is not whether a person can perform various feats of elocution or mild acrobatic *tours de force*, but whether he is in a fit condition to pursue his ordinary daily vocation in life', and continued that 'nine times out of ten the policeman's diagnosis is correct'. Not surprisingly, press reports of drink-drive cases at the time expressed the view that 'motorists had a feeling of apprehension that they might at any time find themselves charged with a serious offence and that there was no certainty that the tests applied were of such a nature as to give them a fair chance of vindicating their reputation' (BMA 1965:6; originally in BMA 1927).

In response to the evidential difficulties presented by s.40(1), the BMA set up a committee 'to consider and report on the present tests for drunkenness with recommendations as to their modification or improvement'. The Committee included general practitioners, police surgeons, magistrates, scientists and others. In 1927 it issued *Report of a Committee on Tests for Drunkenness* (BMA 1927, 1927a) to guide doctors who were called upon to give evidence in court, which sought to provide uniform tests to be used in such cases. These tests would cover general behaviour (such as speech and self-control), memory and alertness, writing ability, pulse, temperature, skin condition, muscle condition, reflexes, and so on. Yet confusion remained. The *Law Times* (163:173) in February 1926 was moved to say that it did not think that 'the Report … carries the matter any further in the way of incisive definition'. It is, said the same editorial, 'Really, wholly a matter of common sense, and the sole difficulty that arises in adjudicating upon cases of this description is to differentiate between the effects of alcohol on the one hand, and of illness, excitement, or shock, on the other'. Meanwhile, the courts were hearing of all sorts of novel tests being utilised, such as that put forward by a medical witness at the London Sessions 'that a good test for sobriety was to get a man to lace up his boots' (*JPN* 93:427), and the recital of various 'tongue twisters' of the 'truly rural' and 'Methodist episcopal' variety (*JPN* 89:6).

The last few years of the 1920s saw endless definitions of drunkenness being put forward which served only to add to the confusion; and, of course, then as now, everyone had his or her own definition too. The point was, however, soon to be rendered academic, as in 1930 the word 'drunk' was to be removed from the definition of the offence (although it was not to be so easily disposed of).

The crucial question of how best to establish whether the necessary condition of intoxication existed in the accused, remained to be addressed. Scientific work in this area was starting to produce results and in 1927 the clinical significance of tests of body fluids and breath in order to establish consumption of alcohol was placed on the agenda by The True Temperance Scientific Committee in the Presidential Address given by Sir James Crichton-Browne FRS on the 'riddle of alleged inebriety' (Crichton-Browne 1927). The matter was discussed by the BMA later that year, and taken further in a lecture on the methods and pitfalls of *Tests of Drunkenness in Motor Accidents* given in January 1928 in London by a lecturer in forensic medicine from Sheffield University, who was also a senior police surgeon. In addition to detailing the traditional tests and their strengths and weaknesses, he outlined a case in which he had successfully presented details of the alcohol content of urine as a guide to the amount of alcohol a man accused of manslaughter and being drunk in charge had consumed. This type of test was, of course, to become crucially important in future years.

Drunken driver or drinking driver?

Aside from the evidential difficulties was the fact that if the provisions of the 1925 Act were narrowly and strictly construed, so that only those found to be 'drunk' could be successfully prosecuted, it would leave untouched the person who although under the influence of alcohol could not be said to be drunk in the generally accepted meaning of falling about and being incoherent (or to use the medical terminology - in a state of motor incoordination bordering on the paralytic); but who was recognised even in 1925 as capable of being a danger on the road. The courts were soon called upon to adjudicate on the matter. In *R v Presdee* (1927) 20 Cr App R 95 the appellant was charged under s.40(1) of the 1925 Act with the offence of being 'drunk while in charge ... of any mechanically propelled vehicle'. The jury was unable to reach a verdict, returned to the court, and explained that some of them thought the defendant drunk and some thought him not. The Chairman replied to the jury: 'Don't be frightened by the word drunk. I suggest you ask yourselves was he unfit to drive a motor car, and was that brought about by alcohol?'. The jury then returned the verdict - 'guilty of being incapable of driving a motor car brought about by alcohol, but he was not drunk - not drunk to the extent we would call a drunken man'. The defendant was convicted, sentenced to one months imprisonment and lodged an appeal. In the Court of Criminal Appeal counsel for the appellant argued that 'Here the offence is drunkenness: the motor car, so to say, is a mere aggravation'. It was, he said, for the jury to decide whether the defendant was drunk and in this case they had in their own words, when delivering the verdict, said he was not. Despite arguments for the Crown that there was a higher standard of sobriety expected of a man in charge of a motor car, the Lord Chief Justice had little option but to hold that 'No ingenuity or argument can get rid of the plain words "he was not drunk". That is - not guilty'. As Greer J. put it '"Drunk" is what an ordinary reasonable person would consider such'. As early as 1927 we have the distinction being made between the 'drunken driver' and the 'drinking driver'. The latter, even though clearly capable of being a danger to others, fell, due to the courts interpretation of the enactment, on the right side of the law.

The case for reform

There was an urgent need for new legislation. The number of vehicles and road accidents had escalated and the law was hopelessly outdated. Figures on prosecutions and convictions for drink-drive offences were published from 1928 as a return to the House of Commons and from 1929 convictions were shown separately for each offence. In 1929 1,730 offences are shown, with 1,724 prosecuted (99.6 per cent) and of those 1,232 findings of guilt (71.4 per cent); the figures for 1930 are similar (see Appendix 1 Table 5). This represented a rate of 560/550 findings of guilt per million motor vehicles licensed (see Appendix 1 Table 8).[3]

A second Royal Commission on Transport reported in 1929. Its first report stated: 'we cannot sufficiently emphasise the urgency of the questions involved in this Report' (Home Office 1929:3). It considered that the safest place in the world was 'an English railway train, the most dangerous a London street'. On drink-driving, the Commissioners felt that 'a difficulty has arisen since juries are often unwilling to convict drivers for this offence owing to the uncertainty of the meaning of the word "drunk". We are of the opinion that a new definition is necessary in order that this most serious and dangerous offence may be adequately dealt with' (para.25). The proposed definition was 'under the influence of drink or drugs as to be incapable of having proper control'(para.25). Suggested penalties were a fine not exceeding fifty pounds, or imprisonment not exceeding four months, or both, with suspension of licence for at least 12 months. The Commission's report marks the end of Chapter 1, which has taken us from Cugnot's eighteenth century steam carriage and the early development of 'road traffic law', to the mechanised industrial society which had developed by the end of the 1920s. The English landscape had changed considerably during this period, particularly in the first two decades of the twentieth century.

By 1930 motor transport had become firmly established, car ownership had widened considerably, and there were 2.3 million licensed vehicles in Britain (see Appendix 1 Table 3). Little open hostility remained towards the car *per se*, but concern was growing over the rising numbers of road casualties: death had topped 7,000 and injuries stood around 185,000 (see Appendix 1 Table 4). However, while the period witnessed a dramatic increase in technical development and other vehicle related matters, road traffic law had become little more sophisticated than it was fifty years before. In particular, legal policy in relation to the drink-driver effectively had not changed since the provisions of the Licensing Act 1872. Indeed, as the 1925 Act, unlike the 1872 Act, conferred no power of arrest, the provisions in this respect were weaker than under the old law.

Two principal difficulties needed to be addressed. First, the law required a driver to be drunk to establish guilt; secondly, no acceptable and accurate test for drunkenness existed.

Notes

1. As the offence carried a maximum penalty of four months imprisonment the defendant had a right to jury trial.

2. In a lecture entitled 'Drunkenness: Its Tests and Medico-Legal Aspects' (*Law Times* 159:47).

3. It should be noted that throughout this book figures for policing and court proceedings are for England and Wales, while those for motor vehicles licensed and casualty rates are given for Great Britain. Thus in Table 8 absolute rates cannot be trusted, but trends should be valid.

2 The incapable driver (1930-1960)

As well as the predictable increase in the volume of motor vehicles and traffic casualties the period 1930-1960 saw an expansion of scientific research and investigation into the relationship of alcohol and road safety. Legislation did not keep pace with these developments, and the enactments which did appear contained vague and uncertain provisions which lawyers zealously exploited in the courts. The introduction of a fixed blood-alcohol level was resisted and Parliament instead made several unsuccessful attempts to define the necessary physical condition which amounted to the commission of an offence. The original requirement of being 'drunk' was replaced in 1930 by the need to show that the driver was 'under the influence of drink... as to be incapable of having proper control', and in 1956 by 'unfit through drink', but no definition of or accurate test for the level of intoxication for the commission of the offence were provided. The result was that the law was unable to escape from its association with 'drunkenness'.

Road Traffic Act 1930

Before 1930, drunken driving had been a summary offence. It could be prosecuted under the Licensing Act 1872 or the Criminal Justice Act 1925. The latter provided for higher penalties, but unlike the earlier Act, gave no power of arrest. Both Acts applied only to drunken driving, leaving the drinking driver, who might still be a danger on the road, unaffected. Parliament intended to rectify this by dispensing with the word 'drunk' and providing a new definition for the offence.

The Road Traffic Bill, introduced in the Lords in November 1929, was almost entirely in accordance with the recommendations of the Royal Commission (Home Office 1929). While its introduction had been quick and easy, the Bill's passage was slow and tortuous. As Willett (1964:74) observed: 'few bills of a non-political nature could have had such a prolonged examination and so much amendment, mainly because of the non-party but controversial issues of the abolition of the 20 mph speed limit for cars and motor cycles, the introduction of compulsory third-party insurance, and the increased penalties for dangerous and for drunken driving'. Plowden (1971:256-7) tells us that the passage of the Bill was plagued with party political and ideological class based conflict. For example, in committee 'a debate about how to treat drivers who were merely in, and not in charge of, their vehicles, degenerated, via a discussion of drivers being chauffeured home, into crude partisan abuse'. For Plowden the reasons for the conflict were clear. By the 1920s the pro-motoring lobby had been joined by an equally vociferous opposition; which, unlike the resistance of the early days of road traffic, was becoming well organised and had a membership influential enough to challenge the power of the motoring organisations. These pressure groups, on the side of the cyclist and pedestrian, had powerful ammunition at their disposal as 'for the first time the casualty rate was seen as an urgent political problem'.

The Bill's provisions relating to drink-driving were less contentious. Provisions were introduced designed to avoid the problems created by the strict interpretation of 'drunk' in *Presdee* (above). The new offence was to be driving, or attempting to drive, or being in charge of a motor vehicle on the road or other public place 'under the influence of drink or a drug to such an extent as to be incapable of having proper control of a vehicle' (s.15(1)). Moving the Bill's Second Reading Earl Howe described the new wording as being 'the first time that we have had a really satisfactory definition of when a person is drunk' (*Parl.Debs.*(Lords) 76:152). There were in fact three separate offences - driving, attempting to drive, or being in charge of a motor vehicle 'under the influence of drink ... as to be incapable of having proper control'. The accused had to be charged with one of them, although the same penalties were available for each offence. The new offences were triable summarily or on indictment. The penalties on summary conviction were a maximum fine of fifty pounds or imprisonment for a maximum of four months, and in the case of a subsequent conviction, a maximum fine of one hundred pounds, imprisonment for a maximum of four months, or both; on conviction on indictment the penalty was a maximum term of imprisonment of six months, an unlimited fine, or both. In either case there was a mandatory disqualification from driving for a minimum of 12 months, unless special reasons (relating to the offence rather than the offender) not to disqualify could be proved.

The Act 'toughened up' the law. The police were given a power of arrest without warrant and maximum fines were increased; also, more significantly, the requirement that the defendant needed to be drunk was abolished. It was now an offence to drive, attempt to drive, or to be in charge of a motor vehicle 'under the influence' of drink or drugs so as to be 'incapable of having proper control' of it. 'A very proper change. I think everyone will admit' opined Sir Robert Wallace (*The Magistrate* 2:411). But how successful would the Act be in practice?

The 1930 Act in practice

The Act generated many problems of interpretation. Much case law followed on 'in charge' and 'public place'. Interpretation of the words 'public place' followed the case law from other enactments, but a particular question which arose, not surprisingly, under s.15(1) was whether a parking enclosure at the rear of an inn was a public place. The matter was heard by way of case stated in the King's Bench Division in *Elkins v Cartlidge* [1947] 1 All ER 829 and decided in the affirmative.

The use of the words 'in charge' caused more difficulty. A motion had been moved during Second Reading of the Bill in the Lords to remove the words 'in charge'. The House was told of the 'pathetic case of a lady who, finding herself in an unfit condition to drive, subsided in the car and waited until she had recovered. That seems to me a perfectly proper thing to do in the circumstances. I think it would be rather hard to make anyone in such a case subject to a penalty'(Earl Howe *Parl.Debs.*(Lords) 76:152). In reply, it was said that the police felt that a great many prosecutions would not be obtained if the 'in charge' provisions were removed. The provision survived this and a further challenge in the Commons, but went undefined, giving rise to many problems of interpretation. The leading cases on 'in charge' were *Leach v Evans* [1952] 2 All ER 264 and *Haines v Roberts* [1953] 1 All ER 264. In *Evans* the Divisional Court had to decide if a driver walking towards his vehicle with the intention of driving could be held to be in charge of that vehicle. The court held unanimously that he could. In *Roberts* the question to be decided was whether a person remained in charge of a vehicle left in a car park - the Divisional Court held unanimously that a person remained in charge of his vehicle 'if he has not put the vehicle in (the) charge of somebody else' (Goddard, L.C.J., 345 F). *Evans* was generally felt to be correctly decided, as had the police not intervened the accused would have driven his vehicle. *Roberts*, on the other hand, was widely thought to be harshly decided as it meant that a person who had no intention of driving could be guilty of the offence, unless the vehicle had been put into the charge of another person; which in effect meant that 'the driver who habitually left his car outside his house ... and who, in the privacy of his own home, then had too much to drink would be guilty of an offence' (Cassel & Havers 1956:674). It may happen of course that a person who is in charge of a vehicle and has been drinking may have no immediate intention of driving but may change his mind. Should such contingencies form the basis of criminal liability? It is interesting to note that the Divisional Court judgments in both *Evans* and *Roberts* were delivered by the then Lord Chief Justice, Lord Goddard, who had strong views on the subject of drink-driving. For example, during the Parliamentary debate on what was to become the Road Traffic Act

1956 Goddard expressed the view that 'for people to drive motor cars under the influence of drink is almost as serious an offence as attempted murder. These people are mad dogs' (*Parl.Debs.*(Lords) 191:89).

The wide interpretation placed by the courts on 'public place' and 'in charge' were thought to operate unfairly in some cases. The most often quoted example was that of the person who had been drinking, but had no intention of driving, who decided to 'sleep it off' in the back of the car, yet could be convicted under the Act. It is interesting to note that this is one of those rare occasions when the law relating to drink-driving was widely thought of as too strict.

Of central importance to the operation of the Act were the problems of interpretation associated with the words 'under the influence' and 'incapable of having proper control'. These words were intended to move the law away from the old concept of drunkenness. But the use of the word 'incapable' was too closely associated in legal parlance with drunkenness ('drunk and incapable') for this to be successfully achieved. For Havard (1967:152) 'this was an extremely poor piece of parliamentary draftsmanship as the offence inevitably became confused in the minds of the police, the jury and even the bench, with drunk and incapable'. It was 'therefore not surprising that a jury composed of lay persons may not convict unless medical proof is forthcoming of intoxication to an extent far greater than that required to impair driving ability' (BMA 1960:26). This view was widely subscribed to and linked with other factors postulated as affecting the decisions of juries in these cases. So that:

> juries particularly tended to interpret 'incapable' as if it meant 'drunk and incapable', but no one really knows why juries decide as they do, and I suggest that unjustified acquittals are probably due to sympathy with a man in a situation in which a juryman realizes he might have been himself, and unwillingness to risk such a person being sent to prison, rather than to any misapprehension as to what the law requires. (Smith 1963:300)

Another point concerning juries was put forward by a senior police officer. He argued that juries tended 'to attach too little weight to the evidence of the occurrence itself, becoming confused by a mass of medical evidence and of advocacy arising out of that evidence' (Simpson 1963:51). Grave doubts were being expressed about the reliability of jury trial in these cases (Heath 1955) - attributable variously to the 'there but for the grace of God go I' notion; the existence of imprisonment as a sentence; difficulties of proof (Cornish 1968); and, perhaps most significantly, confusion over the degree of intoxication required for the commission of the offence.

Conviction rates in drink-drive cases differed dramatically before magistrates and juries (see Appendix 1 Table 7). In the ten-year period 1953-1962 the conviction rate in the higher courts averaged 49 per cent, while the comparable figure in the magistrates' court was 91 per cent; and there were even greater regional variations. For example, Cohen et al. (1958) took a five-year average in Lancashire and found that only 37 per cent of cases before juries resulted in convictions, as compared with over 90 per cent by magistrates. The differential rate of conviction between the courts was far higher than for other offences triable in both the lower and higher courts (Butler 1983). For example, reckless/dangerous driving offences for magistrates' and higher courts drawn from Home Office Returns for the same period (1953-1962) show a conviction rate before magistrates of 82 per cent and 76 per cent before the higher courts. These figures generated significant concern.

The numbers of cases committed for trial can be seen from Appendix 1 Table 6. Both in absolute terms, and as a percentage of total prosecutions, committals for trial remained very low until the 1950s (some 150 cases - around 5 to 6 per cent); then rose steadily up to the mid-1960s and the introduction of the breathalyser (some 1,800 cases - around 17 per cent), no doubt encouraged by the greater chances of acquittal. However, with the introduction of the breathalyser in 1967 the percentage dropped dramatically to 3.7 per cent until the right to jury trial was eventually abolished in 1977 (see Appendix 1 Table 6).

Accepting these figures, what was to be done? The dilemma can be illustrated by two contemporary, conflicting views. On the one hand, that put forward by the Recorder of London, speaking to a jury at the Central Criminal Court on 21 May 1958, that everyone would welcome a short Act of Parliament which would deprive drivers accused of being under the influence of drink of the right to be tried by jury, and on the other, the castigation of this view by the *Solicitors' Journal* (102:88) as being 'a bad beginning to single out so serious an offence for a denial of that right'.

Even before magistrates, a very high level of intoxication was required for a guilty verdict. This was attributable to the problems of definition and evidence discussed above. Willett (1964:95) gives the example of *Dryden v Johnson* [1961] *Crim LR* 551. Here the divisional court allowed an appeal by way of case stated against the acquittal of a defendant who had been arrested at midnight, smelling of drink and unsteady on his feet. At a clinical examination he was unable to walk a straight line, tie his shoes, speak coherently or write legibly. A urine test showed he had consumed a minimum of five pints of beer. Nevertheless the magistrates had acquitted him. 'Mr Justice Salmon said that the argument on the accused's behalf would not have deceived an ordinary child of twelve, let alone a bench of magistrates' (Willett 1964:95).

Drunken driver or drinking driver?

The central issue for the 1930 Act matched that faced by previous legislation - did the law encompass the drinking as well as the drunken driver? (Weeks 1931; Vernon 1937). The prevailing legal view of the degree of intoxication required for the offence can be illustrated by reference to the first edition of Wilkinson (1953:46) which, when discussing evidence under the 1930 Act, stated that 'Ordinary witnesses may give their opinion as to the accused being drunk'. Although it did continue: 'The offence, of course, is being under the influence of drink, not necessarily drunk'. These same words appear in the second (1956) and third (1960) editions, although the later editions do carry the new tests set out by the BMA in 1954 - which by then referred to 'intoxication', rather than 'drunkenness' (see below).

Evidence as to the accused's condition was adduced from witnesses on the manner of driving and from a doctor (whether a police surgeon or not) as expert evidence. In 1934 it was said that 'The doctor is called by the police to give an opinion, not whether the accused is fit to drive a car, but whether he is under the influence of drink to such an extent as to be incapable of having proper control of the vehicle. This involves an examination to discover whether he is affected by illness, or not' (*The Magistrate* 1:841). The doctor would put the accused through the series of tests as laid down by the BMA in 1927 (see above); reinforcing, of course, the notion that drunkenness was necessary as these tests had been devised for 'drunkenness'. The use of the term was common in discussions of liability under the Act. Various articles containing advice for magistrates in these cases appeared under such titles as 'Conflicting Medical Testimony in Cases of Drunkenness' (McCormack 1937) and 'The Drunken Motorist' (Thomas 1937); while research reports throughout the period carried similar titles, for example, 'Drunken-Driving and Drunk-in-Charge' (Christian Economic and Social Research Foundation 1959).

At a meeting of the Medico-Legal Society in 1939 on traffic accidents, one of the speakers, a police surgeon, was concerned that he was constantly being asked to determine whether a person was drunk, not whether that person was fit to be in charge of a motor car - and even in response to this question he would, he said, be very grateful if anyone could tell him what drunkenness was, as the BMA tests for drunkenness - although the best currently available - were by no means a perfect tool for the medical witness in court, whose task was often made even more difficult by 'clever barristers (who) sometimes pulled medical evidence to pieces'(PJC. 1958). Lawyers, of course, had a duty to defend their clients to the best of their ability. So when faced with vague definitions, unscientific tests and conflicting medical evidence they had little alternative but to exploit the situation in their client's interest. Nevertheless, criticism of the way in which lawyers conducted themselves in these cases was widespread. As the BMA put it - in view of the difficulties of medical proof it was 'easy for an enterprising defence counsel to discredit medical evidence in the eyes of the court' (BMA 1960:26). In 1954 the *Solicitors' Journal* (98:722) was talking of 'Tilting at drunkenness tests (as) an old-fashioned sport of advocates in the criminal courts'. By the early 1960s it was being said that 'the difficulties of proving incapability ... are notorious' (Smith 1963:301).

The 1930 Act aimed to encompass the drinking as well as the drunken driver, but failed. The way in which the Act was framed, the interpretation placed upon it and the evidential difficulties experienced in the courts did nothing to change the fact that only drunken drivers rather than drinking drivers were convicted (Davies 1955). Drunkenness was in effect still the test for liability. So that while the number of convictions increased under the new law - from 1,232 convictions in 1929 (560 per million vehicles licensed and 71 per cent of offences prosecuted), to 1,966 in 1935 (756 per million vehicles licensed and 80 per cent of offences prosecuted) and 2,261 convictions in 1950 (513 per million vehicles licensed and 80 per cent of offences prosecuted) - this was as

Mannheim (1950:178) put it 'far below their actual occurrence, because they represent only those cases that were *obviously* due to drink or drugs'.

The period witnessed not only the failure of the Road Traffic Act 1930, but also a rapid increase in the incidence of road traffic accidents. In 1930 the number of deaths on the road was 7,305 (Appendix 1 Table 4) and road accidents were becoming a major public concern (Weiss 1938). Alcohol was increasingly being talked of as a causative factor, while evidence to scientifically establish a link was being developed and disseminated.

The period 1930-1960 is characterised by an increasing public awareness concerning road casualties and rapid advances in the scientific investigation of the relationship of alcohol to traffic safety; which by the end of the period would set the stage for radical reform. Three principal factors fall to be considered - government enquiries, public opinion (influenced by both official and pressure group campaigns) and advances in scientific knowledge.

Government enquiries

By 1930 motoring and traffic safety had become politically important issues, giving rise to several influential official enquiries. In December 1937 a select committee of the House of Lords was set up to enquire into *The Prevention of Road Accidents* (1938 HL.35) - it received important information on blood-alcohol testing. Among those called to give evidence was a Dr Weeks, who represented the Parliamentary Temperance Group. The Temperance movement had grown considerably during the 1920s and 1930s and had been instrumental in raising concern over problems of alcohol abuse. Dr Weeks described the effect of alcohol on mood, coordination and performance; the limitations of clinical tests; and evidence from several other countries, including the US, Sweden and Germany, on the testing of blood-alcohol concentrations and their relation to accidents, injuries and deaths. He concluded by putting the case for the introduction of such tests in England and Wales.

In view of the evidential difficulties being encountered by the Road Traffic Act 1930, the issue of blood-alcohol testing raised by Dr Weeks was of fundamental importance - further evidence on this issue was presented to the Committee by a member of the Council of the BMA who detailed the mechanics of a method of blood-alcohol testing pioneered in Sweden. The Committee (1939 HL.2:52) called for 'drastic action' on road safety, and criticised the Ministry of Transport for showing 'a lack of vision, of initiative and of driving force'. Recommendations were made for road and vehicle improvements to facilitate accident reduction. In particular, the Committee recommended a programme of propaganda 'to train and fortify public opinion in the condemnation of persons who drink and drive', and to educate the public and the courts that 'under the influence' does not necessarily mean intoxication - 'for driving skill is affected long before a man is consciously under the influence of alcohol'. However, the Committee rejected the suggestion that jury trial should be unavailable in these cases, preferring instead to recommend that clear directions should always be given to juries as to the meaning of the words 'under the influence of drink'.

An especially significant recommendation was that blood-alcohol testing should be introduced, albeit on a voluntary basis - as the 'time has not yet come when the imposition of compulsory blood tests would be sanctioned by Parliament' (para.42). The attitude of the Government in relation to blood-alcohol tests had been expressed some five years previously by the Home Secretary in answer to a Parliamentary Question when he stated that he doubted the value of such a test and, in any event, had 'no power to require any person to submit to it' (*Parl.Debs.*(Commons) 285:521). Even so, the Committee held out the hope 'that at a later date the public will be so educated so as to agree that tests should be made obligatory in appropriate cases' (para.42). As to blood-alcohol level, the Committee considered that a level of over 150mg per 100ml would render a driver incapable of having proper control of a vehicle (a level which subsequent investigation was to prove to be much too high). The Committee concluded with the hope that their report would be acted upon and not join others to be placed merely 'in the pigeon holes of Whitehall'. The outbreak of war ensured that this is exactly what did happen, albeit temporarily, to their report.

Propaganda and pressure groups

The post war period saw an increase in the number of motor vehicles, an end to petrol rationing and 'motoring began to boom again ... so did deaths, injuries, motoring offences, and the inevitable letters of complaint to the press' (Willett 1964:75). The main allegations were of the law being flouted by selfish and dangerous motorists; excessive leniency being displayed towards motorists by magistrates; and the failure of juries to convict in cases of motor manslaughter and driving under the influence of drink.

The apparent failure of the criminal law to arrest the increase in road traffic casualties led to attempts being made to change attitudes to motoring offences and to educate the public into obeying the law (as recommended by the House of Lords Select Committee in 1939). In 1943 a Ministry of War Transport Committee was set up to consider the Select Committee report. Drawing on wartime experience, the Committee recommended a programme of road safety propaganda. This was launched by the Minister of Transport in 1945 under the slogan 'Keep Death off the Road'. It was aimed at juries, magistrates, the police and others with a part to play in the legal process; as well as motorists. In particular, there was an attempt to re-educate the public, so as to make drink-driving socially unacceptable, and to remove any sympathy which might attach to a drink-driver - who, although not thought of as being on the right side of the law, was not regarded as being 'really criminal'. The campaign was to complement the efforts already being made in this direction by the Royal Society for the Prevention of Accidents.

The drink-driving laws were a particular target for campaigners and emerged as a major factor in road safety debates. The main thrust of the anti-drink-drive lobby was in the direction of harsher punishment, particularly increased use of imprisonment. Yet, while this may have been a symbolic way of stressing the serious nature of the offence, and carried with it ideas of improved deterrent effect, it would do nothing to ensure the apprehension and conviction of the drink-driver; indeed, juries might be even less likely to convict. What was needed was a clearer definition of the offence, accurate methods of adducing evidence, and increased apprehension on the part of the drink-driver that he would not escape arrest and conviction.

In October 1950 a demonstration was held in London, organised by the Cyclists' Touring Club and the Pedestrians' Association. A unanimous resolution was passed calling for the road safety laws to be strictly enforced against the drink-driver: by both the police and the courts. The meeting was presided over by Lord Trevot, who called for prison with hard labour for anyone who 'misused the roads after being once convicted', while Professor A.L. Goodhart claimed that the 'feebleness' of magistrates in drink-drive cases was demonstrated by the fact that in 1949 out of 1,682 convictions for driving under the influence of drink or drugs only 54 prison sentences were passed without the option of a fine (see Appendix 1 Table 9). A year later Lord Goddard, the Lord Chief Justice, made an emphatic pronouncement on the subject in the Divisional Court. He said that he wished to express in court what he had been saying to magistrates' benches throughout the country on the proper sentence for cases of driving under the influence of drink. The offence, he felt, was one of the worst that it was possible to commit, and should never be mitigated by the fact that no one was injured. It consisted of doing a dangerous and wicked thing which placed others in danger; the question which magistrates should ask themselves was whether there existed any reason *not* to send the offender to prison. Drunken drivers, he concluded, 'were as great a menace as mad dogs and ought to be dealt with by severe sentences' (*The Times*, 13 October 1951). Professor Goodhart, another influential shaper of legal policy, spoke out later the same year at a conference, *Alcohol and the Road User*, organised by the Pedestrians' Association. Describing the drunken motorist as 'a major social problem', it was, he said, time that the sympathy felt for the drunken motorist was transferred to his victim. He went on to stress that it was the drinking as well as the drunken motorist, who may not appear drunk, but could have increased confidence and impaired ability that should be tackled. It was 'unfortunate that the popular phrase is "drunk in charge"'. Commenting on Goodhart's remarks, a leader in the *Law Times* (212:211-2) considered the subject of 'vital interest to all those engaged in the administration of the law or concerned with its content'.

In 1954, Sir Carleton Allen, a distinguished legal academic, speaking at a conference on *Road Safety and the Law*, said that 'Punishment of alcoholic offences was profoundly unsatisfactory'; in 1952 out of 2,349 convictions 'for driving while drunk' only 233 were sent to prison, and 640 disqualified for more than 12 months' (use of the word 'drunk' illustrates how deeply ingrained the notion of drunkenness was, even among those who professed to know better). The following year, the Royal Society of Medicine was addressed by the Chief Constable of Surrey, speaking on *Police Problems in Drunken Driving Cases*. Detailed statistics were presented for 1951 which included the 'number of casualties and accidents under the influence of drink or drugs', 'days on which drink accidents occurred', 'times at which drink accidents occurred', and 'results of police action' - both arrests and court verdicts (Simpson 1953). The presentation of these figures and the call for the introduction of a 'Scandinavian system' made by the President of the Society in his summing-up of the meeting attempted to move the debate on from the over-simplified solution of harsher penalties.

By the early 1950s, despite strong pressure for reform, it was clear that any changes would be slow and hard fought. As one commentator put it: 'facts and figures about maiming and death on the roads, terrifying though they are, never seem to shake those in authority into doing more than tinkering with the problem' (*Solicitors' Journal* 94:1).

Alcohol and traffic safety - the early work

The first publicly available information on the relationship between alcohol consumption and road traffic safety came as a result of a request in 1935 by the Minister of Transport, Mr Hore-Belisha (of 'Belisha Beacon' fame), who announced in the House of Commons on 30 January 1935 that he intended to ask the BMA whether it could usefully make any observations on the place of alcohol in the causes of road accidents (*Parl.Debs.*(Commons) 297:341). In response the BMA re-appointed its special committee (which had produced *Tests for Drunkenness* in 1927) to investigate the relationship between alcohol and road traffic safety in terms of the effect which alcohol has on driver efficiency. *The Relation of Alcohol to Road Accidents* was published in 1935 (BMA 1935). The report, after reviewing the available evidence and research, concluded that even small amounts of alcohol, less than would give rise to liability under the 1930 Act, could have a deleterious effect on driving ability. 'The Report heralded the beginning of one of the most important campaigns to have been fought by the BMA' (Havard 1985:3). A campaign which continues today. The report described the scientific tests which had been developed to quantify the amount of alcohol in blood or urine and the advances made in explaining the ways in which alcohol could affect driving skills in terms of impairment of mental processes (judgment, concentration, self-criticism, power of estimating risk) and neuromuscular coordination (of eyes, hands and feet):

> alcohol in no greater quantity than that contained in three ounces of whisky has been found to affect appreciably the mental processes and neuro-muscular co-ordination of individuals, it must frequently affect the driving capacity of the driver who takes alcoholic liquor in small amounts. After taking alcohol he may believe himself to be driving better, but, in fact, his body works less effectively. (BMA 1935:59)

The first country to have made practical use of these advances, by making it a criminal offence to drive with a blood-alcohol concentration above a prescribed limit, was Norway in 1936 (50mg/100ml). Other Scandinavian countries followed Norway's example. Blood-alcohol testing became known as the

'Scandinavian system' (Ross 1975; Andenaes 1984). A campaign for the introduction of similar legislation in England and Wales was launched the year after the BMA report was published. The United Kingdom Alliance at its 1936 annual general meeting passed a resolution calling for the introduction of scientific testing for blood-alcohol concentration and Winterton, who led the campaign, has recorded the part played by the temperance movement in the years up to the passing of the Road Safety Act in 1967 (Winterton 1968). But the desirability of scientific testing was not apparent to everyone. For example, some lawyers felt that the system was not able to perform the task which it set itself, as measurement of the level of alcohol in the blood was not the same thing as measurement of the effect which the alcohol had upon capability and conduct. Comparative experience was usefully utilised in response to such arguments. This was facilitated by the first of many international conferences on alcohol and road safety held in Stockholm in 1950. These conferences provided the opportunity for those working in different countries to come together and share their knowledge and experience.

In the light of advances which had been made in international scientific research the BMA Council once again re-appointed its special committee to revise and bring up to date the BMA publications of 1927 and 1935. The 1927 report was replaced by *Recognition of Intoxication* in 1954, in which alcoholic intoxication for the purposes of being 'under the influence of drink' was defined as 'the condition produced in a person who has taken alcohol in a quantity sufficient to cause him to lose control of his faculties to such an extent that he is unable to safely execute the occupation on which he is engaged at the material time' (BMA 1954:5). The report went on to detail an updated series of clinical tests which could be used to establish whether a driver was in such a condition. It also revised the view on blood-alcohol testing put forward in 1927, which had read that 'analyses of the blood, urine and cerebro-spinal fluid for estimating the amount of alcohol consumed are not practicable in connection with the examination of persons charged with "drunkenness" owing to the conditions limiting their application' (BMA 1927:55). In line with this revised view the 1954 report included details of 'The Determination of Alcohol in Body Fluids' (BMA 1954:23-9). The presence or otherwise of any amount of alcohol in the body fluids did not, of course, amount to the offence, but could be used along with the results of the clinical examination to determine the state of intoxication of the accused. The Home Secretary, in a Parliamentary reply, said that in 1954 there were 1,020 tests for alcohol in the urine carried out in the combined police laboratories, and 964 of the persons concerned had been prosecuted for offences under s.15 of the 1930 Act (*Parl.Debs.*(Commons) 548:297).

The BMA report stressed that a person need not be 'drunk' in the everyday meaning of the word or even to have committed an offence under the Act to be a danger on the road; but that many motorists were ignorant or heedless of the possible consequences of drinking and driving. The report called for a public education programme.

As was to become the pattern, the publication of the BMA report led to public (in the press and on radio and television) and legal as well as medical debate on the drink-driver. Yet despite attempts to impress on the public and the courts that even small amounts of alcohol could be dangerous and constitute an offence, the idea of 'drunkenness' had become so ingrained into the provisions of the 1930 Act that the new tests were used, as were the ones they replaced, in relation to drunkenness on the part of the defendant. Further legislation was necessary.

Road Traffic Bill 1954

The Queen's Speech in 1954 expressed concern at 'the grievous toll in death and injury that is taken by road accidents (by 1953 road deaths had risen above 5,000 and injuries stood at 227,000), the inadequate road system and increasing vehicle numbers' (in 1953 licensed motor vehicles stood at 5.3 million). An expanded programme of road construction and improvement, and a Road Traffic Act were promised (*Parl.Debs.*(Lords) 190:4). The Road Traffic Bill was introduced in 1954. It contained 24 clauses and three schedules. When it eventually reached its final stages in 1956 it had expanded to 55 clauses and nine schedules. However, the provisions on drink-driving did little to strengthen the law. The drafters of the Bill had largely ignored the recommendations of the various committees, the Government's own public education exhortations and the advances in scientific knowledge. The Bill addressed only the problems caused by the 'in charge' provisions (although important, not a central issue) and acceded to the calls for harsher penalties.

Road Traffic Act 1956

The Road Traffic Act 1956 increased the penalties for drink-driving (sentences for other 'moving' motoring offences were also raised), and drew a clear distinction between the offences of driving and of 'being in charge'.

The penalties available for driving or attempting to drive under s.15 of the 1930 Act became on summary conviction for a first offence a fine of £100 which could be imposed in addition to any sentence of imprisonment awarded by the court (maximum four months and six months for a second or subsequent offence); the maximum term of imprisonment for a conviction on indictment was increased to two years (s.26(1)(d)). During the Bill's Second Reading in the Lords the view was expressed that imprisonment should be the automatic penalty for drink-drive offences (one speaker even suggested the re-introduction of hard labour). But much of this was merely rhetoric, as were the demands for lifetime periods of disqualification. And there was always the counter-argument that severe penalties would make juries less likely to convict. A new power was introduced by s.26(4) of the Act. This allowed the court to order that a person who had been disqualified from driving for a drink-drive offence must pass a driving test before having his licence returned. The Act also amended the law in relation to the offence of 'drunk in charge'. This offence, the subject of strong opposition when it was introduced in the 1925 Act, was widely perceived as operating unfairly in two respects. First, although a less serious offence than driving or attempting to drive it attracted the same penalties; and secondly, the very strict interpretation put on 'in charge', could lead to unfair convictions.

To deal with the first point, the words 'when in charge', were repealed from s.15(1) of the 1930 Act and replaced by s.9(1) of the 1956 Act. This section restated the wording from the 1930 Act, but provided that the penalties under the new provisions would stay at the lower level of the earlier Act; and that disqualification, compulsory for a minimum of 12 months on a first conviction under s.15(1), would be compulsory for 'in charge' only on a second conviction. To deal with the second point, s.9(1) provided that a person would be deemed not to be in charge for the purposes of the section, if he proved (and this is one of the exceptional cases where the burden of proof is put on the accused): (i) that at the material time the circumstances were such that there was no likelihood of his driving the vehicle so long as he remained unfit to drive; and (ii) that between his becoming unfit to drive and the material time he had not driven the vehicle on a road or other public place. Apart from the direct effects of this provision, the view was expressed, when the amendment was moved in the Lords, that such a change was necessary as the existing law was an incentive to drive when under the influence (rather than wait to be caught recovering in one's vehicle or nearby); and that the resulting injustice would lead to a lack of public support for the drink-drive laws generally (Lord Reid, *Parl.Debs.*(Lords) 191:106-7).

Post-1956

The provisions of the 1956 Act prompted little change in legal policy in relation to drink-driving. The Act did nothing to remove what were clearly the fundamental obstacles standing in the way of an effective legal response - the absence of a satisfactory definition of the necessary degree of intoxication required for the commission of an offence, and the evidential difficulties which plagued cases in the courts. The years following the 1956 Act saw little change in legal policy, which was basically much the same (apart from the higher penalties) as it had been under the Licensing Act 1872. So, not surprisingly, an analysis of Home Office Statistics relating to England and Wales for 1953-1958 concluded *inter alia* that 'The incidence of the offence has not been affected by the 1956 Act' (Christian Economic & Social Research Foundation 1959:18).

In 1958 the BMA published a revised edition of *Recognition of Intoxication* (BMA 1958) which was basically unchanged apart from amendments designed to improve the practical efficiency of the tests. For example, the provision of suitable receptacles at police stations for urine samples, and a standard form for certificates reporting examinations.

By 1960, the number of motor vehicles had expanded considerably to 9.4 million (see Appendix 1 Table 3) and the motor car was ceasing to be a middle class luxury. The road casualty rate continued to rise with 6,970 killed and 348,000 injured on British roads that year (see Appendix 1 Table 4). The number of drink-drive prosecutions numbered 6,807 and convictions 5,525 (587 per million vehicles licensed and 81 per cent of offences prosecuted - little changed from 30 years before - see Appendix 1 Tables 5). Dissatisfaction was being expressed in many quarters over the perceived inadequacy of the law in regulating the growing number of motorists and the rising tide of road casualties. Much of this concern was focused on the part played by the drink-driver. Parliamentary Questions continued to be asked on the subject of drink-driving, and time and again the Government was called upon to take action, but this was refused pending, according to Government replies, the necessary scientific evidence on the link between alcohol and road casualties.

The Drew research In 1953 the Committee on Road Users, appointed jointly by the Medical Research Council and the Road Research Board of the Department of Scientific Research, commissioned a study 'to investigate the effects of small amounts of alcohol which would produce concentrations in the blood below those regarded in a number of countries as evidence of intoxication and within the range of those reached in ordinary social drinking' (Drew 1959). The study was designed to test scientifically the link between driving skills and the consumption of alcohol. The work was carried out by a team led by a professor of psychology at Bristol University (Professor Drew) with the subjects being 40 volunteers drawn from the staff of the Road Research Laboratory (Road Research Laboratory 1963). The study involved these men and women undertaking a series of laboratory tests on an experimental task which resembled the driving of a vehicle on the road. The work was not completed until 1958.

For most of the 1950s, all Parliamentary Questions on drink-driving were met with the reply that the Government awaited the report of this research, which finally became available in 1958 (Drew et al. 1958). It confirmed that driving skills such as ability to judge distance, speed and movement were impaired by consumption of alcohol. Yet, even after its publication the Minister stated, in a written reply in February 1959: 'I am not yet in a position to say what action my Department will take in this matter' (*Parl.Debs.*(Commons) 599:149-52).

Road Safety Bill 1959

The necessary scientific evidence was available - other studies, both before and after Drew had come to similar conclusions (e.g. Cohen et al. 1958; Walls 1958; Jeffcoate 1958; Haddon & Bradess 1959); and public opinion supported reform of the drink-drive laws - for example, a Gallup opinion poll carried out in 1955 showed 75 per cent of those questioned felt that motorists involved in accidents should be tested for alcohol consumption (Gallup 1977:346-7). Yet the Government still refused to act.

On 11 November 1959, Graham Page (Chairman of the Pedestrians' Association) introduced a private members Road Safety Bill (House of Commons Bill 1959/60, No.24), containing provisions for the introduction of a blood-alcohol limit and chemical testing. It got as far as its Second Reading in April 1960, but was badly timed and was lost. The Bill attracted a spirited debate at

Second Reading and much support. Opposition speeches were mainly limited to pointing out that drink-drivers were not the only danger on the roads - the problems caused by dogs and drunken pedestrians being referred to several times. There was little constructive opposition to the Bill's provisions which was not effectively answered by reference to the scientific evidence provided by the Drew and BMA reports (*Parl.Debs.*(Commons) 622:563-656). With one important exception. Drew had presented evidence on the adverse effect of alcohol on 'skills resembling driving', using a driving simulator. During the debate it was put several times whether evidence could be produced to show 'a direct association between road traffic accidents and the amount of alcohol taken below that necessary to make a person drunk or intoxicated' (e.g. Hall, ibid.,571); and the 'precise percentage of accidents that drunkenness causes' (Cooper, ibid.,610-1). As yet no such evidence was available.

Road Traffic Act 1960

The Page Bill had alerted the Government to the wide cross-party support that such measures could command; and calls for reform were now of such intensity it seemed they could not be ignored. Yet the Road Traffic Act 1960 did just that. The best that the Government could offer was an Act designed merely to consolidate the existing law on drink-driving. The Road Traffic Act 1960 simply brought together the provisions of the Acts of 1930, 1934 and 1956. This was seen by many as a lost opportunity to tighten up the law (Willett 1964). So that the old 'drunken driving' law was still effectively in force - its inadequacies becoming steadily more apparent as lawyers' techniques and arguments developed in these cases. The law was struggling to come to terms with the part it could play in controlling the drink-driver. So far it had not done well. Mostly the law had been concerned with technical definitions and increased punishment. The massive advances in knowledge on alcohol and traffic safety which had been made since 1930 had largely been ignored. But by the beginning of the 1960s it was no longer possible to do so.

Alcohol and traffic safety - a developed science

Rapid advances had been made in the scientific study of alcohol and traffic safety. A body of experts had emerged - including psychologists, doctors, traffic experts, chemists and biologists - and a circuit of international conferences had allowed for the exchange and dissemination of information. A comprehensive summary of available knowledge was distilled into a revised edition of *The Relation of Alcohol to Road Accidents*, published by the BMA in 1960. It was instrumental in bringing about reform of the law.

The report provided an authoritative analysis of the relationship of alcohol to road accidents; surveyed the available research; and concluded that official figures considerably underestimated the number of accidents caused by drivers who had been drinking alcohol, particularly in fatal accidents involving pedestrians. Further, it was pointed out that relatively low concentrations of alcohol caused a deterioration in driving performance and increased the likelihood of an accident; yet existing legislation came into effect only when much higher levels had been reached. Thus, the report concluded, existing measures could do little to prevent accidents caused by alcohol consumption. The report stressed that clinical examination was not sufficiently sensitive or reliable, in the absence of bio-medical tests, to detect deterioration of driving performance to the degree required; although clinical examinations were a necessary part of any examination of a suspected drink-driver, 'since it is the only way of detecting physical illness and the presence and extent of any injury' (BMA 1960:33). A wealth of comparative material was presented, including details of legislation, which was of two types. First, that which made it an offence to drive a car when impaired by alcohol, the type in force in England. This approach was said to suffer from legal and medical drawbacks which caused the deterrent effect to be weakened 'by the realization that a substantial number of persons charged with the offence are never convicted' (p.28). Secondly, legislation which made it an offence to 'drive motor vehicles with the presence of a certain proportion of alcohol in the body fluids, irrespective of the presence or absence of any impairment of driving ability demonstrable by clinical examination' (p.28). The latter provisions rest on the assumption that impairment can be linked to a quantifiable amount of alcohol in the body. If a greater chance of apprehension and conviction can be shown, then it should follow that a greater deterrent effect will be present. It would also signify that the crime is drinking and driving rather than drunken driving. The Committee believed 'that a substantial reduction in the number of accidents caused by alcohol has been achieved where it has been made an offence to drive a motor vehicle when the concentration of alcohol in the tissues is in excess of a certain level' (p.33).

The report advocated the introduction of legislation of the second type in England - subject to agreement on the level of alcohol which constituted impairment and how this could be measured in a reliable, practical and acceptable way. On the second point, the report mentioned the 'conventional methods' of measurement by taking blood or urine samples and then went on to note that 'an apparatus is now available for taking samples of breath from which the concentration of alcohol in the tissues can be rapidly and accurately estimated' (p.33). There would be obvious advantages, not least in terms of 'minimal invasion of the person', in breath testing over the taking of urine or blood samples.

The setting of the permitted blood-alcohol level generated much debate (as it still does today). A concentration of 50mg of alcohol in 100ml of blood was put forward by the report as 'the highest that can be accepted as entirely consistent with the safety of other road users':

Taking into consideration (1) the investigations performed in recent years on the effect of alcohol on different functions in laboratory experiments, (2) the results of statistically designed practical tests on drivers, air pilots, etc ... and (3) the statistical evidence from the few adequate studies existing on alcohol and road accidents, the inference cannot be avoided that at a blood-alcohol concentration of about 50mg/100ml a statistically significant impairment of performance is observed in more than half of the cases examined. (World Health Organization 1954)

The BMA report argued that since 1954 additional work had made the case for a 50mg/100ml limit even stronger and that 'alcohol has been shown to impair driving ability at concentrations as low as 10mg/100ml', but 'it is probable that other factors not yet subjected to adequate scientific experiments (e.g. the normal range of fatigue, irritability, climatic changes, etc. may effect no less a degree of impairment than does alcohol at such a low concentration' (p.31). Particularly noteworthy, in the light of later developments, was the reference to the work of Drew et al. (1958, 1959) who 'have shown that there is no level below 80mg/100ml at which a sudden deterioration can be shown to occur, and that at concentrations between 10 and 80mg/100ml deterioration in driving ability is proportionate to the amount of alcohol consumed' (p.31). The report therefore considered it necessary to fix the level pragmatically, as, for example, with the speed limits, eyesight tests and driving hours. Various factors would have to be taken into consideration, including 'questions of the liberty of the subject' (p.32). Consequently, the report did not put 50mg/100ml forward as a recommended limit, but merely offered the figure as a conclusion based on scientific work. However, the Committee went on to say that in some circumstances this level may not in individual cases lead to a significant reduction in driving ability, although it was stressed that at levels in excess of 100mg/100ml rapid deterioration occurs and that 'the Committee cannot conceive of any circumstances in which it would be considered safe for a person to drive a motor vehicle ... with an amount of alcohol in the blood greater than 150mg/100ml'. The discussion of blood-alcohol levels in the report aroused considerable controversy. In particular, they were seen as seriously understating the effects of alcohol on driving ability (Havard 1960); and the BMA did in fact alter its position quite substantially in its subsequent report (BMA 1965). Nevertheless, the report provided the first comprehensive and accessible details of a 'Scandinavian system' suitable for introduction in Great Britain.

The case for change

Several factors came together in 1960 to produce an irresistible case for reform of legal policy.[1] There was an impressive literature on alcohol and traffic safety, as well as detailed procedures for accurately relating, testing and measuring alcohol intake to driver impairment; the publication of the BMA report generated much public and legal interest; the drink-driver had become a particular target in the popular press; traffic offences and road casualties continued to cause public concern; figures were released which showed a high level of fatalities over the Christmas period, when alcohol consumption was known to increase (Road Research Laboratory 1960); claims of excessive leniency and inconsistency on the part of the courts continued; and the motorcar was no longer a middle class luxury, motoring for the masses had arrived, bringing with it a rapid expansion in road traffic. This, coupled with continued pressure from groups such as the Pedestrians' Association, together with the dissemination of scientific advances in alcohol and traffic safety studies by the BMA made legislation inevitable. For as one commentator put it: 'The present position is highly unsatisfactory, whether it be looked at from the point of view of the police, who desire to obtain a conviction, of the public, who desire to be safe on the road, of the lawyers, who desire justice, or of the medical practitioners, who are asked on many occasions to do the impossible' (Camps 1960:6).

Policing the motorist

The approach of the police to drink-drving has, historically, been rather ambivalent. While the police were understandably frustrated at the way in which drink-drive cases were handled in the courts they appeared, for several reasons, to be less than enthusiastic about the actual policing of the offence. First, at an individual level, officers seemed to share the common conception of the motoring offender as being 'not really criminal', and many were of course motorists themselves. As Willett (1964:310) found: 'The results of this inquiry leave little doubt about their general attitude: the police do not, on the whole, see even *serious* motoring offenders as criminals. Hence their evident reluctance to prosecute unless the case is nearly flawless, especially where drunken driving is concerned'. Secondly, the police may have been reluctant to pursue drink-drive prosecutions, because of the high likelihood of an acquittal and the possibility of a drubbing from a 'clever lawyer'. Willett (1964:120) again: 'A certain amount of dissatisfaction was expressed by police officers over the difficulty of convincing benches, and even more so juries, of the credibility of police evidence in cases of speeding and drunken driving'. And thirdly, the police were experiencing great difficulty in coming to terms with the rapid increase in the number of motor vehicles; particularly as many of the 'respectable middle classes', upon whom the police had traditionally relied for support, were now finding themselves on the wrong side of the (albeit motoring) law. For Willett (1964:106): 'Few inventions can have influenced relations between the police and the public more than that of the internal combustion engine. The image of the policeman has changed from that of a friend and protector of all but a small criminal minority, to that of a regulator and supervisor who is in close contact with all who use the roads'.

The problem of traffic policing adversely affecting police/public relations has been said to date from the introduction of the 20 mph speed limit in 1905 with its 'speed traps' (Willett 1964; Critchley 1967) and is certainly evident in early police literature. For example, in 1935 a sergeant (Bristol City Police) wrote:

The suggestion - which originated in the distant days when every mechanically propelled vehicle was, by law, limited to the speed of the man who preceded it on foot, with a red flag, and which has been revived periodically ever since - that the motorist is harassed, pestered, persecuted, and oppressed by the police, has again been brought forward of late ... the enforcement of the laws, by-laws, and regulations relating to the use of mechanically propelled vehicles is having the very serious effect of alienating from the police the sympathy and valuable goodwill of a large, and ever increasing, section of the public. (Cook 1935:350-1)

And as an Assistant Commissioner at New Scotland Yard writing in *The Police Journal* in 1936 put it - 'traffic law must be enforced by the police and the power of the police is entirely based upon public goodwill' (Alker-Tripp 1936:97). The need to maintain this goodwill was felt to be necessary, not only for the effective enforcement of road traffic laws, but for policing generally. Yet while the Chief Constable of the West Sussex police was of the opinion that: 'The police have proved themselves both courteous and efficient instruments for the enforcement' of road traffic law (Wilson 1938:437), others disagreed and thought that the police, while effectively maintaining general order, were 'quite inadequate to secure that a code of law for promoting the safety and convenience of the road-using public is even tolerably complied with' (Tarry 1938:185). The establishment of general order was seen to flow from the goodwill and cooperation of the public, which Tarry asserted did not exist in the case of road traffic law - 'which is evaded and infringed by all and sundry'.

The 1929 Royal Commission on Police Powers and Procedure expressed the view that the main problem facing the police was 'to find means to restore the relationship between the police and the public' (quoted in Whitaker 1964). Although in the 1930s and 1940s the police seemed to feel that police/public relations were good. For example, a serving officer observed in a note to *Police Review* in 1946 that: 'foreigners visiting us so often pay spontaneous tribute to the mutual confidence which exists here between Police and public'. However, the post-war period witnessed increasing concern over police/public relations. Several factors were identified as problematic - including the enforcement of traffic laws (e.g. Wilson 1940; Jones 1946). Attempts were made to devise strategies to address these issues. One proposal for more effective road safety measures, without alienating the public, was the designation of 1951 as 'Road Courtesy Year' and the introduction of the 'Courtesy Cop'. For while 'much of the work of the police is, naturally, unpopular with the persons involved ... experience has shown that a carefully worded bit of advice from a highly trained police driver ... will be well received and generally acted upon' (Anon 1951:3).

This approach may have had something to commend it in the case of minor infringements of the law, but was of little use when dealing with more serious breaches such as drink-driving offences. It was in any event short lived; but the idea of special traffic police was pursued. The plan being to hive off the traffic part of police duties to a separate 'Traffic Corps' which would allow the 'ordinary' police force to remain untainted and maintain its traditional public support. By the end of the 1950s concern was such that one commentator in supporting the introduction of such a corps felt able to assert:

Not the least important of the issues ... is the strained relationship between Police and public. As long as the motorist regards the Policeman as a potential enemy ... that spirit of co-operation and good citizenship which should exist between them - and did in the days before motor-cars were considered necessities - will be perpetually endangered. The help which could often be given in matters of crime will be withheld, and the Policeman will go on being the subject of caricatures in cartoons and on stage and television. (Bendix 1959)

By the end of the 1950s, as the police moved into what Reiner (1985) has termed the period of 'politicisation of the police', it seemed to have been generally agreed that public support for the police had diminished and that 'restrictions on road usage are the favourite whipping boys' (Elmes 1959). Although this view was by no means universal:

The safety and convenience of all who use the roads is one of the most difficult problems of the day. It is a constant and increasing strain on the resources of the police upon whom the responsibility of keeping traffic on the move and at the same time enforcing standards of safety falls. It is in the discharge of these duties that the suggestion is made that relations between the police and the public have deteriorated throughout the country. We have found no evidence to support this view. (Her Majesty's Chief Inspector of Constabulary 1960:60)

It was recognised that other factors were involved in the deterioration of police/public relations. And, according to Critchley (1967), had been since the mid-nineteenth century. The most important of these was an increasing feeling of public unease over allegations of police brutality and corruption, to which the media had begun to accord extensive coverage. In response to the worsening situation the Police Federation, in 1959, requested a meeting with the Home Secretary on police/public relations and issued the following statement:

There are a few black sheep in every service ... but the Police Federation is greatly disturbed at the way in which these few black sheep have been used in recent months to weaken the good relationship which has always existed between police and public. (Joint Central Committee of the Police Federation of England and Wales statement, 30 July 1959)

The statement continued that the Home Secretary would be informed that the nature and extent of such incidents had been greatly exaggerated and that police enforcement of legislation 'which the public is out of sympathy with - e.g. street betting, gaming, liquor licensing laws and many of the regulations concerning road traffic' (ibid.) were the cause of a diminution of public sympathy with the police. The Police Federation deputation met with the Home Secretary on 17 September 1959. It was reported that the Home Secretary pledged his support for the police and agreed to consider any proposals designed to improve relations between the police and the public. At a press conference following the meeting a member of the Police Federation deputation reported that 'the present trouble was felt to come from two main sources: recent adverse publicity, and the lack of sympathy among the public towards certain laws enforced by the Police - legislation concerning betting and gaming and certain aspects of the traffic laws particularly' (*Police Review* 67:644).

Whether bad publicity and unpopular laws were responsible rather than any serious problems with brutality and corruption remained to be seen; but it is perhaps understandable, if not acceptable, that the police were grateful to use the 'whipping boy' of road traffic laws as the more palatable explanation for diminishing public confidence and support. In any event issues of police/public relations had become inextricably linked with the question of effective enforcement of road traffic law. The Royal Commission on the Police, the Royal Warrant for which was signed in January 1960, was to examine these issues, which are considered further in Chapter 3.

Notes

1. Other jurisdictions were in a similar position - for Europe see Lasok 1962 and for Canada see Ward Smith 1960.

3 The impaired driver (1961-1966)

The world had changed considerably between 1929 and 1960, yet for practical purposes legal policy in relation to the drink-driver remained much the same - the offence still looked for drunkenness rather than any lesser form of intoxication on the part of the defendant. This becomes all the more remarkable when it is remembered that the position in 1929 was, in practical terms, little different in relation to drink-driving than it had been under the Licensing Act 1872.

Motoring law had developed significantly by 1960, as had many other areas relating to motor transport, such as vehicle production and road systems (Wilkinson 1960; Willett 1964; Plowden 1971), but extensive public concern continued over the problems caused by motoring, particularly road casualties, which had risen dramatically during the 1950s. Pressure for the reform of motoring law was strong. As mentioned above, various factors had come together to precipitate this pressure - the dramatic increase in the number of vehicles; the fact that motoring was no longer the sole domain of the privileged or even the middle classes; the increase in scientific knowledge regarding alcohol and traffic safety; the work of the Road Research Laboratory (established in 1946) in producing valuable information on traffic safety (Road Research Laboratory 1963;1965); the World Health Organization consideration of both alcohol and road traffic accidents as serious public health issues (Norman 1962); and the development of sophisticated media and communications systems which allowed the wide-scale dissemination of information. The last of these was particularly important - road accidents and casualty figures (together with special attention at Christmas and Bank Holidays) became regular features in the media, and 'the drink-driver seemed to become a particular target in the popular press during 1960 and 1961' (Willett 1964:77).

While Chapter 2 had witnessed little or no change in legal policy in relation to drink-driving, it had seen the development of scientific techniques which allowed the links between drinking, driving and traffic safety to be postulated. This was a crucial prerequisite for policy change. For while the relationship of alcohol to road casualties had been assumed for many years it was not until the 1950s that the necessary scientific evidence linking alcohol consumption to driving skills was established. However, there was still no conclusive statistical evidence which demonstrated the number of accidents which could be associated with levels of alcoholic intoxication. Chapter 3 saw this 'missing link' established.

Public and Parliamentary opinion had been tested and the experience of other countries considered - in particular, a working party of Ministry of Transport and Home Office officials, and police had visited Sweden in 1960. A working party was set up to examine the evidence on fixed limits and compulsory tests, but the proposals met with the disapproval of the Attorney General, with the result that they did not find their way into the 1962 Act.

During 1960 many Parliamentary Questions were asked on road safety, several on the number of drink-related accidents, deaths and injuries; others demanding tougher laws. The Government could no longer answer that it was awaiting the Drew report, and Parliamentary frustration over legislative inaction was becoming apparent. For example, in his address in reply to Her Majesty's Speech for the 1960-61 session, which had promised 'legislation designed to promote greater safety on the roads', Lord Silkin asked if the Government had 'made up their minds on the question of drivers who drive under the influence of drink, and what tests, if any, they propose to make, either on the lines that are being carried out in Scandinavian countries or elsewhere' (*Parl. Debs.* (Lords) 226:157). The Government continued to prevaricate. The Lord Chancellor replied that 'the Minister of Transport, the Attorney General and myself have been considering that point, and he (Silkin) need not think that it will be omitted from consideration in the (Road Safety) Bill. As to the final provision, I would ask him, again, to wait a little while' (ibid.,201).

Road Traffic Bill(s) 1961

The Bill was first introduced into the Lords on 21 March 1961. It received a Second Reading the following month at which Lord Chesham outlined what the Government hoped to achieve by the Bill:

Last year saw 6,970 people dead on the roads; it saw around 90,000 people seriously injured; it saw a further 240,000 injured to some lesser extent; and, if that is not enough to ram home to us not only the crushing, needless, wasteful cost in terms of human suffering and human misery, then we should look to the future. On the same basis the sixties may well see one

44

million people dead or seriously injured, and perhaps 20 million accidents. (*Parl.Debs.*(Lords) 230:340)

This, he continued, should be kept in mind by those 'who conceive it their duty to guard and preserve sectarian road users' rights'. However, on introducing the clauses in the Bill on drink-driving (clause 1 - new definition for the offence and clause 2 - introduction of blood-alcohol testing), Lord Chesham, while recognising the value of the work which had been carried out by the Medical Research Council and the BMA showing that even small doses of alcohol affect driving skill and judgement, noted 'but as the Medical Research Council has pointed out, none of the work establishes an unassailable case' (ibid.,345). This point was taken up by several speakers during the debate. For example: 'It seems to me that the important point is that we have no simple and comprehensive set of data establishing the exact relationship between drink and road accidents' (ibid.,345). And, although Baroness Wootton drew the attention of the House to the Evanston and Toronto studies referred to by Drew (1959), it was not until the publication of the Grand Rapids Survey (below) that the necessary evidence was finally to be made available. The rest of the debate on clauses 1 and 2 (which dominated the Bill's Second Reading) dealt mainly with problems of definition of the offence, other factors responsible for accidents, and doubts about, together with a lack of understanding of, the scientific evidence surrounding chemical testing. Many speeches questioned whether the Bill went far enough to ensure that 'it gave the hard evidence that the courts require' (ibid.,430). Compulsory chemical testing and the establishment of a blood-alcohol limit were debated. While all speakers expressed the view that the Bill was a non-party measure, the House seemed to divide instead on whether or not it accepted and fully trusted the available scientific evidence. This was clearly demonstrated at Committee where long debates on the nature and accuracy of the scientific evidence, particularly the breathalyser,[1] were conducted: 'None of us has seen this mysterious apparatus. Is it a thing like a chemical apparatus, or is it like a set of bagpipes? Is there any method by which the mouthpiece can be cleaned? Could a caste Hindu submit himself properly to this test or not?' (Lord Hawke, ibid.,1031).

The Bill was sent to the Commons on 13 June 1961. However, the Minister of Transport announced (19 July 1961) that there was insufficient Parliamentary time available for the passage of the Bill that session. This provoked strong objections as the 'purpose is to save lives so how many will be lost by delaying to the next session?' (*Parl.Debs.*(Commons) 644:1241). Further, as Baggott (1988:71) has put it: 'This, more than anything else, reflected the relatively low priority which the Bill had in the Government's legislative programme. Indeed there is no evidence of a conspiracy against the Bill within Government or Parliament since it was enacted in the following session, and became law in 1962'. The Bill was reintroduced, substantially unaltered, in the 1961-62 session on 1 November 1961. The debates largely followed the pattern of the earlier Bill. There was an attempt to include a blood-alcohol limit ('as prescribed by the Minister') at the Common's Second Reading, but this was defeated 199 to 159. The Bill received the Royal Assent on 1 August 1962, some 21 months after it had originally been introduced.

The Act aimed to overhaul motoring law and to 'toughen it up'. The latter was to be achieved by extended use of the penalty of disqualification from driving. Mandatory disqualification for a minimum of one year was proposed for a list of six offences - manslaughter, causing death by dangerous driving, reckless or dangerous driving if committed within three years of a similar offence, driving under the influence of drink or drugs, driving while disqualified and racing on the highway; discretionary disqualification for a further twenty offences; and compulsory disqualification for a minimum of six months for a third or subsequent conviction for any of the twenty-six offences ('totting-up' as it came to be called). Some of these proposals were, of course, already law. For example, in the case of drink-driving mandatory disqualification for a minimum of one year had been introduced by the Road Traffic Act 1930. But never before had the motorist faced such extensive possibilities of losing the right to drive. Not surprisingly, the proposals relating to disqualification were met with strong opposition, not only from the motoring organisations, but also from less partial sources. Willett (1964:78), writing at the time, said of the Act 'For British motoring law it is severe, and it is a more formidable measure than any before Parliament since 1903'.

The proposals for reform of the substantive law on drink-driving received much support, including a unanimous resolution at the annual conference of the Association of Police Surgeons in 1961 to 'support the Minister in his efforts to secure greater safety on the roads', but also met with considerable opposition, particularly from the motoring organisations; which challenged the provisions both on the new definition of the offence and the proposed introduction of blood-alcohol testing. Nevertheless, the proposals were enacted and became part of the Road Traffic Act 1962.

Road Traffic Act 1962

The drink-drive provisions of the Road Traffic Act 1962 (which became law on 20 December 1962) drew heavily for inspiration from the BMA report of 1960 and aimed to facilitate the conviction of guilty motorists. This was to be achieved by removing any confusion with drunkenness from the law; by the introduction of a clear standard for liability; and by solving problems of proof in these cases.

Impairment

To deal with the first two of these, the Act replaced 'incapable of having proper control' as the test for the purposes of 'unfitness to drive' under s.6 of the 1960 Act, with 'a person shall be taken to be unfit to drive if his ability to drive properly is for the time being impaired' (s.1). The new wording was intended to separate the drink-driving offence from the concept of 'drunkenness' by removing the word 'incapable' with its misleading association with 'drunk and incapable'. This, it was hoped, would avoid the problem of juries confusing the driving offence with drunkenness and acquitting anyone who could not be proved to have been drunk. Having said that, it was not clear what impairment actually meant. So that initial speculation ranged from a fear that the new test would 'For the majority of people mean that one drink would be an offence' (*Solicitors' Journal* 105:13) as the test was 'much less demanding than the older requirement that the offender should 'be under the influence of drink or drugs to such an extent as to be incapable of having proper control' (Willett 1964:78-9); to doubts as to 'whether it (the proposed new law) will make any significant impact on the tragic problem of road accidents' (*Solicitors' Journal* 105:13). Past experience of attempts to implement a workable definition for the offence led a leading criminal lawyer to comment that it 'would seem that the change in definition makes no difference at all in law; if a man's ability to drive properly is impaired, he is incapable of having proper control, unless there is some subtle distinction between proper driving and proper control' (Smith 1963:301). Others shared the view that the change in wording would make little difference to lay magistrates and juries as it was still the case that 'guilt depends on a matter of opinion (impairment) rather than on a matter of fact, since no minimum consumption of alcohol (or drugs) is specified' (Willett 1964:94). A commentator in *The Magistrate* (19:17) described s.1 as 'lawyers' law' which 'it is difficult to imagine will result in any noticeable change in this branch of the administration of justice, since all it does is to substitute one definition for another'.

It was, of course, inevitable in the absence of any guidance or indication as to what 'impaired' was to mean that uncertainty and confusion would result. (This may also have been the case if the Act had attempted guidance on the meaning of the word.) In order to establish whether or not the accused was in an impaired condition (whatever this meant) the court was to have regard to various factors, which could be offered as evidence. These were the way in which the car has been driven (the observation of witnesses, including police officers could be used), the defendant's physical and mental condition (ascertained by a clinical examination) and the amount of alcohol taken by the defendant as shown in a blood, urine or breath test (see below). Of these, the courts still favoured the clinical examination based on the BMA's tests, which received judicial approval from the Court of Criminal Appeal in *R v Somers* [1963] 3 All ER 808. Yet the clinical examination, which had been the main focus of attention for establishing the necessary degree of intoxication under previous legislation, had been declared inadequate. And its defects were by now well documented (e.g. BMA 1960; Anon 1964; Hirsh 1965). There were three main failings. First, the tests were too 'coarse' to indicate the mild stage of intoxication when a person may be in an unsuitable condition to drive; secondly, the tests were not standardised, so that one doctor's assessment of the degree of intoxication, as well as of the signs observed, may have differed from that of another; and, thirdly, the examination was conducted some time after the alleged offence was committed. As the Metropolitan Police Commissioner observed in 1962:

it is unlikely that a medical examination of a prisoner will start less than half or three-quarters of an hour after arrest and often not for one or even two hours. During this time the prisoner may, by shock and self-control, have sufficiently overcome some of the defects which led to his arrest, so as not to display them to any marked degree during a clinical examination. (Simpson 1963:50)

Further, the police claimed that some defendants could 'pull themselves together' for the examination, only to relapse into a state of severe intoxication 'as soon as heat was off'. This was said to result from a physiological and psychological 'alarm' reaction induced by the crisis in which the driver found him/herself. Indeed 'it is not unknown for a driver to satisfy the police surgeon only to have to be assisted from the police station after the crisis has passed and the symptoms of intoxication have re-asserted themselves' (Goldberg & Havard 1968).

By the 1960s some police forces were dispensing with the presence of a doctor altogether, unless the accused specifically requested that one should attend. This practice was criticised by some medical practitioners who, while fully acknowledging the limitations of the clinical tests, argued that although the police were in most cases better able to recognise intoxication, they would be less able to diagnose injury or illness. One suggestion put forward was that a medical officer should not be 'allowed to express an opinion on the question of intoxication but merely certify medical fitness' (Camps 1960:5). By 1964 this system was being operated by some police authorities who relied 'entirely on police evidence as to incapacity to drive, leaving the doctor to say only that the accused was, or was not, suffering from any illness which may have affected his driving' (Willett 1964:94). But when the police 'fortified by the BMA report ... began to dispense with medical evidence for the purpose of proving unfitness to drive. The courts ... were unwilling to acquiesce in such a change and criticised the police for failing to call medical evidence on the issue of fitness to drive' (Havard 1967:153-4).

The courts and the legal profession were generally still in favour of the use of clinical examinations, despite attempts to inform them of the tests' shortcomings. Typical of the mood of the lawyers was a leader in the *Solicitors' Journal* (106:152) which argued strongly that the defence should be supplied with a copy of the doctor's report and also that of the analyst where one had been obtained - 'What cannot be tolerated is the proposition that the prosecution can choose what evidence is to be available' and further, 'if the defendant had been fit to drive when he arrived it would be relevant in mitigation'. Willett (1964:95) found that police doctors were asked 'to say whether or not they thought the accused was fit to drive; and, if the delay was substantial and the driver had sobered, the doctor had to say so and the result was usually an acquittal'. The evidential difficulties encountered with previous drink-drive legislation were, it seemed, to similarly afflict the concept of 'impairment' under the 1962 Act. But the Act had made provision for this.

Evidence of impairment

The third aim of the Act, to deal with problems of proof, was covered by s.2 which required the court to have regard to the proportion of alcohol or drugs in the driver's body tissue as ascertained by a test of his blood, urine, or breath. The Act further provided that refusal to submit to such a test should be treated as support for the prosecution, unless reasonable cause for refusal could be shown.

Despite the Minister of Transport's enthusiastic welcome for statutory recognition of the results of chemical tests as evidence in court proceedings dealing with drink-drive charges (Marples 1963), it had been strongly opposed, particularly on the point that although the tests were voluntary, refusal to submit to one could be used against the accused unless he or she could show reasonable cause for that refusal. What constituted reasonable cause was not laid down in the Act. Wilkinson (1963:102) advised that reasonable cause to refuse a blood test might arise from religious beliefs or 'even a genuine fear of the needle', as 'One recalls the collapse of many parties, stout and thin, at inoculation parades in HM Forces'; while reasonable cause to refuse a urine test might arise, *inter alia*, from a physical inability to pass water or a physical disgust at the idea. On the question of breath tests Wilkinson (1963:101-2) advised that '(until) the Home Office have approved a breathalyser, the court must still have evidence of its accuracy, reliability and proper use on each occasion'. However, the provision in the Act relating to breath tests under s.2(6) was yet to come into force. The Home Secretary stated in Parliament that it could not be brought into force until 'the Government were satisfied that suitable arrangements could be made for taking and analysing breath samples (and) a working party was considering whether certain equipment used in Australia was suitable'.

Admissibility of the results of analytical tests (s.2(2)), and of refusal to submit to them, as evidence in court had at last moved the determination of a driver's fitness towards an objective scientific basis, but no maximum permitted level was included in the Act and no guidance was given on the level which might impair driving ability. And, 'in the absence of an agreed figure, there has been a general tendency to argue the case around 150mg/100ml ... and to dismiss 112mg/100ml unless supported by other strong evidence' (JTM. 1963:64). Also, as had been the case prior to the 1962 Act, chemical tests were to be used only as part of the evidence, along with other matters such as the observations of the arresting officer and the findings of the doctor called to examine the suspect; so that in practical terms the law was much the same as before the Act. Although a leader in *The Magistrate* (19:18), while criticising the absence of a fixed blood-alcohol limit, felt that s.2 'does a great deal more (than s.1) to put the drunken motorist on the spot'. And it was to be hoped that 'the statutory recognition of the tests will encourage their use and emphasize their value to the court' (Smith 1963:301). Others were less optimistic, as it soon became clear 'that the courts were not ready to accept blood-alcohol concentration as evidence of impairment of driving ability' (Havard 1967:155). Perhaps understandably, the courts felt uneasy with medical

49

calculations which they did not fully understand, and wanted to be told the amount of alcohol consumed by the defendant in terms which they did understand. So rather than relying on the results of the analytical tests, the courts almost invariably wanted to know what these tests meant in terms of how many alcoholic drinks the defendant had consumed. This information was available in the conversion tables contained in the BMA report of 1960.

The courts were not alone in wishing to have the permitted level of alcohol intake spelt out to them in terms which they recognised. When the BMA report was published, the press gave a high profile to the tables and in particular the figures of 1.5 and 4 pints of beer which were equated in the report with 55mg/100ml and 147mg/100ml respectively. The practice of translating blood-alcohol levels into measures of alcoholic drinks received judicial approval in the Court of Criminal Appeal in *R v Somers* [1963] (3 All ER 808) in which the analyst estimated, as a result of a urine sample, and the accused's statement that he had not had a drink for some two hours, a consumption of eight and a half pints of beer. The accused had admitted to drinking only six pints.

These calculations are inherently problematic, dependent as they are on a number of variables. When drawing up the tables the BMA had allowed all of these variables to operate so as to give the *lowest* possible alcohol consumption equivalent for each blood-alcohol concentration. This was done as the many varying factors, such as absorbtion rates, which had to be included in the calculations, could give rise to a wide variation in results, for the same number of drinks in different people, and in different situations. Further, from the results of these calculations were then taken the lowest possible number of alcoholic drinks which could correspond with the resulting blood-alcohol concentration. So that by using this method of assessing the number of alcoholic drinks a person had consumed, the courts would almost always arrive at a figure much lower than was actually the case. The difficulties inherent in producing accurate conversion tables led the BMA to omit them from its later reports.

Havard is highly critical of the courts' cautious approach to the results of analytical tests as evidence (Havard 1967, 1985), but it should be noted that the conversion tables, used by the courts, were produced by the BMA in the same spirit of caution and desire to resolve any doubt in favour of the defendant as was employed by the courts. Why did the BMA, in the light of the great advances made in scientific investigation between 1954 and 1962, not produce more realistic, updated conversion tables? Presumably, because it did not want to encourage the courts to depart from the analytical evidence, which was in line with its campaign to have a 'legal limit' of blood-alcohol concentration introduced, and also because, as has been said above, conversion tables accurate enough to be relied upon for the purposes of imposing criminal liability could not be produced. It was 'essential to educate courts and juries to understand that it is the amount of alcohol in the blood that is important, not the amount drunk' (Tryhorn & Smith 1963:289).

However, the main argument had now become clear, at least to some people - that while there were large variations in the effect which different numbers of alcoholic drinks produced on different people, in different circumstances (as the amount of alcohol getting to the blood varied), 'there is a relatively constant relationship between blood-alcohol concentration and ability to drive properly' (BMA 1965:14). This was the factual criterion which was needed, and it could be objectively measured. Although this approach could be subjected to the criticism that 'a quantity (of alcohol) that will cause impairment in one person will not do so in another, and we are then back to relying on opinion unless it is decided to give the 'reasonable man' a tolerance level and make anything in excess of that evidence of impairment' (Willett 1964:94).

Legal obstacles

As we have seen, the legal profession contributed to the failure of the early legislative attempts to control the drink-driver. Lawyers argued that they had a duty to act in the best interests of their clients, even if this meant discrediting medical evidence. Further, due to the adversarial nature of court proceedings, and the way in which 'differences of opinion which are often of no scientific significance may be brought out' in court:

A public image is created of the doctor called by the police giving medical evidence to try to get the accused convicted, and of the doctor giving evidence for the defence trying to get him acquitted. Experienced doctors are well aware of the dangers inherent in such a situation and are at great pains to emphasize and preserve their position as impartial witnesses. (BMA 1965:26)

While this approach could in some ways be understood as a traditional reluctance by the legal system to accept the findings of scientific techniques with which it was unfamiliar, there seems to be no explanation for the quite exceptional way in which the courts dealt with admissibility of evidence in drink-driving cases. The question of the exclusion of evidence was dealt with in a way which is quite exceptional in English law (tax evasion cases are another example). Rarely do judges exercise their discretion to exclude evidence improperly obtained - concentrating more on the relevance of the evidence to the issue rather than the means employed to obtain it - yet in *R v Court* [1962] Crim LR 697, the court held that when a driver had consented to an examination by a police surgeon and he had been told before he consented that the results would not be used in evidence, then they could not be. This ran contrary to authority, for it had been decided by the Privy Council that evidence (other than a confession) was not rendered inadmissible if obtained illegally or by a trick: *Kuruma v R* [1955] PC 197. When considering the point in the later, and similar, case of *R v Payne* [1963] 1 All ER 848, one commentator observed:

The scrupulousness of the court to be fair to the accused in these cases contrasts strangely with such cases as *R v Rumpling* [1962] 2 All ER 233 where it was held that an intercepted letter was admissible against the accused ... Would the evidence in the present case have been excluded had it been relevant to a charge of murder? It is thought that it is very likely that

51

it would have been admitted. And yet, surely the graver the charge, the more strictly ought the rules to be applied in favour of the accused. (1963 Crim LR.:288-9)

This approach, on exclusion of evidence in drink-drive cases, which may have been adopted because lawyers still believed that the accused was in effect giving evidence against him/herself, is considered further in Chapters 4 and 6. The medical world was firmly committed to effective measures against drink-driving, so too appeared to be the police (subject to their reservations regarding police/public relations). But what of the lawyers? The Oxford jurist A.L. Goodhart (1963:89) had concluded his address to the Third International Conference on Traffic Safety in 1962, by saying:

What a valuable part the members of the legal profession could play in bringing about an essential reform of the law if they would help to sweep away some of the existing misconceptions. This will not be an easy task, but until it is accomplished the enforcement of the law against driving while unfit through drink will continue to be haphazard and difficult.

In answer to his question 'why is the law unable to play a more efficient part in dealing with this evil?' Goodhart gave a threefold reply. First, there was the problem of confusion with the need for drunkenness, even when high levels of alcohol intake were proved.[2] The only solution to this problem was, he said, the introduction of a fixed limit. Secondly, the reluctance of juries to convict; and this too would be greatly alleviated by the introduction of a fixed limit, for 'scientific evidence has a great effect on the modern jury'. The third problem he saw as evidential, with the solution being the introduction of compulsory blood tests. These had been debated in the House of Lords during the passage of the Road Traffic Bill in 1962, where Lord Hailsham, the Minister for Science, had claimed that such tests would be dangerous to persons suffering from haemophilia. A view described by one doctor as 'blithering scientific nonsense from the Minister of Science'. Goodhart also dismissed what he called 'a more serious objection to the test, that it is said to violate the basic principle of the English common law that no man shall be compelled, directly or indirectly, to give evidence against himself', by distinguishing the tests as a 'case of physical evidence, where it is not the person speaking, but the fact itself'. In support, he quoted with approval the decision of the United States Supreme Court in *Breithaupt v Abram* which had rejected such an argument in a similar case in 1957. He also pointed to the fact that 47 US States used chemical tests, including blood tests, in drink-drive cases.

Blood-alcohol limit

The 1962 Act achieved very little. A matter of months after it was passed the Minister of Transport indicated at an international conference that he was having doubts as to how effective it would be (Marples 1963). As a contemporary legal journal put it: 'If these doubts are realised it is to be hoped he will do better than to offer once again his personal solution - to drink himself and to let his wife drive (for) road traffic is itself the killer of the 20th century - mixed with alcohol it becomes even more lethal' (*JPN* 126:580).

Questions were asked in Parliament about the effectiveness of the Act, particular concern being voiced about the relationship of alcohol to Christmas accident figures. When the Road Research Laboratory (1964) figures for Christmas 1963 were published they 'reinforced the main conclusions of the 1959 report by the Road Research Laboratory that drink is the main cause of the increased accident rate at Christmas' (Lord Chesham, *Parl.Debs.*(Lords) 258:6638). But Lord Chesham continued by advising that the 1962 Act had to be given 'time to work' and that in any case 'alteration of the law is not by itself enough'. He announced the launch of a publicity/education campaign 'to make it plain to all that it is dangerous to drive after drinking even small doses of alcohol' (see below). But this did not silence the Act's critics and questions continued to be asked. Five questions were asked on the Christmas and New Year road accident figures on 3 March 1965. Interestingly, in reply to these the Government stated that it was not against the introduction of a blood-alcohol limit, but that it was waiting for the latest Road Research Laboratory findings before it could commit itself. Also, as Graham Page had put a second Bill before the House (see below), the Minister would take the opportunity of putting the Government position during the passage of the Page Bill.

The House of Commons had rejected the idea of a fixed blood-alcohol level on four grounds. First, it was felt that if a maximum limit was to be set, there would be some people who would be impaired below this limit and it would be extremely difficult to prosecute them successfully; secondly, it might give the impression that it was safe to drink up to the limit, which would not be the case; thirdly, the existence of a limit might lead suspects to refuse to submit to a test; and fourthly, the idea of compulsion would probably not get the support of public opinion. The first two arguments were rather weak, and would, in any event, be largely defeated with the introduction of a realistically low blood-alcohol level. The third could be dealt with by making it an offence to refuse to take a blood-alcohol test, and, lastly, the law can lead public opinion.

There was by now comprehensive scientific evidence on the relationship of driver impairment to blood-alcohol content (Havard 1962, 1963a). And 1962 saw drink-driving given a high profile in Britain with the holding of the third international conference on alcohol and traffic safety in London. The conference attracted some 220 delegates from 22 countries. The proceedings, published in 1963 (Havard 1963), run to more than 350 pages and contain a definitive account of the state of knowledge at the time. The conference was a highly prestigious event. Prince Philip was its Patron, the Minister of Transport its President, and the world's leading authorities presented papers. The conference/conference proceedings were widely reported/reviewed and did a great deal to stimulate debate on the issues. In particular, international comparisons were made widely available for the first time. However, despite an acceptance of the relationship of blood-alcohol content to impairment, there remained a further argument to put against the introduction of a blood-alcohol limit. This was that such an objective arbitrary level could lead to a person

53

being convicted, not because that person was unfit to drive, but because somebody else might well have been in the circumstances. To meet this point more evidence of the relationship between blood-alcohol concentrations and traffic accidents was needed, for although 'powerful and impressive evidence was available as to the effect of alcohol at various concentrations on impairment ... there was very little about its effect on actual risk of involvement in an accident' (Havard 1985:6).

The Grand Rapids Survey This was remedied in 1964 with the publication of what has become known as the *'Grand Rapids Survey'* (Dale 1964). This was the largest and most detailed study which had then been conducted of the relationship of alcohol to traffic accidents. The study was carried out over a three-year period in Grand Rapids, Michigan. It involved studying the case histories of thousands of drivers. The survey concluded that above 50mg/100ml both accident involvement and responsibility increase rapidly and that compared with a level of 10mg/100ml a person with 60mg/100ml was twice as likely to be responsible for causing an accident. At a blood-alcohol level of 100mg/100ml a person would be six to seven times more likely to be involved in and responsible for an accident, and this would rise to 21 times at a level of 160mg/100ml This study was to have major international impact and would be extensively cited in the forthcoming White Paper (Ministry of Transport 1965 - see below).

There now existed a comprehensive body of international literature on the relationship of alcohol to traffic safety. The link between alcohol and vehicle crashes had been made. The necessary response to the drink-driver could now be implemented. It consisted of the introduction of a blood-alcohol limit together with compulsory chemical testing. This information now needed to be acted upon. To this end two initiatives were taken. First, the introduction of the Road Safety Bill 1964, and secondly, publication by the BMA of *The Drinking Driver*.

Road Safety Bill 1964

Graham Page introduced a Bill in the House of Commons on 17 January 1964, which would make it an offence to drive a vehicle or to walk unaccompanied on a road above a specified blood-alcohol level. The Bill commenced its Second Reading on 28 February but after some debate it was adjourned to 24 April, then deferred to 8 May and again to the 26 June and then lost. Page reintroduced the Bill in the next session (1964-65), under the new Labour Government returned in October 1964, on 4 December. After being twice deferred it commenced its Second Reading on 18 June 1965. It was in this debate that the Grand Rapids evidence was used for the first time. The strength of this evidence combined with an administration sympathetic to making the drink-drive laws more effective finally provided the political climate necessary for fundamental reform of the law. The Minister of Transport pledged support for the Bill and expressed the Government's intention to introduce a fixed limit and the breathalyser. In view of this statement, Page withdrew the Bill. The political stage was set for the introduction of a blood-alcohol limit and chemical testing.

The Drinking Driver 1965

In 1964 the terms of reference of the BMA's Special Committee were redrafted: 'To advise the Council on the medical aspects of the prevention of traffic accidents with reference to the part played by alcohol or other drugs, and to keep up to date the reports which have so far been published by the Association on the subject'. The Committee surveyed the scientific literature relating to alcohol and traffic accidents and published it in *The Drinking Driver* in 1965. The report provided a comprehensive and accessible account of the state of scientific knowledge at the time. In it the Committee surveyed its own previous publications and updated them in line with current thinking. In particular, while supporting its previous contention (BMA 1960) that the clinical examination of the defendant after his arrest is essential in order to help establish whether his behaviour was due to any factor other than intoxication, such as illness or injury, the Committee stressed that the court should no longer rely on the clinical examination to determine whether ability to drive properly has been impaired by alcohol as, 'in the absence of chemical tests of the concentration of alcohol in the tissue' the test 'is neither sufficiently sensitive, nor reliable enough to detect deterioration in driving ability unless it is considerable' (BMA 1965:15).

While a definition such as 'impairment' remained, the report suggested that it should be measured by other methods, such as those discussed above. But the report put forward a very strong case for the abandonment of such subjective definitions and the introduction of a fixed blood-alcohol limit. The offence would involve driving with a blood-alcohol level over a fixed limit, no other evidence, including clinical examination would be required or permitted. At what level should the limit be set? The Grand Rapids Survey had demonstrated the link between blood-alcohol level and accident responsibility. From this the report argued that the limit should be fixed at a level which reflected the findings of this work. Examples from other jurisdictions were considered by referring to a table of comparative legislation contained in a previous BMA report. Some countries had a level as high as 150mg/100ml, several others had adopted a level of 50mg/100ml, the lowest was Czechoslovakia at 30mg/100ml (BMA 1960:38-44). Further guidance was available from an international conference held in Rome which had unanimously resolved that in no circumstances could a blood-alcohol concentration in excess of 50mg/100ml be permitted in drivers of motor vehicles on the public highway. The Committee believed that this evidence confirmed the conclusions reached in its previous report that 'a concentration of 50mg/100ml is the highest that can be accepted as entirely consistent with the safety of other road users' (BMA 1960:31-2). At 60mg/100ml the report noted that drivers are twice as likely to be responsible for causing an accident. Yet the report did not recommend that a limit of 50mg/100ml should be introduced in Britain, rather, it seemed to be persuaded by the fact that 'The recent evidence ... shows that, although the degree of impairment and risk of accident involvement varies between different individuals at concentrations in the blood up to 80mg/100ml, the variable factors responsible for these differences are dominated by alcohol in concentrations above this concentration' (p.10).

This 'recent evidence' seems to be exclusively that of Drew et al. (1958;1959). So that although the Committee felt it necessary to qualify the view expressed in its 1960 report on the higher levels of 100mg/100ml and 150mg/100ml, it went for what can only be described as a rather weak compromise for the maximum permitted level: 'there is now adequate scientific evidence to support legislation making it an offence ... for a person with a blood-alcohol concentration in excess of 80mg/100ml to drive a motor vehicle on the public highway'. This was to prove highly influential when Government legislation was finally introduced. The Minister had said during the Second Reading of the Page Bill in June 1965 that when he had first considered the introduction of a fixed limit he had started at 100mg/100ml, 'then last Christmas' he decided that 50mg/100ml was the figure to introduce, but in view of the BMA report he had now adjusted this upwards to 80mg/100ml. The report did stress that a level of less than 80mg/100ml was in no way an indication that a person's ability to drive was not impaired. A decision was taken to recommend a limit which would not be so low as to catch unimpaired drivers, but would allow some impaired drivers to escape liability. The wrong decision was taken. A limit of 50mg/100ml may have brought in some drivers who were not substantially impaired, but it would not have allowed substantially impaired drivers to escape liability, as the Committee acknowledged a limit of 80mg/100ml would (we shall return to this later).

Having established a case for a blood-alcohol limit, the report moved on to the question of how the new offence was to be proved. At the time of publication the provisions of the 1962 Act relating to breath testing had yet to come into force (in fact they were never used under the 1962 Act); nevertheless, the report recommended breath testing over taking blood or urine samples. Details of breath testing procedures, together with examples of apparatus used in other jurisdictions were presented, and a recommendation was made that a procedure for taking breath 'should be introduced as soon as possible'.

The BMA in previous publications had favoured the use of urine tests for the purposes of blood-alcohol estimations, being easier to collect than blood (BMA 1953); but the Committee now favoured blood or breath as they had proved more reliable. The taking of urine had always caused problems For, in the words of then Director of the Metropolitan Police Laboratory: 'Particularly in Great Britain there is an instinctive dislike of admitting any knowledge at all of the existence of urine' (*JPN* 128:545). However, the taking of blood had been met with particular reluctance; and matters were not helped by the method of obtaining a sample - a 'deep puncture' in a disinfected ear lobe or finger tip was to be made with 'a sterile, dry, sharp lancet so that the blood oozes out spontaneously' (BMA 1965:34). In the absence of an approved breath analyser the less reliable method of testing of urine would continue. If compulsory testing was to be introduced it would be essential to be able to utilise breath testing.

Would compulsory evidential blood-alcohol testing be introduced? The Government had acknowledged the influence of the BMA's previous report in the creation of the Road Traffic Act 1962 and it seemed likely that the 1965 report would be similarly influential. The Minister of Transport in a written answer stated that he expected to receive soon the BMA's latest report (which was at that date yet to be published) as well as the report of a Home Office Working Party on breath-testing equipment; and that 'the Government accept in principle that it should be an offence to drive with more than a prescribed amount of alcohol in the blood'. He went on to promise a Bill to this effect 'at the first convenient opportunity'. A White Paper was published later the same year, a Bill introduced the following year and the Road Safety Act passed in 1967.

Build-up to the Road Safety Act 1967

By the early 1960s the large number of motoring cases coming before the courts, coupled with the seemingly ambivalent attitude of the criminal justice system towards them, became a cause for concern. Further, the degree of moral turpitude attributed to motoring offenders appeared to be low. There was also a commonly held view that the motoring offender was an otherwise law abiding citizen (a view supported by the motoring organisations, which were still seen by the Government as important indicators of the state of opinion among motorists). Little was actually known about motoring offenders, for although there had been much research conducted into various aspects of motoring (e.g. the scientific research on alcohol and traffic safety) minimal work had been done on the motoring offenders themselves. The first domestic attempt to provide some of this information was Willett's study, *Criminal on the Road*, published in 1964.

Willett directed his attention to what he called the 'serious motoring offender', and set out to test some of the assumptions commonly surrounding them. He identified six offences for inclusion as serious - causing death by dangerous driving, and manslaughter; driving recklessly or dangerously; driving under the influence of drink or drugs; driving while disqualified; failing to insure against third party risks; and failing to stop after, or to report, an accident. Willett conducted a comparative literature review; a survey of the law and its historical development; an examination of the relationship between the police and the motorist; and an empirical study of 653 offenders drawn from police files, supplemented by interviews with 43 offenders. The resulting material being 'a mixture of fact and impression'. The work generated much interest and was widely reviewed. Two of Willett's findings were singled out for particular comment. First, that contrary to what everybody had apparently thought, motorists who break the law are not otherwise law abiding citizens from across the driving spectrum - rather, they are likely to be male, semi-skilled or un-skilled, in their early twenties with convictions for non-motoring offences.

Secondly, that the drink-driver was an exception to this - being likely to be a middle aged, middle class man with extensive driving experience.

However, a later analysis of Willett's data challenged these assertions, pointing out two fundamental problems with Willett's study. First, Willett had neglected to re-weight his data to take account of different sample sizes among the six offences; and, secondly, Willett's conclusion that all six types of motoring offender were tearaways who also committed other offences such as burglary and theft was wrong - for if the offenders were split into two groups - 'dishonesty offences' and 'moving offences' - that aside from the two 'dishonesty offences' (driving while disqualified and failure to insure against third party risks) '"driving" offenders', according to their social characteristics, 'were not criminals on the road, but average motorists' (Steer & Carr-Hill 1967:224). Despite this quite justified critique by Steer & Carr-Hill and the fact that much of Willett's work, in particular its desire to establish whether the motoring offender is an otherwise respectable and law-abiding citizen now seems rather dated, Willett's work was important. In the long term, because it was a pioneering piece of research which stimulated others to take an interest in motoring offences, and in the short term, because it generated debate and provided information for pressure groups and policy makers.

In relation to the drink-driver Willett (1964:92) observed that 'of all serious motoring offenders, the drunken driver is one of the most controversial and least popular, and the impression is that he has now replaced the 'road hog' as a target'. If true, this may have been due in some part to the continuing efforts at propaganda being carried out by the Government. Dismissed by many as a cheap high-profile way of doing nothing very much, efforts in this direction nevertheless continued. In November 1964 the Government launched what it claimed to be the largest ever publicity campaign on road safety. It was to reach its peak at Christmas and its aim was to make drink-driving socially unacceptable by creating an awareness of the dangers of mixing the two. The Road Research Laboratory (1964) evaluated the campaign with a *before* and *after* survey of public attitudes towards drink-driving, which 'confirmed the findings of previous reports that alcohol was one of the main reasons for the above-average accident rate over the holiday period' (Ministry of Transport 1965a).

The Government considered that a major difficulty with drink-drive legislation had been the fact that many people seemed to feel that it was not the law's business to tell them how much they could or could not drink. Also, despite the obvious danger of combining alcohol with driving, there was a widely held belief that it was 'the other driver' who was a menace, the person who was not a good driver anyway. For these reasons the Ministry of Transport was 'anxious not to be thought to be preaching' (*JPN* 128:799). It directed the campaign towards increasing public awareness of the legal and medical facts about drink-driving. The number of drinks which would reach the generally accepted level of impairment of 50mg/100ml was given and this was said to be as little as one and a half pints of beer or three single whiskies. (It is interesting to note that 80mg rather than 50mg/100ml was eventually put into the 1967 legislation.)

By 1965 disillusionment was being expressed with the Government publicity campaign. It was widely felt that 'mere exhortation' was not enough to discourage drink-driving. Although the Ministry of Transport expressed the view that its half-million-pound campaign in the winter of 1964 had 'accelerated the change which was already taking place in the attitude of the public on the subject and made drivers better informed about the problem' (Ministry of Transport 1965:16); it had to qualify this by admitting that 'there is little evidence that it affected the behaviour of those who drink before driving'. This, together with what was now being termed the 'Christmas slaughter' on the roads; the availability of evidence on the ineffectiveness of existing legislation; the fact that 'the colloquialism "drunk in charge" dies hard in the folk memory' (*JPN* 128:799); the increasing public and media preoccupation 'with this social menace on our roads' (Doherty 1965); and the availability of scientific blood-alcohol testing, meant that some form of statutory blood-alcohol level was the only way forward. Also published in 1965 were the road casualty figures for 1964 (7,952 killed and 398,000 injured), 'the worst ever in Great Britain in peace time' (Ministry of Transport 1965).

There had been several significant developments since the 'compromise' Act of 1962. First, the Grand Rapids Survey had provided the final scientific evidence needed to link alcohol and traffic casualties; secondly, the evidence supplied by the BMA and Road Research Laboratory had reduced resistance to reform, even from the motoring organisations; and thirdly, a change of government in 1964 brought with it a new Minister of Transport who was sympathetic to the case for reform of the law and an administration more likely to carry it through - it is to say the least doubtful whether the previous Conservative administration would have passed the Road Safety Act.

A review of the law was jointly undertaken by the Home Office and the Ministry of Transport in 1964/5. It accepted the need for a fixed limit, but outlined two issues which remained to be resolved. The first was the level at which the limit should be set, and the second was how it should be enforced. As discussed above, the BMA had come out strongly in favour of a limit of 80mg/100ml. This was accepted by the Government. More contentious was the issue of police enforcement powers. A White Paper was published in 1965.

White Paper - *Road Safety Legislation* 1965

The White Paper set out the background to the Government's programme of road safety legislation on drink-driving and goods vehicles. Drink-driving was identified as one of a number of factors which combine to cause road accidents, 'but it is a serious one (that) can be avoided more easily than others'. The case against drink-driving was put by a review of the scientific evidence on alcohol and traffic safety and an account of the findings of the Grand Rapids Survey. The latter was crucial, as it had provided the evidence necessary to link blood-alcohol levels with accident risk and involvement. The view was expressed that:

The prevention of road accidents caused by drink is largely a social problem. Many people have grown accustomed to drive to and from places where they consume alcohol and, as the ownership and use of private transport increases, the problem will grow, unless steps are taken to solve it. If the deaths and casualties caused by alcohol are to be prevented, social habits must change. People must either severely restrict the amount they drink before driving or they must arrange their social lives so that they do not need to drive after drinking. There is no other alternative. (para.15)

The role of legal policy was considered and the existing law examined and found wanting. In particular, problems generated by the term 'impairment' were illustrated by reference to figures for acquittals at Quarter Sessions in the Metropolitan Police District in the last quarter of 1964. A third of the drivers committed for trial who had been shown by urine analysis to have blood-alcohol concentrations over 200mg/100ml had been acquitted, as had nearly half of those with levels between 150 and 200mg/100ml. The law was 'clearly unsatisfactory'. The White Paper recommended that a blood-alcohol limit be introduced, set at 80mg/100ml - based on Drew (1959); BMA (1965). To deal with drivers below this level 'the existing law should be retained ... where evidence of "impairment" can be shown'. It was further recommended that 'the Minister of Transport should be empowered to vary the prescribed concentration, subject to affirmative resolution of both Houses of Parliament, if this appears desirable in the light of experience'.

The question of enforcement was also considered. Under existing legislation the police could arrest only those drivers whom they considered to be impaired by alcohol or other drugs. In practice this meant those whose driving ability was *obviously* affected. These would be the worst cases of drink-driving. The introduction of the fixed limit would ensure that if apprehended these drivers would no longer be able to escape conviction. But without a change in police powers only these *obvious* cases would be stopped and tested - thus allowing those who were impaired and 'over the limit', but who showed no outward signs of this, to escape arrest. This would not only allow many drivers to escape conviction, but would also have an adverse effect on the deterrent value of the law. The White Paper put forward two possibilities for strengthened police powers, both of which involved roadside screening checks by use of a portable breath test device. The first was to empower the police to make spot checks by stopping vehicles at random and requiring the driver to submit to a screening breath test. There would be no need for the officer to suspect that the driver had been drinking. The second was to empower the police to stop and breath test only in cases where the officer had grounds to suspect that the driver had been drinking alcohol. These tests 'would tend to be made outside places where drink was known to be consumed, such as public houses, hotels and clubs'. Of the two: 'The Government considers that random checks would be preferable. These checks would be completely fair and undiscriminating ... They would be the most effective deterrent since any driver would be liable to be stopped at any time to see whether he had exceeded the statutory blood-alcohol level' (para.32). If a driver refused or was unable to take a breath test it was recommended that this should constitute an offence, unless the driver could show 'reasonable grounds' for refusal. The White Paper recognised the 'drastic' nature of its proposals, but felt them necessary to make the law effective.[3] Despite favouring breath analysis it recommended that further work was necessary to produce breath-test apparatus reliable enough to be used for evidential purposes. Consequently, in the meantime, blood/urine tests were to be utilised.

The White Paper attracted a good deal of attention, both in the popular and technical press. Most of the editorial space given to the proposals in the legal press was very positive. But the proposed roadside breath tests attracted adverse comment. Lawyers were quick to point out the vagueness and uncertainty of some of the terms used in the White Paper, while the press extensively debated the civil liberties implications of the police having power to stop and test the breath of any motorist, whether or not that motorist was suspected of having consumed too much, or even any, alcohol. Strong opposition to random testing was mobilised. The Law Society came out against it, as did the motoring organisations. It was eventually dropped. Baggott (1988,1990) has examined the political machinations which led to the dropping of random testing from the legislative provisions. The main attack came from the motoring organisations, but while these had traditionally exerted influential pressure on the Ministry of Transport, which felt the need to secure their support to publicise new measures, the Home Office, which was responsible for the White Paper, did not feel subject to the same pressure and was determined to press ahead with the measures. The motoring organisations therefore took their attack into Parliament. Here they had strong support from the Conservative Parliamentary Transport Committee. The Labour Government, with a majority of only four in the House of Commons, feared the possibility of an embarrassing defeat, and also had to take notice of the fact that the police, while keen to see the law on drink-driving tightened up, were concerned about the resource implications of random testing, and the possibility of generating adverse public reaction. Added to this was a further impediment concerning Barbara Castle, the newly-appointed Minister responsible for the legislation. She had become personally associated with the measures, as she had with the 70 mph speed limit, which had attracted strong opposition, a short time before. And 'conveniently symbolic was Mrs Castle's own inability to drive a car ... she was widely attacked as an unsuitable appointment to Transport on that score (which) helped to sharpen the opposition to the new Road Safety Bill which she introduced in 1966' (Plowden 1971:356).

Road Safety Bill 1966

The Road Safety Bill was introduced on 27 January 1966. Following the White Paper, it contained provisions relating to goods vehicles and drink-driving. Only the latter will be considered here. At Second Reading the debates ranged over most of the issues contained in the White Paper; mainly on technical details, the setting of the blood-alcohol level and the issue of random testing. The most contentious provisions were, as expected, those dealing with random testing. Seven Members spoke in favour of random testing and nine against. Many of those who spoke against based their opposition on what they saw as a threat to fundamental civil liberties; although it is interesting to note that the provisions in the Bill relating to the random testing of goods vehicles were not questioned in any of the debates. Most of the opposition came from Members associated with the Conservative Transport Committee and 'significantly one of the most vociferous of those speaking against the measures was the RAC's Parliamentary consultant, Sir Richard Nugent MP' (Baggott 1988:75). However, Nugent was also the Vice-President of RoSPA and his contribution to the debate was well matched by Graham Page, who was Chairman of the Pedestrians' Association.

The Bill passed its Second Reading but was interrupted by a General Election in March and lost. The Labour party was re-elected and Barbara Castle continued as Minister of Transport; but when the Bill was reintroduced (9 August 1966) it had been toned down. Random testing had gone and the police were to have only limited testing powers (but as to whether the police actually wanted increased powers see below). Drivers could be required to submit to a test only if they appeared to be under the influence of alcohol; had committed a moving traffic offence; or had been involved in an accident. Moving the Bill's Second Reading Castle referred to the dropping of random testing and said that in the original Bill it had 'aroused more than just disagreement. It aroused in some quarters almost hysterical and irrational opposition'. Despite this, the Minister retained the view that random testing would provide the most effective deterrent, but that the main objective was to change attitudes to drink-driving. This would not be achieved, Castle claimed, by 'legal procedures which are widely regarded as unfair to those affected by them'. So that:

> Though the opposition to this proposal totally failed to convince me that our plans were wrong it did convince me that enough people thought we would in some sense unjustly persecute completely innocent motorists to make me think again. It is on the basis of this analysis of public opinion, as well as on other reasons on which I will touch, that the Bill had been changed. (*Parl.Debs.*(Commons) 735:985)

Castle denied that the pressure had come from organised lobbying. It had not been the motoring organisations which had changed her mind, she said, it had been public opinion 'that came into Members of Parliament and the Department of a strength of feeling which was genuinely held in some quarters, quite apart from the motoring organisations' (ibid.,986). This is difficult to accept, as the evidence from opinion polls suggested the opposite. In a poll in January 1966, 59 per cent of those asked were reported to favour random testing (Gallup 1977:849) and in early 1967 some 71 per cent were said to believe that 'the Government's measures are not strong enough'. As for the 'other reasons', these were not forthcoming. However, during the Lords' debates on the Transport Bill 1981, Lord Houghton referred back to this issue and to 'the longest discussion in the Cabinet that I remember in my time' - he attributed the loss of random testing to the Minister of Transport who 'feared not only that we would have the motoring organisations against us, but also many of our own supporters too' and the then Home Secretary, Roy Jenkins, who was 'concerned about relations between the public and the police'. As Jenkins had embarked on a programme to modernize the police, which included a massive re-organisation involving a reduction in the number of forces from some 120 to around 50 and the introduction of unit-beat policing, Jenkins was not prepared to risk any adverse effects on his plans caused by alienating the police and/or damaging police/public relations at such a crucial time.

Despite Castle's denials, it is clear that the organised opposition to random testing (consisting chiefly of the motoring organisations, the Police Federation,[4] the licensed trade[5] and the Conservative Transport Committee[6]) had taken the opportunity provided by the loss of the original Bill to mobilise their forces. And they had won a 'significant victory. Random testing had been dropped to save the rest of the legislative package' (Baggott 1988:76). There was some surprisingly fierce press reaction:

> Plans to allow random testing were abandoned because the motoring lobby claimed that it would be a gross infringement of individual freedom. Of course it would. It would attack the freedom of the motorist to kill and injure innocent people through their own lack of thought. It would attack the freedom to roar off from the public house in a spurious glow of confidence and speed fearlessly through a built-up area. It would attack the freedom to saturate the reactions with so much alcohol that all judgement, timing and driving skill is lost. Are these freedoms worth preserving? (Leader, *Daily Mail*, 28 December 1966)

During the passage of the Bill through the Commons an attempt was made to introduce an amendment to insert random testing. This provoked a lengthy and heated debate, during which it was said that: 'The real issue is not how many drunken drivers the police may pick up but how many drivers we can prevent from reaching that drunken condition' (general deterrence is still the main argument put forward in favour of random testing today - see below). As expected, the amendment was withdrawn as 'I recognise that my right hon. Friend is breaking new ground with the Bill and that this is a highly contentious and difficult sphere. I hope that she will give further thought to the matter and may possibly even arrange for a suitable Amendment to be introduced in another place' (Hooley, *Parl.Debs.*(Commons) 741:1233). An amendment was moved at the Lords' Committee stage, by Baroness Wootton, who in an excellent performance stressed that the 'real deterrent to any offence, is not so much the severity of the punishment as the certainty of detection' (a view shared by many penologists and, in its modern form, originating with Bentham). Wootton went on to point out that clear agreement on the potential effectiveness of random testing had emerged during the debates in both Houses and that it had only been dropped due to the opinion of the motoring organisations or of a wider public. Feeling it necessary for the House to give a clear statement of its opinion in favour of random testing, and fearing that Members would vote not on their opinion, but out of party loyalty, Wootton reluctantly withdrew the amendment.

It was clear from the debates during the passage of the Bill that the relationship between alcohol and road accidents was accepted. Extensive references were made to the scientific studies outlined in the White Paper, particularly the Grand Rapids survey. There was debate on the blood-alcohol level - some thought it too low, more thought it should be 50mg or less, but most were content to accept it at 80mg on the 'recommendation of the BMA and bearing in mind the views put forward by the Medical Research Council' (*Parl.Debs.*(Commons) 735:982). Although there was 'provision for the Minister of Transport to lay down a different level by regulations should the existing prescribed limit prove unfair or unsatisfactory' (*Parl.Debs.*(Lords) 281:303-4). The Bill was on the whole generally welcomed by both Houses. It received the Royal assent on 10 May 1967.

Despite its failure to introduce random breath testing powers The Road Safety Act nevertheless represented a radical change in legal policy in relation to the drink-driver, changing completely the basis on which the law operated. For the first time in England and Wales an objective criterion had been laid down governing the relationship between alcohol consumption and driving - removing difficulties surrounding the definition of the offence and the subsequent problems of establishing the offence in the courts. Also, chemical testing and the compulsory provision of a sample of breath and blood/urine were introduced. The biggest impact on the public and the media was provided by the provision for roadside testing using the 'breathalyser'. This instrument though it has been considerably modified remains the symbolic heart of legal policy and the drink-driver. Subsequent developments in legal policy have refined the law introduced by the 1967 Act but the basic principles remain; and in October 1992 the 'breathalyser' celebrated its 25th anniversary. The impact and effectiveness of the new law is considered in Chapter 4.

Policing the drink-driver

Before moving on to the introduction of the Road Safety Act it is appropriate to return to and look more closely at the role and attitudes of the police in relation to legal policy and the drink-driver; which can affect the way in which drink-driving is actually policed by individual officers, the operational policies formulated by each Constabulary and the success or otherwise of proposed changes in the law.

The police position was that a conflict existed in policing motoring offenders between protecting public safety and fostering police/public relations. For example, the 1961 annual report of the Chief Constable of Kent found it 'rather disconcerting that when concerned in traffic law enforcement (he had) many critics and few supporters'; a position made worse, according to a *Police Review* (70:853) leader of 1962, by inconsistent enforcement policies between force areas (158 at the time). As mentioned at the end of Chapter 2, the police appeared somewhat coy in their approach to motoring crime. And as seen in Chapter 3 the Police Federation opposed the introduction of random testing in the Road Safety Bill. Such opposition is highly influential - for how is one to argue successfully for police powers which the police themselves say they neither want nor need? How can this uncharacteristic reluctance to take on increased powers be explained, especially in the light of the strong support coming from other quarters? It is clear from contemporary police literature, that the prospect of the introduction of the breathalyser generated fears that it 'would aggravate rather than improve what we are constantly being led to believe are the already bad relations between the Police and the motoring public' ('Ebor' 1964). Was this the case?

Information on the road user and the police is not readily available. As Brogden et al. (1988:74) comment 'lesser attention has been given to the development of, say, traffic departments' than to other specialist functional departments such as the CID and Special Branch. So that although there is a huge and ever expanding literature on the police it is usual to find no mention of 'motoring' or 'road traffic' in the index of published works (e.g. Morgan & Smith 1989; Brogden et al. 1988; Benyon & Bourn 1986; Reiner 1985). The reasons for this omission are unclear. It may be that this area of policing is considered unexciting, not overtly political and/or comparatively non-contentious. Yet when one considers the scale of the police traffic operation, and the deaths and injuries which occur on the roads these reasons appear less than sufficient.

For many people motoring situations provide their only contact with the police. As discussed above, this has important ramifications for police/public relations - and may help to explain police attitudes to motoring offenders. Indeed, the 1960s witnessed an increasing general interest in all aspects of the relationship between the criminal justice system and the public. For example, the *Criminal Law Review* produced a special issue with five articles written around the theme (June 1961). The need for law to be 'good law' i.e. to command public support was examined by Silvey (1961). And it is interesting to ponder the paradox that while public opinion polls produced evidence supporting the introduction of more restrictive drink-drive laws, the police were expressing the view that the public resented the enforcement of such legislation.

The historical development of policing has been well documented. Reiner (1985) charts three phases in its evolution in Britain. First, 'the establishment of professional policing 1829-1856'; secondly, 'the depoliticisation of the police 1856-1959'; and thirdly, 'the politicisation of the police 1959-1981'. Despite the need to be wary of considering that there existed perfect police/public relations up to the end of the 1950s, most writers agree with Reiner that 'As far as police acceptance by the public is concerned, the 1950s seems a 'Golden Age' of tranquillity and accord, with only hesitant harbingers of coming crisis'. Benyon & Bourn (1986) examined three factors which they see as important in shaping police/public relations. First, police effectiveness in tackling crime; secondly, the extent to which citizens identify with the police; and thirdly, the opportunity for public participation in policing. The policing of motoring crime is obviously highly relevant to the second of these. Could it be that the traditional common interest of a large part of society with that of the police may have evaporated with the expansion of motoring? Stevenson & Bottoms (1990:5) have noted during this period that 'in the Home Office's meetings with the Central Conference of Chief Constables, chief constables' anxieties about some of the social features of the age were expressed: these included ... perhaps especially, the apparent damage to police/public relations caused by the growth of motorised traffic'.

It is also worth noting that the 'immediate trigger' (Reiner 1985:62) for the setting up of the Royal Commission on the Police did not involve obvious corruption or brutality, but a more subtle blend of these arising out of a road traffic situation - a case of speeding by the comedy actor Brian Rix in 1958 which was followed by an alleged police assault on a civil servant who became involved in the incident (Morris 1989). The Royal Commission (1962) produced two reports. The first on pay and conditions of service; the second on wider constitutional issues, including road traffic issues. These ranged over general problems of traffic control, complaints about too much police time being spent 'on traffic work, and too little in dealing with crime', and a chapter on 'The Police and the Public' including a section on the 'motoring public'.[7] Increased car ownership was seen as bringing 'the constable into contact with sections of the community with whom previously, he had few if any dealings' and the Morton-Williams survey had shown that *both* the police and the public 'regard traffic duty as the least popular and acceptable part of police work'.

The survey demonstrated that police/public relations were best with older people and non-motorists and worst with young people and motorists. The survey evidence suggested that neither the police nor the public were fully committed to rigid enforcement of road traffic law - the police seeing traffic law enforcement as unpopular and less important than 'real crime', and being keen to maintain good police/public relations; while the public appeared to be motivated by self-interest, which put the possibility of being criminalized higher than that of being killed or injured. For the police, despite some positive results from the survey, concern that their public image was at risk had been confirmed, and underlying police anxiety persisted; but it was still not possible to establish with any certainty the exact part played by revelations of brutality and corruption and that played by enforcement of traffic legislation. Yet to rely exclusively on either, or even both, of these explanations would be to over-simplify a complex issue. Nevertheless, motoring law enforcement was now *perceived* in many quarters as having the potential to harm police/public relations. And as the policing of the motor car did bring the police into contact with people they otherwise would not be involved with, it was a practical possibility. As the HMCIC Report (1965:72) put it: 'For some reason the enforcement of traffic legislation designed for the safety and convenience of road users arouses a degree of resentment quite unknown in other fields. Traffic Regulations must be enforced, otherwise the law of the jungle would rapidly prevail with dire results for all concerned'. But the strategic advantages to the police of advancing road traffic as a cause of deteriorating public relations must be recognised and, as the 'politicisation' phase of policing developed, it became clear that issues of a much more fundamental nature than that of a law abiding person becoming disgruntled because he has been 'stopped for speeding' were involved. Nevertheless, police/public relations appear to have played an important part in the dropping of random testing from the Road Safety

Bill. Similar considerations will appear in the later history of legal policy in relation to drink-driving.

Chapter 3 ends with road casualty figures at their highest since the end of World War Two. Yet despite attempts to improve the legal response to drink-driving the number of drink-drive offences dealt with in 1966 - 11,329 which resulted in 9,859 findings of guilt (a rate of 587 per million vehicles licensed and 87 per cent of offences prosecuted) - was in relative terms no higher than before. The percentage of cases committed to the higher courts reached an all time high of 15 to 17 per cent and the conviction rate ranged from 50 to 56 per cent; compared to 92 to 96 per cent in the magistrates' court. However, hopes were high that the legal response would be dramatically improved with the introduction of a fixed blood-alcohol limit and chemical testing. Yet legal policy in relation to the drink-driver was still far from settled. In particular, as will be seen in Chapter 4, the interpretation by the courts of the new legislation was to bring not only the drink-drive provisions, but also the law in general into disrepute.

Notes

1. The word 'breathalyser' is used in Britain as a generic term to cover the various screening instruments which have been developed. In fact the Breathalyser is the trade name of a more sophisticated device designed and developed in the US by R.F.Borkenstein in 1954 - see Borkenstein & Smith (1961).

2. Goodhart cited cases (decided under the 1960 Act) to support this contention - one defendant admitted to consuming six double whiskies and was acquitted by a jury, so too, was another, who had drunk eight pints of beer.

3. By 1966 several countries had introduced similar legislation - including Norway, Sweden, Denmark, Switzerland (which had for some time allowed compulsion with force), France and Belgium - for an interesting contemporary account of comparative legislation see Bowden (1966).

4. Arguing that there were insufficient officers available to make the checks effective and that random checks were likely to harm relations between motorists and the police.

5. Which feared loss of business - although a high profile campaign against the provisions was avoided as self-interest in maintaining sales might be seen to conflict with a responsible attitude to road safety.

6. Which took up the motoring organisations' claims that unfettered police powers would represent an infringement of civil liberties - the 'civil liberties issue introduced an ideological, party political element into what had been hitherto an essentially cross-party consensus that "something must be done"' (Tether & Godfrey 1990).

7. Further contemporary information on the state of police/public relations is to be found in *The Police and the Public* (Rolph 1962). Although somewhat overshadowed by the publication of the Royal Commission, reviews of this book make interesting reading. They appeared in publications as diverse as *Police Journal* and *Men Only* and are reviewed in Muir (1963).

4 The excess alcohol driver (1967-1975)

In terms of popular culture 1967 was undoubtedly the year of the breathalyser - 'B for Breathalyser Day! ... the introduction of the social revolution ... for which I am responsible' (Castle 1984:307). Introduced by the Road Safety Act which became law at midnight on 9 October 1967,[1] this strange device was received 'amid prophecies that it would bring about a minor revolution in social drinking habits' (Boney 1971) and 'leading brewery shares promptly slipped a shilling on the stock exchange' (Sayce 1969).

Road Safety Act 1967

The Act sought to overcome the problems which had previously limited the law's effectiveness - the conceptual vagueness of the term 'impairment', evidential problems and the reluctance of juries to convict - by defining the offences in objective scientific terms and by making provision of the necessary evidence by the defendant compulsory, with penalties for refusal.

Three new offences were created - driving or attempting to drive, or being in charge of a motor vehicle, with more than 80mg of alcohol per 100ml of blood (s.1); refusing to take a breath test on the approved breathalyser (s.2); and failing without reasonable excuse to provide a specimen of blood or urine for laboratory test after arrest (s.3). The Act did not repeal or significantly amend the 'unfit' provisions of s.6 Road Traffic Act 1960 and ss.1,2 Road Traffic Act

1962, so that two sets of offences were available. Conviction under the 1967 Act was automatic, if the necessary preliminary steps were taken. These were:

* that the defendant had been arrested, either under s.6(4) of the 1960 Act (on suspicion of being unfit to drive through drink or drugs) or s.2 of the 1967 Act (a breath test taken under s.2(1) or s.2(2) being positive or the defendant refusing to take a test);
* where the arrest was under s.2: (i) the defendant was driving or attempting to drive and was required to take a breath test because he was suspected of having committed a moving traffic offence or of having alcohol in his body (s.2(1)); or (ii) that the defendant had been involved in an accident (s.2(2)); and that in either case the breath test was positive or the defendant refused to take it;
* at the police station, after arrest under s.6 or s.2, the defendant was offered a breath test, that breath test being positive or refused;
* (i) in a case of refusal to provide a blood or urine specimen, warning of the consequences under s.3(10) of the 1967 Act and compliance with s.3(6) of the Act as to requests for blood or urine and effluxion of time thereunder; and (ii) on a charge of driving or being in charge with more than 80mg of alcohol per 100ml of blood that the specimen of blood or urine was properly given in compliance with s.2 of the 1962 Act (division of sample and offer of container).

A conviction under s.1 of the 1967 Act depended entirely on the analysis of a specimen of blood or urine which showed an excess of 80mg of alcohol per 100ml of blood or 107mg of alcohol per 100ml of urine. On a charge under s.6 of the 1960 Act 'evidence of analysis of a properly taken specimen of blood or urine voluntarily and duly given is admissible as part of the prosecution's case, whether above or below 80mg' (Wilkinson 1970:121). Under s.6 the court was free to acquit a defendant above this figure or convict below it, having satisfied itself from all the evidence as to the defendant's fitness or unfitness to drive. It was not necessary for the purposes of s.6 to show that all the preliminary steps as laid down for the 1967 Act had been taken - provided the specimen was voluntarily given and s.2 of the 1962 Act had been complied with (see above). The penalties available under the 1967 Act were unchanged from those available under the 1960 legislation.[2] The controversy which preceded the Act continued after its enactment. The law was considered to be 'very strict (although still lenient in comparison with some foreign laws on the subject) and bitterly resented by some persons, as being the un-English, arbitrary, and oppressive invention of a set of kill-joy zealots' (Elliott & Street 1968:26). The new law was attacked on several grounds - principally, the reliability of the scientific methods utilised and the fairness and clarity of the provisions.

Scientific method

The Act required the utilisation of several pieces of scientific equipment to take samples of and analyse breath, blood and urine. Liability depended on the results of these tests (BMA 1974). As one commentator put it 'the enforcement of an alcohol limit will introduce, for the first time on a relatively wide scale, the use of a chemical test as the sole basis for conviction of an offence carrying heavy penalties' (Wright 1967:660). The accuracy and reliability of this equipment was the subject of considerable resistance and suspicion (Wright 1967; Pole 1969; Fitzgerald & Pole 1969), as were the practical problems encountered in their use (Ched 1968; Robinson 1975). A *Daily Mirror* leader in 1968 expressed the fear that 'many innocent motorists may have been wrongly fined and disqualified from driving because of certain inaccuracies in breath and blood tests'(27 September 1968:16). Both the accuracy of the equipment and the nature of its operational procedures were questioned.

Fairness

Civil liberties It was claimed that the new law encroached upon civil liberties - especially freedom from arbitrary arrest and the provision of self-incriminatory evidence and the erosion of the presumption of innocence. As one commentator put it:

> The Act makes great demands upon and requires surrender of some of the cherished privileges of the public. Thus it allows the police wide powers to set enquiries in motion, demands submission to rather humiliating tests, virtually forces or at least induces the accused to supply evidence upon which alone he may be convicted, and permits the luxury of non-co-operation only in exchange for conviction of an offence virtually identical with that in regard to which co-operation was refused. These inroads upon the liberties of the subject could only be justified if they were acceptable to the public and resulted in a marked diminution in the toll of road accidents. (Walls & Brownlie 1970:132)

Against this it was contended that if a driver was suspected of having consumed alcohol then as with any person 'who is suspected of a serious crime (he/she) has always been subject to arrest, and has always been obliged to 'testify against himself' by allowing his clothes to be examined for stains, his pockets turned out, his features scrutinised by eye-witnesses' (Elliott & Street 1968:32). But this did not answer the case if the defendant had committed a moving traffic offence or had been involved in an accident; for then there needed to be no grounds to suspect that the person had alcohol in the blood. Two main issues underlay the objections to the new law. First, despite the view advanced by Elliott & Street, for many people the label 'serious crime' was not attached to drink-driving offences. Secondly, there was a general concern that the police might abuse their powers under the Act.

The fixed limit Fears were expressed too concerning the fairness of setting a fixed blood-alcohol limit. First, it was argued that one individual may be less affected at a particular blood-alcohol level than another person at the same level, so that what might be unsafe in one driver would not be in another. A not uncommon lay observation. For example, 'I know of a lady with whom I would not drive round the block after she has consumed a glass of sherry, and I know a gentleman with whom I would drive to Timbuctoo after he had consumed half a bottle of whisky' (*Parl.Debs.*(Commons) 622:652). Or, more scientifically, as Cohen and Preston (1968:119) found in their study - 'the safest driver had a much higher blood-alcohol level than the most dangerous driver'. They argued, that according to their evidence, equal amounts of alcohol did 'not by any means signify equal degrees of dangerousness'. Cohen & Preston argued that there were psychological measures of driving capacity available which would produce much more accurate assessments of driving capacity, but that these were much too time consuming and elaborate to introduce as a practical device. Consequently, they recognised that 'the pharmacological measure is justified (but) only by the fact that it is more expeditious, not because it can measure that which it is claimed to measure'. This line of argument can, of course, be put against any road safety measure. It rests simply on the fact that some drivers are better than others. But, however good or bad the driver, that person will become more of an accident risk if he/she drives a vehicle with defective brakes and steering, at excessive speed, after consuming a large quantity of alcohol. A 'good' driver who voluntarily makes himself more of an accident risk cannot, if prosecuted, then plead unfairness by claiming still to be less of an accident risk than other less good drivers who have not voluntarily made themselves a greater risk. This is not to say that more effective measures should not *also* be considered to improve the skills of, or eliminate from the roads, those who do not come up to a required standard of competence.

The second argument put against the fixed blood-alcohol limit was that destruction rates, the rate at which the body eliminates alcohol from the blood, vary from one person to another. So that when tested unfairness might result, as some people would have faster elimination rates than others. And aside from the issue of unfairness between different people, the destruction rate argument highlighted a more fundamental defect in the practical application of the provisions - that of clarity.

Clarity

Despite the maxim *ignorantia non jus excusat*, it is a basic principle of English law that the content of any criminal offence should be ascertainable. But, although the provisions of the Act relating to the basic offence itself were clear - driving or attempting to drive with a blood-alcohol concentration exceeding 80mg per 100ml - for the average motorist the law was much less clear in practice. So far as proving the offence was concerned, this could be established by the application of the scientific tests referred to above, but for the motorist who drove after having consumed alcohol, it was impossible to tell with any certainty whether the limit of 80mg per 100ml had been exceeded; as the offence, described in terms of blood-alcohol concentration, meaningless to most lay people, does not give any clear indication as to what a person can and cannot do. How was a person to know the consumption of alcohol necessary in his or her case to reach this level? No simple formula exists - any calculations have to take account of such factors as varying strengths and absorbtion rates of different alcoholic drinks, the sex, body weight and stomach contents of each person, the period of time over which the alcohol was consumed and individual destruction rates (Department of the Environment 1976; Bierness 1987). So that as Pole (1969:147) put it: 'the driver may be in honest error and therefore caught unawares'. This point was put and answered several times during the passage of the Road Safety Bill through Parliament. The consensus seemed to be that:

> the large majority of the population not only knows that they are affected by alcohol at much lower levels (than 80mg per 100ml), but also have serious doubts about their ability to drive. If, in spite of this, they drive, because of social pressures and because they think (again perhaps rightly) that they can compensate for their disability, they cannot complain if they are caught and penalised. (Wright 1967:631)

While this might be a morally reasonable position, it still does not cover the point. If the law allows drivers to travel at 30 mph on a particular stretch of road, they are entitled to do so. Similarly, if I am allowed to drive with 79mg per 100ml, then I am entitled to do so. I can check my speed on the speedometer, but how am I to check my alcohol level?[3] There is, of course, the offence of impaired driving still available under the old provisions, but what if impairment could not be shown? Then a person who honestly tried to stay within the law and who could not be shown to be impaired for the purposes of the old law could be found guilty of an offence. Realistically, however, it is difficult to see how the law could be otherwise and remain effective. The difficulties of reliable self-estimates, the wide variations of blood-alcohol concentrations possible in different drivers with the same amount of alcohol, and even in the same driver in different circumstances, 'were well known to the Government, which consequently declined to give any guidance, except that those who intended to drive should not drink at all' (Saunders 1975:850). However, research suggested that most drivers thought that they knew how much drink it was safe for them to take before reaching the limit (Sheppard 1968). Although whether they actually did or not was, of course, another question.

Effectiveness of the Road Safety Act

Countering the criticisms levelled against the new law was the claim that the Road Safety Act would be an effective measure against drink-driving and would bring significant reductions in road casualty figures.

Significant reductions

In its White Paper *Road Safety - A Fresh Approach* the Ministry of Transport (1967) estimated that the new provisions would save between 150-240 deaths and 2,000-3,000 serious injuries each year. A projection borne out by the casualty figures for 1967 which showed significant reductions compared with 1966. The number of road users killed fell by 8.3 per cent, seriously injured by 6.1 per cent and the number receiving slight injuries was down by 5.5 per cent; while the index of motor traffic had risen by nearly 5 per cent over 1966. RoSPA (1969) in its 1967 report cited the reduction in the December 1967 death toll from 980 in 1964 to 654 in 1967, as further evidence of the effect of the Act. Barbara Castle (1984) was certainly pleased with these figures, as her diary entries for February 1968 revealed - 'the papers are full of more glowing tributes to the success of my breathalyser ... we sailed through Question Time with ease, considerably helped by the latest figures of the post-breathalyser accidents. The December figures are so dramatic that I was rapidly raked in for two tv interviews'.

In 1968, the first full year of the new law, road casualties fell by some 20,000. Deaths were down 7 per cent compared with 1967, serious injuries 5.5 per cent, and slight injuries 5.6 per cent. The index of motor traffic rose by almost 4 per cent. Casualty figures for 1968 were the lowest since 1962, despite the volume of road traffic rising by 48 per cent. For the Ministry of Transport (1969): 'the main reason for this dramatic fall in casualties was almost certainly the new drink and drive legislation'. Casualty savings were highest between 10pm and 4am, when fatal and serious casualties fell by 33 per cent (40 per cent on Fridays and Saturdays) compared with 4 per cent during the rest of the day. As these were the periods when it was thought that drink-drivers were most likely to be on the roads, this was seen as added evidence of the effectiveness of the new law in reducing drink-driving. Further evidence pointing to the success of the Act came from Coroners' Reports (Codling & Samson 1974). From December 1966 Coroners had been asked to take a blood-alcohol analysis of all drivers/riders of motor vehicles who died within 12 hours of injuries received in a road accident. Of these, in the 10 months prior to the Act, 28 per cent had blood-alcohol levels above 80mg per 100ml; in the 12 months after this had fallen to 15 per cent (cf. Ross 1973).

However, the 1967 Act had not been subjected to the same sort of rigorous scientific research as had the studies which facilitated its introduction. In particular, no attempt had been made to assess the role of other factors which may have contributed to the drop in road casualties. These included the introduction of the 70mph overall speed limit in 1966; minimum tyre tread depth and safety belt legislation introduced in 1967; driver education programmes; better street lighting and other road improvements; the permanent adoption of British Standard Time in the Spring of 1967, which made rush hour traffic safer; the reduction in the volume of two wheeled traffic; and weather conditions.

In fact casualty figures had started to drop six months before the introduction of the Road Safety Act (Leeming 1969). Also, there was no clear picture of how the Act was working; sales of alcohol actually rose in the first 12 months following the Act. Were more people drinking at home (night-time traffic volume fell by 3 per cent over the period)? Were potential drink-drivers enlisting other people to drive them? Or were they driving more carefully to avoid detection and thus having fewer accidents? In any event, by the end of 1968, the figures were again rising. The Minister of Transport, Richard Marsh, addressing the

RoSPA Congress in October 1968 expressed himself aware of this, but was sure that 'we are on a winner with the drink-drive laws' which even 'the most blinkered critics' had to concede were effectively reducing casualty figures. If the new law had been responsible, at least in part, for the initial reduction in casualty figures, declining effectiveness was perhaps to be expected as the novelty of the breathalyser wore off, the attendant publicity started to fade and the 'panic' which the Act had aroused among drink-drivers abated. However, although casualties rose by 4 per cent in the period October to December 1968 over the same period in 1967, they were still 13 per cent lower than October to December 1966, despite traffic having risen by an estimated 9 per cent over the two years (Ministry of Transport 1969).

Data from other studies were not so optimistic. The Automobile Association conducted interviews with a sample of drivers in Northamptonshire at the time of the introduction of the new law and again a year later. While the drinkers among the drivers originally reported reducing their drinking dramatically and expressed the intention to go to fewer parties, pubs, etc. and to use public transport more, a year later most had returned to their pre-breathalyser social patterns and many admitted to driving 'over the limit' several times during the year. These findings fitted with a national postal survey carried out by the Association of 850 of its members - the most significant findings of which were first, that people had come to accept the law and generally to agree with it; and secondly, that their anticipated behaviour (for example, drink less when driving - 26 per cent; walk to 'local' - 24 per cent) differed a year later from their actual behaviour (drink less when driving - 17 per cent; walk to 'local' - 18 per cent). Pubs and restaurants also reported that their level of custom, which had dropped immediately after the 1967 Act, had soon returned to pre-breathalyser levels; while taxi companies enjoyed a boom in business for some three months only (Automobile Association 1968).

Short-lived gains

The significant gains of 1967 and 1968 were not continued for 1969. The total number of road casualties was 1 per cent up on 1968 (motor traffic rose by some 3 per cent). Worse, the number of deaths rose by 8 per cent and serious injuries by 2 per cent. The Government singled out several factors as relevant. First, there was a need to improve driving standards. Initiatives included the publication of a driving manual; the mounting of a television series based on the manual; and the introduction of HGV driver licensing and testing. Secondly, it was felt that a road safety publicity campaign and education measures were necessary. And, thirdly, the Department expressed concern over the continued effectiveness of the Road Safety Act (Department of the Environment 1971).

Further, the Department of the Environment was concerned that by the end of 1968 the Act had 'begun to run into some difficulty', as a result of a series of court decisions in which motorists escaped conviction despite the fact that they had clearly been driving while over the statutory blood-alcohol limit. This, it was said, cast serious doubt on certain aspects of the working of the Act, and made it difficult for the police to enforce the law with confidence - reflected in the monthly breath test statistics, which for the first time began to fall below the figures for the corresponding months a year earlier. The policing of the Act is discussed below, as are the court decisions referred to here.

The Ministry of Transport interpreted the 1969 figures more optimistically - commenting only on 'a small increase in the total number of casualties commensurate with the normal growth of motor traffic' (Ministry of Transport 1971:2). And in its Report for 1970 the Department of the Environment also adopted a more optimistic as well as realistic approach. In 1970 the death toll rose by 2 per cent and the number of seriously injured by 3 per cent over 1969. Motor traffic (measured in terms of vehicle mileage) was estimated at 6 per cent higher. However, the Department's report pointed out that car driver casualties at the end of 1970 were 10 per cent lower in the 10pm to 4am period than over the last comparable 12 month figure before the Act. The report recognised that it was not possible to isolate fully the effects of breath testing from other road safety measures, and that this difficulty increased the longer the period since the Act, but that figures 'suggest that the Act continues to make a significant contribution to road safety, particularly in the context of late night road injuries' (Department of the Environment 1972:20).

This confidence in the continuing effectiveness of the Act was less apparent in the Department's by now annual assessment of the Act for 1971. In 1971 the overall casualty rate fell by 9 per cent over 1970, although the number of deaths increased by 2.5 per cent. The report again stressed the difficulty of isolating the effect of the Act and also identified conflicting evidence about the extent to which the effect of the Act was wearing off. Night-time casualties remained below their 1967 levels, while day-time rates did not; but Coroners' Reports, of drivers with a blood-alcohol level exceeding the statutory limit, which had recorded a drop from 25 per cent in the 10 months prior to the Act to 15 per cent immediately after its introduction, rose to 20 per cent in 1970, and in 1971 showed a return to the pre-Act level of 25 per cent (Department of the Environment 1973:14-5). While for riders and drivers aged between 20 and 29 years of age 40 per cent were found to have a blood-alcohol level over the legal limit (Department of the Environment 1974:10). And in 1970/71 the number of fatalities exceeding the limit between 10pm and 4am on Saturday nights rose to 70 per cent.

The picture seemed clear: the 1967 Act had led initially to a dramatic reduction in road casualties; but its effect had quickly decayed, so that by the early seventies casualty figures had regained their pre-Act levels. Would scientific evaluations confirm this picture and if so how could it be explained?

Evaluating the Road Safety Act

Initial assessments of the 1967 Act tended to attribute changes in accident rates as flowing simply and directly from the change in the law, which had reduced the incidence of drink-driving. An unproblematic operation of simple deterrence .

Deterrence is a subjective concept and the key question is whether it will deter the targeted population. Two methods for investigating deterrence can be used - ecological studies (statistics) and field studies (experimental or otherwise). The first of these can provide extensive information, from which inferences can be drawn (Lewis 1986). However, the usual reservations relating to official statistics apply; and, generally, statistics are only correlations, they do not reveal whether any individual has been deterred, providing only objective rates. However, field studies can be used to ask people whether they have changed their behaviour.

It was some years before the first scientific investigations were conducted (Ross et al. 1970; Ross 1973,1984; Codling & Samson 1974; Sabey & Codling 1975). Ross (1973) conducted a detailed statistical analysis, applying the technique of interrupted time series analysis to casualty rates for the period 1961-1970, which led him to confirm that 'the Road Safety Act had a sharp, immediate effect in diminishing deaths and injuries on British roads'; with the effect being particularly noticeable on weekend nights. Ross also corroborated the view 'that the strong effect of the legislation on casualties was only temporary' (ibid.). Ross's findings were supported by other investigations. For example, Phillips et al. (1984) 'confirmed Ross's conclusions'; but found that the Act 'only accounts for 2.7 per cent of the variance in road casualties' - miles driven and rainfall were said to account for 48.8 per cent and alcohol consumption 4.2 per cent. There was a consensus that the casualty rate had declined significantly after the passing of the Road Safety Act 1967, but that this improvement had been short lived.[4] What was not so clear was exactly what had caused this phenomenon, how it had operated and why the effect had decayed.

Had it been the Act, its propaganda campaign, the attendant publicity, a variety of other factors (as described above) or a combination of all or some of these that had led to the reduction in casualties? (Phillips 1984; Votey 1984; Snortum 1984b). An attempt was made to 'assess what combined effects the new law, the campaign and other related influences such as speeches, editorial comment, etc. were having' (Sheppard 1968). The Central Office of Information, on behalf of the Ministry of Transport, commissioned the Road Research Laboratory to conduct a survey of motorists and non-motorists just before the start of the campaign and again shortly afterwards. The results showed that after the introduction of the new law drivers drank away from home as often as they did before, but were less likely to drive back; an increase in knowledge of the law was reported, but most drivers felt that they knew how to drink within the law and their degree of tolerance to drink-driving seemed not to have changed. The report concluded 'that drivers' behaviour has been affected favourably by the new law and the publicity campaign, but that attitudes to drink and driving have hardly changed' (Sheppard 1968:37). As to the future, 'the evidence of increased knowledge of the law from the survey suggests that the extent to which the law is enforced is likely to be important'. It is to the policing of the Act and its treatment in the courts that we now turn.

Policing the Act

Police powers

The Act laid down three situations in which a police officer *might* require a driver to submit to a breath test. First, if involved in an accident, whether that person was to blame for the accident or not; secondly, if a reasonable suspicion existed that the driver had committed a moving traffic offence; and, thirdly, if there was reasonable cause to suspect that the person had alcohol in his/her body. In the first two cases an officer would request a breath test if there was something which led to a suspicion of the driver having been drinking, such as the smell of alcohol on the driver's breath. The third was less clear-cut, as the cases on 'reasonable suspicion' discussed below demonstrate. What kind of driving behaviour, falling short of a moving traffic offence, raised a reasonable suspicion of a drink-driver - erratic driving; wearing fancy dress; leaving a public house?

Policing practice

It was probably the case in the first few months of the Road Safety Act that motorists 'were uncertain what to expect and were particularly temperate until the nature of police action was more fully understood' (Denney 1970:23). The publicity and controversy which accompanied the Act's introduction raised in drivers' minds a real fear of being caught. The breathalyser was described as 'a new gadget in the hands of the police and a new terror in the hearts of the citizen' (*Daily Telegraph*, 28 November 1967). Whether such fears would be justified depended on the effectiveness of the enforcement provisions in the Act and the police response to them. As has been seen, the random testing provisions of the original Bill had been dropped, would the powers which remained be adequate? Operational implementation of the Act depended on force instructions issued by individual chief constables. To assist chief constables in this regard, and to attempt a degree of geographical uniformity of enforcement, the Home Secretary issued to chief constables a circular (Home Office 129/1967) detailing the powers of the police under s.2(1)(b) of the Act and advising forces to take advantage of the random element in the discretionary powers conferred by the Act. This brought protests from various bodies, particularly the motoring organisations, that it was a way of introducing random testing by the back door - a view also held by the Police Federation. The matter was raised in Parliament and in a written answer it was stated that the Circular 'merely described the power conferred by Parliament and drew attention to its deterrent effect' (*Parl.Debs.*(Commons) 758:399).

The question was whether the police would be rigorous enough in their enforcement to give full effect to the law without abusing their powers under the Act. A meeting held in December 1968 between chief constables and the Home Secretary to assess the working of the Act at the end of its first year of operation concluded that the police had been exercising their new powers in 'a fair and sensible way'. However, for Ross (1984:27) 'fair and sensible' could be better described as 'sparing and restrained'; as evidenced by the less than expected number of tests being carried out, and the high percentage of positive results. That the police were using their powers sparingly seems clear and they did not appear to have changed their patterns of policing (Ross 1973). This may have weakened the deterrent effect of the law as driver's perceptions of the chances of being caught adjusted to the actual risk. It may also have been that 'the manner in which the police have enforced them has done much to allay fears of unnecessary police interference with the motoring public and to ensure public acceptance of the regulations' (HMCIC 1968:51).

Policing policy

The extent to which the police shared the generally perceived public antipathy to the 1967 Act is unclear, but resource implications were certainly a serious concern, as was the fear of further damaging already deteriorating police/public relations. For, as Elliott & Street (1968:70) put it: 'in motoring matters the public's attitude towards the police is one of hostility, rather than the usual admixture of apathy and vague approval'. There was a more general feeling about at the end of the 1960s that motorists were being hounded by rules and regulations - concerning among other things parking meters, traffic wardens, seat belts, breathalysers and the 70 mph speed limit - and that this was not good for police/public relations.

Not surprisingly, the police developed an enforcement strategy that was not the most effective in terms of resources - they failed to target high risk areas such as pubs and clubs - where they could have reasonable cause to suspect that a person seen leaving would have consumed alcohol. This may have been for fear of being thought 'sneaky' or of not 'playing the game'; or because the legal validity of such a suspicion had then not been directly tested in the courts. (Barbara Castle in introducing the 1966 Bill in the Commons had said that there was no intention that the police would 'lie in wait' for motorists near drinking establishments.) Generally, the police appear to have acted well within their powers. This is understandable, for though the Act made it easier for the police to secure convictions in the courts, they needed to tread carefully until the range and scope of the new law was clear and they had gained some experience in its implementation. Also, the police remained conscious of the police/public relations issue discussed in previous chapters, and of the particular difficulties associated with the novel nature of the Act's provisions and the controversy over the extent of their powers (see, for example, *Police Review* 1967:965). And, while the police may be willing to test the limits of their powers with certain types of legislation, the motoring public was perhaps too large and politically influential a group to risk alienating.

'The Cheshire Blitz'

Before leaving policing it is worth considering the implications for *per se* laws of the initiative taken by the Cheshire Constabulary in 1975. As mentioned above, policing policy for individual forces is set by the Chief Constable for that

79

force, within the authority given by Parliament and the resources provided by the Government. In early 1975 the Chief Constable of Cheshire decided to apply strictly the provisions of the 1967 Act. He removed discretion from his officers and ordered that a breath test was to be applied for all moving traffic offences and every accident between 10pm and 2am each day. A pilot run of a week was carried out (with no attendant publicity), the result was that double the usual number of drink-drive offences was discovered; a longer experiment, with extended hours (9pm to 4am and 2pm to 5pm), was planned (again without publicity) for the month of September 1975. News of the proposed 'experiment' was leaked to the press and there was an immediate political uproar - the motoring organisations complained that it constituted 'back door random testing'. But the Chief Constable went ahead with what was now a campaign rather than an experiment (Ross 1977).

As happened after the introduction of the 1967 Act great success in reducing casualties was claimed. An evaluation by Ross found that although the extent of the claims made by the Cheshire police were somewhat exaggerated, and that the casualty rate quickly returned to its pre-blitz level, the experiment in Cheshire 'demonstrated convincingly the potential for deterrence of the existing legislation when accompanied by an enforcement campaign' (Ross 1984:71).

The Act in the courts[5]

Under the new law a court simply had to decide whether the prosecution had proved that at the relevant time the accused's blood-alcohol level exceeded the prescribed limit. Yet, while the definition of the offence itself was now simple, securing a conviction was not. The Act had included detailed procedural safeguards for motorists - specifically to address fears that the police would exceed their powers under the Act or that the scientific equipment would be wrongly used. A conviction could only be obtained if the police had acted within their powers and had meticulously followed a complex procedure - from inviting the accused to take a breath test to appearance in court. It seemed clear from the start that these rather technical safeguards would be exploited by defence lawyers; especially if past experience with drink-drive provisions was anything to go by. Also, as the defence could no longer challenge the police evidence on impairment, it was not surprising that those whose driving licences were threatened should investigate other methods of escaping conviction. They did not have to look far, as Parliament had presented 'would-be offenders with a statute providing golden opportunities for loop hole seekers' (Seago 1970).

Every new Act attracts a number of cases on interpretation, but the number of cases heard on the 1967 Act was quite exceptional. The Lord Chief Justice observed in *R v Durrant* [1969] 3 All ER 1357 that 'this Act gives untold trouble to magistrates and juries all over the country', since every week brings a new point and they go on and on'. Such was 'the fearful complication of the law and practice relating to drunken driving' (Samuels 1970) that lawyers too were falling foul of the cases which they generated - the Act was, as one criminal barrister put it:

a complicated piece of legislation, around which appellate court decisions have fallen fast, furious, and sometimes in conflict. Many counsel, who have not had time to follow the precise impact of the rapid decisions must have felt, when confronted with a breathalyser brief at five o'clock the previous evening, that they were plunging into a quicksand which has shown itself capable of shifting its position alarmingly almost overnight. (Boney 1971:viii)

For the 1973 edition of Wilkinson (Halnan 1973) the editor said in his preface that 'the number of cases on the Road Safety Act - their number now exceeds those on the Rent Restrictions Acts - has necessitated a large degree of rewriting of the section relating to drink/driving offences'. And by the 1975 edition the drink/driving offences had 'assumed an importance and attracted a body of case law sufficient to justify treatment of these offences separately from the other road traffic offences' (Halnan 1975). What was happening in the courts? Newark & Samuels (1970:59) claimed the high level of legal challenge to the Act flowed from 'The fact that the defendant is frequently middle class and represented and desperate to avoid automatic disqualification'.

Defendants electing jury trial had dropped significantly from 15-17 per cent of total prosecutions before the Act to 3-5 per cent from 1968 (see Appendix 1 Table 6). Convictions had increased from 9,859 (741 per million vehicles licensed and 87 per cent of offences prosecuted) in 1966 to 20,957 (1,455 per million motor vehicles licensed and 92 per cent of offences prosecuted) in 1968 (see Appendix 1 Tables 5,8); but there were some widely publicised acquittals based on technicalities. Motorists who did not challenge the fact of their excess blood-alcohol concentration escaped conviction on procedural points, even if the procedures had been followed in good faith and the defence had not been substantially prejudiced. This was policy adopted on exclusion of evidence for prosecutions under the 1962 Act, but contrary to the well-established rule in *Kuruma* [1955] concerning the exercise of judicial discretion to exclude evidence improperly obtained (considered further in chapter 5). Further, the courts in their interpretation of the 1967 Act now added to the discretion to exclude evidence improperly obtained, the exclusion of evidence which had not been obtained in accordance with the prescribed statutory procedure, as compliance was considered a necessary prerequisite for a conviction under the Act. Why had the courts adopted such an approach?

Could it be, as Ross (1973) has suggested, that the decrease in discretion allowed to the courts - the only discretion was whether to impose a custodial sentence (very rarely used) and the level of the fine to be imposed - influenced the way in which the courts regarded the Act? Or, as Hood (1972:103) found in his study of the sentencing of motoring offenders in the magistrates' courts: 40 per cent of the magistrates sampled did not regard those who committed any of what he defined as the serious motoring offences (which included drink-driving) as 'criminal in the same sense as those who steal, rob, commit violent or sexual offences'; and if the higher courts shared this sentiment, it may go some way to explaining judicial attitude to drink-drive cases. Whatever the reason, guilty drivers (those whose blood or urine sample had proved them to have a blood-alcohol level over the legal limit) were acquitted on technical

81

grounds which were clearly against the spirit of the Act. These cases led to demands for reform of the law from the police associations, the Magistrates' Association, the road safety lobby, the Law Society and the Bar Council. For not only were these cases claimed to be having an adverse effect on the operation of the Road Safety Act, they were also said to be bringing the law more generally into disrepute. In terms of the number of guilty motorists who escaped conviction, these cases were not important - estimated to be about 100 each year compared with some 42,000 convictions - but questions were raised concerning the justice of allowing well-off defendants to employ advocates and escape conviction by the exploitation of technical loopholes.

The 'loophole cases'

The 'loophole cases', as they were to become known, were of two types - those which challenged the legality of requests by the police for a breath test and those which alleged failure to follow the technical procedures laid down by the Act.

Challenging police powers to breath test Police powers fell to be challenged in two areas - whether there was reasonable cause for the constable to suspect that the driver had alcohol in his body, and whether the accused was driving or attempting to drive at the time the request for a test was made.

Reasonable cause A person driving or attempting to drive a motor vehicle could legally be required to take a breath test only if a moving traffic offence had been committed, an accident had occurred, or there was reasonable cause to suspect that the motorist had consumed alcohol.[6] In theory, the last of these would give the police wide discretion to test for any sort of strange or unusual behaviour, but in practice the police were reluctant to use the power widely and the courts seemed ready to accept many defence claims that 'reasonable cause' did not exist. For example, in *Williams v Jones* [1972] RTR 4. the fact that the accused had executed one or two dubious manoeuvres did not give the police reasonable cause to suspect that the accused had alcohol in his blood. And a woman driver who twice went right round a roundabout and then hesitantly left by an exit she had already passed, was held not to provide 'reasonable cause', 'she is just a woman driver' (*Hay v Sheperd* [1974] RTR 64). Further, although some commentators felt that the fact of being seen leaving a public house would suffice (e.g. Seago 1969), the issue had not been tested in the courts.

Driving or attempting to drive It was necessary to prove that the accused was driving or attempting to drive on a road or other public place at the time the test was requested. Obviously, a literal interpretation was not possible, as a person could not be required to take a test while actually driving. If a driver was stopped by the police, who suspected that person of having consumed alcohol, and the driver, still in the driver's seat, was asked to take a test this was clearly within the meaning of the Act. But in less straightforward cases difficulties arose. There were two particular sets of circumstances - where the suspicion of alcohol in the driver arose after the driver had been stopped by the police or where a driver had stopped before being approached by the police; and where a driver had driven onto private property.

The first of these gave rise to the fear that the police could stop a motorist for whatever reason and then, if the constable subsequently suspected that the driver had alcohol in his body, could request a breath test - was this random testing and were such powers given by the Act? The point was considered by the House of Lords in *Pinner v Everett* [1969] 1 WLR 1266 where it was held by a four to one majority that a person who had stopped or been stopped by the police and whom they *then* suspected of drinking was not driving at the time. This decision has been described as 'a high water mark of benignity towards inebriated motorists' (Prentice 1970:113). The decision was followed in *R v Kelly* [1970] 1 WLR 1050. The facts were that a police officer had been following Kelly to question him on a matter unconnected with driving. Before the officer had made contact, Kelly stopped his car and was walking towards a phone box to make a call when the officer intercepted him. The officer then formed the suspicion that Kelly had been drinking and asked him to take a test. The court held, following *Pinner v Everett*, that Kelly could not be asked to take a test as he was not driving or attempting to drive. It seemed that had Kelly been going to make a phone call about driving or his journey then he could have been tested (Seago 1970a); but the court held that as there was no evidence as to the nature of the call, the defendant was to be given the benefit of the doubt and the court would 'assume that it was unconnected with the purpose of driving'(Widgery L.J.).

The second case was where a driver had reached his destination. Here, it was held, the police had no right to arrest a driver under the Act if he had left his vehicle and entered his house as he was no longer on a road or other public place - *Campbell v Tormey* [1969] 135 JP 267. The Divisional Court held that a person ceases to be 'driving' on finishing his journey and leaving his vehicle and in this case a breath test should not have been requested, despite the fact that the driver had been the object of police pursuit when driving. However, the escape route provided for drivers by *Campbell v Tormey* was removed when the case was disapproved by the Court of Appeal in the subsequent decision in *R v Jones* [1970] 1 All ER 209, which decided that if the accused drove on to private land at the end of a chase, then a test could be ordered by using the doctrine of 'fresh pursuit'. This was affirmed by the House of Lords in *Sakhuja v Allen* in 1972 [1973] AC 152, where their Lordships decided that a person need not be 'driving or attempting to drive' - 'so long as the requirement forms part of a relevant single transaction or chain of events'.

Failure to observe technical procedures - the breath test machine In the early days of the breath test several motorists escaped conviction by claiming that no evidence had been produced to show that the appliance used had been approved by the Secretary of State. The case which decided this and which also provided the judgment that opened up many of the loophole decisions which were to follow was *Scott v Baker* [1968] 2 All ER 993. The Divisional Court held that there could be no offence under s.1 of the Act unless an excessive blood-alcohol level could be shown from a specimen taken under s.3, that a specimen was not taken in accordance with s.3 unless the accused had been arrested under s.2(4) and that an arrest could only be made after a valid breath test in accordance with s.2(1). For a valid breath test the procedures laid down by the Act had to be followed precisely, including the production of evidence certifying that the appliance had been approved by the Secretary of State. The Court of Appeal later overruled *Scott v Baker* on the narrow point, holding that the prosecution did not need to prove that the 'Alcotest 80' had been approved, but the general principle - that for a valid breath test the procedures laid down by the Act had to be followed precisely was affirmed.[7] As Lord Diplock later put it, in *DPP v Carey* [1969] 3 WLR 1169, commenting on the Divisional Court decision in *Scott v Baker*:

> As a general rule evidence to prove the commission of an offence is not inadmissible merely because it was unlawfully obtained. But the Divisional court took the view that upon the true construction of s.1(1) the requirement that the proportion of alcohol in the accused's blood should be ascertained from a specimen provided by him under s.3 was part of the offence itself. An analysis of a specimen of blood obtained otherwise than in accordance with s.3 was inadmissible not because it was improperly obtained but because it was not any evidence of the offence created by s.1(1).

However, Lord Diplock carried on to express the opinion that while *Scott v Baker* was correctly decided, the extension of the doctrine in later cases, such as that before him, had 'gone too far' (Bloom 1969a).

Failure to observe technical procedures - the arresting officer If a positive breath test was given or the accused refused to take the test, the officer could effect an arrest. The Act (ss.2,3) laid down detailed procedures which had to be followed; and, as mentioned above, it was decided in *Scott v Baker* that if these procedures were defective in any way, the accused stood to be acquitted.[8]

Failure to observe technical procedures - blood and urine tests[9] If a breath test proved positive (i.e. indicated a blood-alcohol level exceeding 80mg per 100ml) the driver would be arrested, taken to a police station and, if a second breath test proved positive, would be required to provide a specimen of blood or urine.

Some of the more outrageous defences arose out of the fact that the Act did not specify from which part of the anatomy the blood sample should be taken. Some motorists attempted to escape conviction by asking for the sample to be taken from unorthodox parts of their body, such as a thumb (*Rushton v Higgins* 1 Crim LR 1440), but the courts held that such an offer constituted a 'refusal to cooperate' as 'the defendant cannot insist on the blood being taken from a particular portion of his anatomy selected by him (*Solesbury v Pugh* [1969] 2 All ER 1171). Although not expressly provided for under the 1967 Act, the motorist's right under the 1962 Act to have a sample for analysis was maintained. If this sample was incapable of analysis (if too small, clotted or dried up)[10] the police sample would be inadmissible (*Earl v Roy* [1969] 2 All ER 684). Urine samples were used less often - two samples had to be taken within a one-hour period, the first being disregarded. This was to allow the bladder to be cleared and so allow urine in equilibrium with blood to be taken. An adequate portion of the final sample was to be retained by the driver for private analysis. If there was any inconsistency between the two samples magistrates tended to acquit because of the contradictory nature of the evidence.

Closing the loopholes

As has been seen, later court decisions, particularly those in *Jones* and *Carey*, closed some of the loopholes, so that by 1970 the Act appeared to be working more smoothly. The number of screening breath tests carried out rose from 51,000 in 1968 to 73,000 in 1970 (see Appendix 1 Table 10), and convictions increased from 20,957 (1,455 per million motor vehicles licensed and 92 per cent of offences prosecuted) in 1968 to 29,069 (1,937 per million vehicles licensed and 93 per cent of offences prosecuted in 1970) (see Appendix 1 Tables 5,8). But several loopholes remained. For example, the so-called hip-flask defence, where a person involved in an accident consumed alcohol before the police arrived;[11] and the general principle in *Scott v Baker* - that the procedural requirements were an integral part of the offence - remained good law.

By 1969 a lively debate had begun as to whether the problems with the Act stemmed from its drafting, which was designed to offer safeguards for motorists against arbitrary arrest, or from the way in which the courts chose to interpret it.[12] The evidence suggests that both factors were relevant. The position of the courts was well summed up by Roskill L.J. in *R v Holah* [1973] 1 WLR 127;130: 'The difficulties of police officers in enforcing the Road Safety Act 1967 are notorious ... But sympathy with the difficulties of enforcing the Act cannot deflect this court from its overriding duty to ensure freedom of the individual from unlawful arrest'. It is interesting that the courts were taking such a restrictive view of evidence for the prosecution of these cases, because the English courts do not have a tradition of allowing defendants to escape liability on purely technical grounds. For example, in *Smith v Hughes* [1960] 2 All ER 859 the requirement that soliciting for the purposes of prostitution took place *in* a street or public place was held to take effect even though the defendant was outside the street or public place - the defendant sat in a window in a house and attracted the attention of men by tapping on the window pane, and gesturing to them. The Divisional Court applying the 'mischief rule' dismissed the defendant's appeal:

> Everybody knows that this was an Act intended to clean up the streets, to enable people to walk along the streets without being molested or solicited by common prostitutes. Viewed in that way, it can matter little whether the prostitute is soliciting while in the street or is standing in a doorway or on a balcony, or at a window, or whether the window is shut or open or half

open; in each case her solicitation is projected to and addressed to someone walking in the street. (at p.861)

This decision reflects prevailing judicial attitude in such cases. Yet despite the purpose of the 1967 Act being equally clear - to make the streets safer from drink-drivers - the courts chose not to use the 'mischief rule' and to apply instead the 'literal rule' of interpretation. Why was this? Could it be that the civil liberties of drink-drivers were worthy of more protection than those of a 'common prostitute' or other criminals; was the stigma and censure attaching to drink-driving so low as to exempt it from the general rule; or was the offence one with which the judiciary could identify?

The Magistrate carried several leaders and articles in the years following the Act which expressed exasperation at the Act's interpretation by the higher courts. However, as they gained experience of working with the Act, it was reported that Justices' clerks and stipendiaries felt that a new Act was not necessary as 'the present Act is not unworkable and they would very much prefer to get on with it than start the process all over again' (Sixsmith 1970). For others, the only solution was a redrafting of the Act to 'make the kerb-side procedure more intelligible' and to 'clearly articulate the consequences of failing to comply with this procedure' (Prentice 1970).

Re-thinking the drink-driver

By the early 1970s there was once again a pressing need to re-think legal policy in relation to the drink-driver - the early success of the 1967 Act had not been maintained and the loophole cases needed to be addressed. Yet despite widespread disquiet over the provisions of the Road Safety Act 1967 the Road Traffic Acts of 1972 and 1974 consolidated but did not significantly amend the law.

Parliamentary discussion of the drink-drive laws in the 1967-8 Session consisted mainly of expressions of acclamation at the Act's success, but by the 1968-9 Session its diminishing effectiveness had led to the first call to 'beef it up' as 'the deterrent effect is now wearing off'. The Government was reluctant to act, replying that it was too early to be sure that the figures were correct, although by the 1970-71 Session the need for reform of parts of the existing law was recognised. Yet by the end of 1972 the Government still seemed reluctant to face up to the decaying effectiveness of the Act - to the question 'is the Secretary of State for the Environment satisfied with the state of the existing law on drink-driving? the answer was simply 'yes' (*Parl.Debs.* (Commons) 847:419). However, in 1974 the Blennerhassett enquiry was set up and a year later the Secretary of State for the Environment was expressing the Government's dissatisfaction with the effectiveness of the drink-drive laws (*Parl.Debs.*(Commons) 901:617).

The problems which had beset the law before the passing of the 1967 Act - the conceptual vagueness of the term 'impairment', the evidential problems and the reluctance of juries to convict - had been confronted. Certainty of conviction had been dramatically increased - in 1975 there were 65,200 convictions (3,725 per million vehicles licensed and 93 per cent of offences prosecuted). Yet despite the dramatic increase in the number of convictions, both in absolute terms and as a percentage of vehicles licensed, and the increased number of screening breath tests being carried out (up from 73,000 in 1970 to 134,000 in 1975), the casualty figures indicated that many drink-drivers were still operating and escaping prosecution. The deterrent value of the Act needed to be increased.

Deterrence basically involves two factors - the potential offender's perceived chances of the likelihood of being caught and the severity of the punishment available and used for the offence. It seems generally to be agreed that the perceived chances of being caught are of greater significance and the Scandinavian experience with drink-drive penalties supports this contention (Andenaes 1988). The penalties for the offence in England and Wales - mandatory disqualification from driving for a minimum of 12 months, a fine and the possibility of a prison sentence were in any event considered to be severe. The debate therefore centred on the mechanics of police identification of drink-drivers and police powers to demand a breath test. A manifestly drunken driver who did not come across a police patrol could obviously escape being caught; but so too could a driver who came face to face with the police - if that driver, although over the legal limit, showed no outward signs of impairment. An over-the-limit driver who maintained his/her vehicle in good condition, drove carefully and within the law, and was not involved in an accident could well escape detection. And worse, increasing public knowledge of these facts reduced in many drink-drivers the perceived chances of the likelihood of their being caught; thus weakening the deterrent value of the law. Police powers and methods of identifying and catching over-the-limit drivers needed to be reviewed.

Also in need of review were the so-called 'loophole cases'. Whether one took the view of Ross (1984) that the publicity generated by these cases bolstered the deterrent effect of the law, or that of others who felt that these cases served to reduce the laws effectiveness, the imbroglio which they had created needed to be addressed. It is interesting to note, though, that the 'folklore' which has built up over the years around some of the more outrageous defences is in many cases untrue. The most obvious examples are the exaggerated extent of the 'hip-flask' defence,[13] the helmetless policeman defence and the acceptance by the court that the accused did not refuse to give a sample but was reasonable in asking for it to be taken from his penis or big toe.[14]

The Blennerhassett enquiry was set up in July 1974 to carry out a review of legal policy and the drink-driver - its report leads us into the next stage in the development of the legal response.

Notes

1. 'Shortly before midnight on October 8 1967, a car crashed into a hedge on the A38 Bristol-Bridgewater road at the village of Redhill, Somerset. At exactly two minutes past midnight, according to a policeman's watch, the driver was taken to a police station and at 00.15, on October 9, became the first British motorist to be given a breath test'. (*Daily Mirror*, 29 September 1968, 'The Year of the Breath Test')

2. A comprehensive contemporary account of the new provisions can be found in Wilkinson (1970).

3. Over the years several home breath test kits have been marketed, but have not proved successful. There have been problems with reliability and accuracy, the difficulty of not knowing whether blood-alcohol concentration is still rising and the danger that people might try to 'drink up to the limit'.

4. Similar, although less successful results, were achieved in Canada following the introduction of the Criminal Law Amendment Act which came into force in December 1969 - see Carr et al. (1974); Chambers et al. (1974).

5. For a detailed contemporary account see Wilkinson (1973:145-209).

6. Seago (1969) suggested as the most common ground the commission of a moving traffic offence. For example, speeding (*Wall* [1969] 1 WLR 400); defective rear light (*Price* [1968] 1 WLR 1863); driving a zig-zag course (*Skinner* [1968] 3 WLR 408).

7. Magistrates became increasingly bothered by the long line of appeals which followed, both as lay people concerned that legalism was taking precedence over justice and as adjudicators whose decisions were being challenged and overturned - see, for example, Anon (1968), Messer (1969).

8. Several cases were brought on the provision which required the officer to be in uniform when requesting a test. For example, it was argued that if the officer was not wearing his helmet he was not 'in uniform' for the purposes of the Act. However, in *Wallwork v Giles* TLR 28.11.1969. the defence failed when the court decided that a hatless officer was in uniform.

9. Only some of the difficulties encountered will be dealt with here, for a fuller discussion see Seago (1973).

10. On 14 June 1972, Lord George Brown, former deputy leader of the Labour Party was breathalysed after crashing his Jaguar into a brick wall in St John's Wood, London. The case came to court a year later and, despite defence pleas that the blood samples had clotted and were not fit for analysis, Brown was found guilty, fined £75 and disqualified for one year.

11. *R v Durrant* [1969] 1 All ER 1357. (But see Prentice 1970 for a different interpretation to that arrived at by Lord Parker in the instant case) - confirmed by the House of Lords in *Rowlands v Hamilton* [1971] 1 All ER 1089, where the

court deemed inadmissible expert evidence to the effect that, allowing for the extra alcohol consumed, the accused would still be over the legal limit.

12.   With 'an excessively technical approach to its language' *New Law Journal* (1969:986). For a contemporary analysis of the approach of the courts to the Act see Bloom (1969) - 'there is no doubt that the Act if not dead, is in the last throes, and that the cause is an overdose of rigorous interpretation by Lord Parker's court' (of the 17 'loophole' appeals upheld to the date of the article Lord Parker had presided in 15); see also, *New Law Journal* (1969:1155). On the other hand, arguments in support of the lawyers and the courts also started to appear - for example, *JPN.* (1969:762).

13.   The defence had never been available to those who defiantly and to escape the breathalyser took a swig of alcohol when stopped by the police - they were charged with refusing to take a test.

14.   Stories concerning requests that samples be taken from a big toe or the penis are common. The only reference I have been able to find is a story (not a law report - *cf.* Anon 1974) in *The Times* of 14 January 1969, 'Doctor Refused to take Blood Sample', 'From our correspondent - Hertford January 13'. A John Leigh was said to have been found not guilty at Hertfordshire Quarter Sessions of failing to provide a specimen for a laboratory test without reasonable excuse by offering the sample from his penis and nowhere else (jury out for three hours).

5 Re-thinking the drink-driver (1976-1982)

An objective scientific basis for legal policy in relation to the drink-driver had been accomplished. Many of the original bars to an effective policy had been removed, and public opinion had come to accept the new law and its scientific impedimenta. Nevertheless, as has been seen, problems remained. The law needed to be developed further and it was unclear whether the public, which had only just come to terms with the 1967 Act, and indeed the policy makers, were ready to support further changes. However, two developments were apparent which would consolidate the position of those advocating a stronger line against the drink-driver.

First, significant advances were being made in road safety in relation to roads and vehicles; reflected by the fact that despite an increase in motor vehicles licensed from 17.3 million in 1974 to 19.2 million in 1980, the number of people killed on the roads dipped below 7,000 for the first time since 1968 and fell to 6,010 in 1980; while injuries over the same period fell by some 30,000. The public had come to recognise the need to improve road safety and were ready to support advances in road construction (such as improved surfaces and the introduction of crash barriers) and vehicle design (such as improved braking systems and laminated windscreens), but improvements in driver safety lagged behind and were more problematic. Technical advances were less well developed and measures such as more rigorous driving tests, medical examinations and re-tests for drivers (MOTs for motorists), were felt unlikely to command public support. However, measures to address the behaviour of those drivers who acted in a positively dangerous manner were more acceptable; and under this head came the drink-driver.

Secondly, concern over the problems associated with alcohol and alcohol abuse, apparent from the late 1960s and early 1970s, was expanding rapidly. For example, in 1975 an Advisory Committee on Alcoholism was set up by the DHSS and produced three reports; the House of Commons Expenditure Committee made a number of proposals on alcohol in its 1977 report on preventive medicine; in 1979 the Royal College of Psychiatrists reported on 'Alcohol and Alcoholism'; and alcohol-related problems were considered by an Expert Committee of the World Health Organization (1980). Also, an expanding field of alcohol studies was starting to define the social, economic and political dimensions of alcohol use and abuse. Springing from this new body of knowledge, organisations were established which relied neither on the rather untenable moral position of the temperance and total abstinence lobby, nor on the individual pathology of the disease model, but located alcohol problems firmly within a public health and social education perspective. However, there was thought to be great public resistance towards regulation of personal drinking habits, particularly as any harm was likely to be limited, at least directly, to the drinker. But this was not the case with the drink-driver, who was an obvious target for the attention of those concerned with the problems of alcohol abuse - as 'Perhaps the most widely recognised social aspect of alcohol misuse is 'drinking and driving' and the part alcohol plays in road accidents' (DHSS 1981:14).

The threat to public health and safety posed by the drink-driver was a publicly acceptable challenge for both the road safety and the alcohol lobby. Public opinion, and even the motoring organisations, began pressing for the effectiveness of the drink-drive laws to be improved. These developments combined to produce a strong and effective lobby for reform. However, as in the past, the route to reform was to follow a long and tortuous path.

By the mid-1970s it was clear that the *per se* laws (based on the assumption that above a stated level of alcohol drivers are unfit to drive) introduced by the 1967 Act had come to stay. Debate now centred on their effectiveness. Two issues fell to be considered. First, had the introduction of scientific evidence of blood-alcohol content, to replace the opinion evidence of witnesses on the old impairment tests, made the law more effective in securing the conviction of those who were guilty of and had been apprehended for an offence? A conviction rate of over 90 per cent for those failing or refusing breath tests suggested that it had. However, as has been seen, a complex web of case law had emerged which, in a minority of cases, allowed the guilty to escape conviction. Secondly, had the law been successful in reducing the volume of road casualties? Initially it had, but the gains had not been sustained and the effectiveness of the law was being questioned. There was also concern that the operation of the law should not adversely affect the dignity and liberty of innocent citizens by subjecting them to undeserved police attention. The law needed to be reformed, but what was required and what was acceptable? Opinion varied.

These concerns, coupled with an increased interest in alcohol misuse generally and 'official dismay concerning the fate of the (1967) legislation' (Ross 1977:242), prompted the Government to set up a review of the drink-drive laws; and in July 1974 the Minister of Transport appointed a Departmental Committee 'to review the operation of the law relating to drinking and driving and to make recommendations'. F.A.Blennerhassett QC was appointed to chair the Committee. In September 1974 he announced that the Committee would investigate testing methods; the blood-alcohol level; police procedure; related offences; the treatment of offenders; public opinion; and the effectiveness and reform of the existing law. The Committee contained lawyers, members of various government departments, senior police officers, medics, including a specialist in 'addictions', and the Head of the Accident Investigation Division, Transport and Road Research Laboratory. It deliberated for some 18 months. Members visited Northern Ireland and Sweden, and received evidence from a wide range of sources - including the motoring organisations, the Association of Chief Officers of Police, the BMA, lawyers and other organisations and interest groups such as the temperance movement, the Pedestrians' Association, the Royal Society for the Prevention of Accidents and the National Association of Licensed Victuallers. Additionally, two new groups had appeared, which reflected the growing awareness of the need to examine society's relationship with alcohol - the National Council on Alcoholism and the Camberwell Council on Alcoholism. The Blennerhassett report was presented to the Government in December 1975, it was published on 28 April 1976 (Department of the Environment 1976).

Drinking and driving - Report of the Departmental Committee

The Blennerhassett report is generally seen as a watershed in the recent development of legal policy in relation to the drink-driver. It considered the effectiveness of the law and how it could be improved. Recognising that 'drinking and driving is part of a wider problem of alcohol abuse in Great Britain today' the Committee expressed the view that increased consumption and the consequent increase in alcohol abuse' is a major factor - possibly the major factor - in the declining effectiveness of the 1967 Act' (1.4). However, while it is clear that *per capita* consumption of alcohol and total vehicle mileage are obvious factors in determining the incidence of drink-driving, as Ross (1976:258) put it:

Data are available to show a considerable increase in the consumption of alcohol in Britain since 1968, but the early experience of the legislation showed that savings of lives and injuries could be achieved without a decrease in alcohol consumption. There is no reason to rule out the possibility of motorists continuing to separate drinking and driving even if they do more of both, provided there were an effective deterrent to the combination of these activities.

The Committee did not take the consumption issue further, considering it to be outside its brief, but took an uncompromising position on the association between alcohol and traffic casualties:

> Alcohol accounts for at least one in ten of all deaths and injuries on the roads and its share is growing. The success of the Road Safety Act 1967 sharply, but temporarily, arrested this deplorable trend. The proportion of drivers killed in accidents who have a blood-alcohol concentration above the legal limit is higher than it has ever been, and the social cost of road accidents involving alcohol now exceeds £100 million a year. Although numbers of breath tests and convictions have risen, the police and the courts work under handicaps and cannot stem the tide. Our Report analyses this grave situation and proposes remedies.(1.1)

There is no doubt that the road casualty rate was a serious cause for concern. However, the degree of responsibility attributed to alcohol may not be as easily and accurately quantified as the report suggested and to have described its recommendations as proposing 'remedies' was somewhat optimistic. The report also failed to take full account of the huge international literature on drink-driving and contained little of the available statistical and scientific data. In retrospect, and if we compare the Blennerhassett report with its Australian counterpart (Australian Law Reform Commission 1976),[1] it failed to make full use of the available evidence from both Britain and overseas and did not follow the practice of the Law Commission and the Criminal Law Revision Committee of drafting a Bill containing its proposals - which served to weaken the impact of the report (Ross 1976a; Anon 1976a).

Several factors may have combined to produce the Committee's somewhat parochial approach. First, its composition was mainly domestic practitioner, leading to a rather practical perspective located firmly in Britain; secondly, there seemed to be an assumption among the Committee and those who presented evidence to it that the issues were clear and the necessary reforms widely known and generally accepted, so that the case for change was presented rather than strongly argued and fully supported; and, thirdly, the need to address the problems which the drink-drive provisions had faced in the courts led to a technical exercise in draftsmanship rather than a general re-think of the legislative provisions. Nevertheless, the report was generally welcomed and, although not the comprehensive document it could have been, the report is a major landmark in the development of legal policy and the drink-driver. Its recommendations will now be considered.

Improved technical procedures

The report devoted a chapter to the deficiencies of the technical procedures utilised for the purposes of the 1967 Act - the roadside screening procedure was felt not to be sufficiently reliable and the subsequent stages were considered complex and cumbersome, involving considerable delay and being very labour intensive. To increase the reliability of the screening tests it was recommended that the Alcotest device (the trade name of the device used in Britain since the 1967 Act) should be replaced with one of the simpler and more accurate machines that had recently come onto the market. To streamline evidential testing the Committee, on the basis of strong evidence from the BMA and the Association of Police Surgeons, recommended the introduction of evidential breath testing, subject to a suitable machine being selected and field-tested. Blood analysis was to be used as 'a fallback option', but sampling of urine, the Committee felt, should be abandoned.

The blood-alcohol level

The Committee recommended retention of 80mg per 100ml, with Parliament retaining its power to vary this figure. Mention was made of the 50mg per 100ml limit operating in some jurisdictions, but - largely on the grounds of limited police resources and the fact that 'it is certain that many over the present limit avoid detection' - it was felt that the lower limit would be 'of doubtful value', presumably because more people would go undetected, which is not a sound argument. Better surely, if a lower limit was thought necessary, to introduce it *and* make policing of the law more effective.

For some, Blennerhassett's failure to recommend a reduction to 50mg per 100ml was its 'greatest weakness' (e.g. Denney 1986; Strachen 1976a). There was certainly scientific evidence to support the lower level (some of which the Committee had considered), which was increasingly being adopted in other jurisdictions (Flanagan et al. 1983). Blennerhassett's rejection of any change gave those opposed to toughening-up the drink-drive legislation (particularly the licensed victuallers) a virtually invulnerable defence against a lowering of the limit, which survives to this day. However, others, including the BMA in its evidence to the Committee, supported the existing level as they feared 'that a lower level of toleration for alcohol would threaten 'ordinary' drinkers and jeopardize the legislation's hard won popularity' (Ross 1976:259). This is an interesting proposition, as it forms part of a wider movement away from a general attack on drink-drivers towards targeting particular groups of drivers (see Chapter 6).

The 'loophole cases'

The rule in Scott v Baker The flow of drink-driving cases had continued and the principle in *Scott v Baker* 'which provided the foundation upon which a substantial part of the huge and complex legal edifice was built' (Halnan 1977) was upheld 'with reluctance' by the House of Lords in *Spicer v Holt* [1977] AC 987. Legislation was needed and the Committee made recommendations designed to bring drink-drive cases within the usual evidential criteria on admissibility - that the arrest should not be part of the procedure and that the court should be empowered to disregard a departure from specified procedures or instructions where no injustice would result.

The hip-flask defence A driver who took alcohol after an accident, but before the police had required a breath test, could escape liability as it was not possible to ascertain the blood-alcohol concentration at the time of driving. The Committee recommended that the defence of subsequent consumption of alcohol should remain, but that it should be strictly limited to those who did not consume alcohol to avoid liability and who would not have exceeded the legal limit had they not taken the extra alcohol.[2]

Policing the drink-drive laws

In the absence of an accident or the suspicion of a moving traffic offence, a drink-driver who drove carefully stood little chance of being stopped; and if stopped and breath tested could challenge the legality of the police action in requiring a test. For the Committee this had three detrimental effects. First, drivers were acquitted despite blood analysis showing them to be over the limit; secondly, it artificially constrained enforcement policy; and, thirdly, drink-drivers came to think that if they avoided accidents and drove carefully they would not be apprehended. And, as Ross (1976;258) points out, although some 150,000 breath tests were carried out in Britain in 1974, 'this figure represents only one test for each 750,000 miles driven in that year. This degree of risk is one that drivers may well be able to disregard in making drinking and driving decisions'. The Committee identified as one of the principal reasons for the decline in effectiveness of the 1967 Act a growing appreciation among drivers of the low risk of being caught. Blennerhassett was convinced that enforcement should be made more effective, but the difficulty was how to do this 'without losing essential safeguards for the suspect'. The Committee felt that the anomalies in the law which had arisen over 'reasonable suspicion' could not be addressed without the introduction of unrestricted powers to breath test. Any other solution would fall foul of the same difficulties of interpretation as had the existing powers. This argument was supported by a consideration of other motoring laws which allowed unlimited powers to inspect - such as licences, insurance, vehicle mechanical condition and commercial drivers' log sheets - and also by the results of two driver surveys which demonstrated a change in attitude to random testing:[3] those for increasing from 25 per cent in 1968 to 48 per cent in 1975 and those against decreasing from 68 per cent in 1968 to 37 per cent in 1975 (Department of the Environment 1976:5.9). The Committee recommended that police powers to test drivers should be 'unfettered' - 'We believe this to be essential both for the simplification of the law and avoidance of loopholes, and for its better enforcement. It is central and fundamental to the reforms we propose, and accordingly *we recommend* that the circumstances in which a constable may require a specimen of breath for screening purposes should not be specified' (para.5.16).

Trial and sentence

The Committee noted that penalties for drink-driving had changed little in real terms over 50 years, but considered the available penalties to be appropriate.

On method of trial however the Committee suggested that drink-driving offences should cease to be triable on indictment and the penalties available on summary conviction raised.

High-risk offenders

The 'most intractable element ... with which our enquiry has been concerned is that presented by offenders whose drinking is out of control' (7.1). These 'high-risk' offenders were thought, for various reasons, to deserve special attention. First, when given back their licence they were likely to re-offend as 'at least one in ten of those who are disqualified for drink-driving are likely to repeat the offence' (2.11); secondly, they were likely to drink and drive during the daytime, when they would be of more danger to others, especially children; and, thirdly, they were unlikely to be deterred by the threat of legal punishment - 'they are likely to be people with drinking problems, and to be unreceptive to both publicity and deterrent measures'.

General difficulties in diagnosing drinking problems were thought to preclude the possibility of identifying high-risk offenders at the sentencing stage. Some pre-defined objective criteria were thought to be needed. The Committee offered a definition of the high-risk offender as someone convicted twice within 10 years or with a blood-alcohol concentration over 200mg per 100ml - a level which Blennerhassett considered would hardly ever be found after normal social drinking. It was estimated that this would produce some 15,000 high-risk offenders per year. 'Special procedures' were proposed for these offenders which would involve the court in imposing an order over and above the usual penalties. This order would be for an indefinite period and would specify that the offender's licence would not be returned until he had satisfied the court that 'he does not by reason of his drinking habits, present undue danger to himself and other road users' (7.9). It was suggested that advice on where to get help and support with drinking problems should be given to all high-risk offenders.

Education and research

Increased publicity to educate and inform drivers (particularly young drivers) of the effects of alcohol on driving, together with increasing the risk of apprehension were seen by the Committee as central to redressing the declining effectiveness of the 1967 Act. To this effect, several recommendations were made relating to education and research.

Education Increased education at schools and the use of publicity campaigns to provide full information on all matters associated with drink-driving was proposed. The difficulty facing motorists in being able to accurately assess their blood-alcohol level, was recognised by the Committee, but was not thought sufficient to affect the case for having a legal limit. However, the Committee suggested 'that authoritative information should be made accessible to enable drivers to appreciate the factors which account for these variations' (Transport and Road Research Laboratory 1983); but went on to say that practical problems made it inadvisable that breath-testing equipment should be made available for public self-test use.

Research Scientific research had provided the required technical advances and, by linking alcohol with traffic casualties, the necessary political climate to expedite the introduction of the 1967 Act. Research was now needed into other areas including policing and punishing the drink-driver. Of particular concern to the Committee was the need for fuller information on the extent of drink-driving on the roads and on the profile of the drink-driver - 'who are the drinking drivers?' While recognising that drink-drivers can come from all sections of society, the report was concerned to identify any groups which were over represented. Those convicted of drink-driving or killed while intoxicated were said to be overwhelmingly male and predominately young. And the Committee saw a clear link between road accidents and social activities, demonstrated by the high rate of accidents after 10pm, particularly on Fridays and Saturdays. Those involved were almost all male - 'because men both drive and drink more than women'; and this commonsense approach was continued to explain the predominance of young people who 'go out more than others'; while inexperience, both as drinkers and drivers - 'put young men particularly at risk'.

To gain detailed information on the extent of drink-driving and profiles of drink-drivers the report recommended the introduction of 'periodic surveys of blood-alcohol concentrations in representative samples of drivers on the roads, as a separate activity from police enforcement'. Its purpose was two-fold. First, information on the blood-alcohol distribution in the driving population would allow screening tests under the Act to be conducted in the most cost-effective way, and would provide information to monitor the operation of the Act, and any other measures which may be introduced; and, secondly, the characteristics of over-the-limit drivers would allow appropriate penalties to be developed and utilised.

Post-Blennerhassett developments

Changes in the law

Criminal Law Act 1977 Blennerhassett conferred with the James Committee (on the distribution of business between the criminal courts - Home Office 1975) and both Committees recommended that the excess alcohol and impaired driving offences should become triable only summarily. To redress the subsequent diminution in available sentences, the Committees recommended that the maximum penalty on summary conviction for driving or attempting to drive be raised from four to six months; and in view of their less serious nature three months for the 'in charge' offences. Also recommended was a bringing into line of the penalties for refusing to provide a specimen with the offences of driving or attempting to drive and being in charge, as imprisonment was not then available on summary conviction for the offence. The Criminal Law Act gave effect to these recommendations.

The main criterion adopted by the James Committee for the allocation of offences was the seriousness of the offence in the eyes of society. The provisions of the Criminal Law Bill thus adopted this criterion and it was proposed that some offences triable by jury if the accused so wished should become purely summary offences. So much controversy was aroused by the proposal to include theft of under £20 in this category that the clause was dropped from the Bill. However, despite one or two lone voices there was no similar debate over the proposal to remove jury trial for drink-drive offences; for as the Earl of Mansfield put it:

> It is also fair to reflect that trial by jury is also to be withdrawn in what I might call breathalyser cases and I imagine that this will save the superior courts a great deal of work ... I have not detected any outcry about the breathalyser; the public at large seems to be content that breathalyser offences should be heard by magistrates. (*Parl.Debs.*(Lords) 378:815)

The status of drink-drive offences on the scale of seriousness was such that their downgrading went through unopposed. Debate on which offences should be triable only summarily revolved around two points. First, that the possibility of trial in the higher courts was seen as marking the seriousness of an offence; and secondly, that trial by jury should be available for offences which affected the reputation of the defendant. Drink-driving was not seen as a serious offence and a conviction was not seen as affecting a person's reputation. The 1977 Act reflected the notion of drink-driving as a minor offence and reinforced this by 'demoting' it to the magistrates' court.

R v Sang [1980] As seen in Chapter 3 when dealing with cases brought under the 1962 Act the courts adopted a policy of excluding evidence improperly obtained; and adopted the same policy of excluding evidence not obtained in accordance with the procedures laid down by the 1967 Act. This was contrary to the general policy of the courts on exclusion of evidence in such cases.

The issue was considered by the House of Lords in *Sang* [1980] AC 402, a case on entrapment as a substantive defence and as the basis for a discretion to exclude evidence where the House considered the wider question of whether 'a trial judge has a discretion to reject admissible evidence unfairly obtained otherwise than in cases where its prejudicial effect outweighs it probative value?' Against earlier rulings the House answered the question as follows:

* A trial judge in a criminal matter always has a discretion to refuse to admit evidence if in his opinion its prejudicial effect outweighs its probative value.
* Save with regard to admissions and confessions and generally with regard to evidence obtained from the accused after commission of the offence, he has no discretion to refuse to admit relevant admissible evidence on the ground that it was obtained by improper or unfair means.

Cases on drink-driving decided after *Sang* seem to have adopted this very narrow view of the discretion to exclude improperly obtained evidence, and relegated the old cases on the 1962 Act to the limbo of lost causes. For example, in *Trump* [1980] Crim LR 379 the Court of Appeal allowed evidence of the analysis of a sample of blood obtained illegally (without the accused's consent) to be admitted; and in *Birdwhistle* [1980] Crim LR 381 the same court held that an unlawful arrest did not lead to exclusion of the evidence subsequently obtained (Harper 1981).

Morris v Beardmore [1980] However, not all drink-drive cases were brought within *Sang*. While Blennerhassett had been concerned to rid the law of specious procedural defences, and *Sang* had redrawn the law in this area *Morris v Beardmore* [1980] 3 WLR 283 once again presented the courts with a situation where the procedure adopted by the police had been held to invalidate the defendant's subsequent arrest. However, the procedural irregularity was no mere technicality. The facts were that police officers wished to interview the defendant about a road accident. They called at his home and were admitted by his son, who went to tell his father that the police wanted to see him. The son returned and told the officers that the defendant did not wish to see them and they should leave. The officers went to the defendant's bedroom and requested a breath test. The defendant refused and was arrested. The justices dismissed the information and the prosecution appealed on the law to the Queen's Bench Division. The respondent's case was that the protection of property from unlawful invasion was such a fundamental right, that as the Act had not specifically conferred a power of entry in such cases, such an entry must be unlawful and negate the validity of any subsequent proceedings. However, Cummings-Bruce L.J. supported by Neill J. approached the case from the position of the right of the police officer to require a specimen and held that unless the officer's behaviour could be said to be 'oppressive', when the court would have a discretion to exclude any evidence, the officer's conduct would be lawful. The decision was heavily criticised (e.g. Samuel 1980) and subsequently overruled by the House of Lords which unanimously held that any statute which gives the police a power of arrest does not also give them power of entry to private property unless it expressly says so.

The reintegration of drink-drive cases within the general law of evidence may have been precipitated by several factors. First, initial hostility to and suspicion of the new 'breathalyser law' had largely abated by this time and the courts appeared no longer to feel it their same mission to 'protect the citizen' in drink-drive cases; secondly, the 'loophole' cases were attracting very unfavourable publicity and there were worries in the legal establishment that the law in general was being brought into disrepute; and thirdly, after *Sang* the law was much clearer and tighter making it less easy for a court to distinguish drink-drive cases, a line which the judiciary must in any case have began to realise was indefensible. However, that there were still limits to police behaviour was underlined by the House of Lords in *Morris v Beardmore*; so that while the police were freed from the technicalities of the old 'loophole' defences, and the ordinary rules of evidence were applied, they could not breach the fundamental rights of the citizen in pursuit of drink-drive evidence and get that evidence admitted.

Policing policy and practice

The police welcomed the Blennerhassett report and devoted considerable effort to the development of satisfactory evidential testing machinery. However, it is not easy to establish the police position on increased powers to breath test. For example, *The Times* (13 June 1974) quoted a Police Federation spokesman as saying 'The police would not like to see the law changed so that they could carry out random breath tests', while a *Police Review* leader (21 June 1974) put the opposite view, as did the Chief Inspector's Report for 1978 - discretionary testing would 'undoubtedly ... be a powerful deterrent to anti-social driving' (HMCIC 1979:34). Of those who argued against extended powers, the possibility of damaging police/public relations was the most common reason given.[4]

A survey by the Automobile Association (1976) found that 25 per cent of motorists felt that the police/motorist relationship was bad or very bad - three times the proportion for the public generally; and 36 per cent felt that police/motorist relations had deteriorated during the last 10 years - only slightly over that for relations with the public generally. A more detailed study was produced by Dix and Layzell (1983) which was clearly practical in nature, identifying policy issues and topics for future research. Unfortunately, it did not investigate causes and explanations, nor did it differentiate between different classes of road user or types of offences. As Reiner (1985a:96-7) put it:

> The relationship between road users and the police cannot be understood without a consideration of the social structure which exposes different classes of road user both to differential pressures to offend and differential patterns of labelling by the police, or of the organisation and culture of the police force which sees traffic control as subordinate to the "real" tasks of policing.

A full understanding of the nature of the relationship between the police and the motorist still lay to be discovered; as did the effect of motoring law enforcement on this relationship.

Implementing Blennerhassett

Blennerhassett reported in December 1975. The Secretary of State announced in Parliament that he expected to recommend the report 'within a few days'. A month later the Government was still 'studying the Blennerhassett recommendations' and by March 1976 was 'inviting comments with a view to announcing the Government's proposals'. The report was published on 28 April 1976 and, for the Government, it was said that: 'There can be no doubt at all that drinking and driving is one of the greatest social evils of contemporary life, and that measures to halt and reverse this rising trend of wantonly created violent death, injury, physical suffering and emotional pain must be one of the most urgent objects for us all' (*Parl.Debs.*(Commons) 910:101-2). However, due mainly to disagreements over the high-risk offender and unfettered testing recommendations, and technical concerns over evidential testing, it was August 1976 before the Government accepted the report as a basis for legislation, subject to continuing research and consultation on evidential testing and the high-risk offender recommendations. No mention was made of police powers to breath test; although the Government was later said to be 'in constant consultation with the police on the workings of the law, and their views are taken'.

It seems that the Department of Transport supported wider testing powers, but some members of the Cabinet feared adverse public reaction, leading to lost votes; and also doubted that the measure would get through Parliament - a particularly important consideration as, in 1977, the Labour Government had lost its working majority. In 1979 the Labour Government lost a general election. The Conservative Party was elected with a massive majority. The incoming Government took up the issue of drink-driving and in December 1979 published a consultative document. In the accompanying Commons statement the Minister of Transport laid out the Government's position on drink-driving, which he said was 'the largest single factor leading to death and injury on the road' (*Parl.Debs.*(Commons) 976:401-2). This information had been gleaned from a Transport and Road Research Laboratory Report (Sabey 1978) which had persuaded the Minister of the need to act quickly. The great majority of Blennerhassett's proposals were accepted, including evidential testing, the need to escape from procedural technicalities, and the high-risk offender provisions - much of the emphasis being to assist the police in tackling 'their task of enforcement more effectively and economically'. The Government diverged from Blennerhassett in other crucial respects - the definition of the high-risk offender; and police powers.

While agreeing with Blennerhassett on the dangers posed by heavy or problem drinkers and accepting in principle the recommendation to introduce a high-risk category of offender attracting special procedures on conviction the Government saw practical difficulties in operating a high-risk procedure as recommended by Blennerhassett and hoped to be able to introduce a modified version.

The Government, as with its Labour predecessor, seemed unable to resolve the question of increased police powers. Blennerhassett recommended that police 'discretion should be unfettered' and that 'the circumstances in which a constable may require a specimen of breath from a driver for screening purposes should not be specified'. The Green Paper debated this issue (20-25) and concluded that 'indiscriminate testing would be undesirable, but further views are sought on the question of whether the present restrictions on the powers of the police to test drivers at the roadside should be removed'.

The Green Paper's rejection of Blennerhassett's proposals on police powers has been described as difficult to explain in view of the support which it attracted - from the police, the BMA, the National Council on Alcoholism, the Justices' Clerks' Society, the Central Policy Review Staff (CPRS 1982), the

101

motoring organisations and the public (Baggott 1990). There was, however, strong opposition from a number of MPs - 'both the Transport and Home Affairs Backbench Committees were hostile and opposition to discretionary testing was embodied in a number of resolutions at the Conservative Party Conference in 1980' (Tether & Godfrey 1990) - and from the drink's industry. Also, it has been said that 'the Government decided not to introduce 'random testing' because of the effect it would have on police/public relations' (DHSS 1981:49).

The Minister of Transport stated in the Commons on 24 April 1980 that he had received over 100 responses to the consultation document - including comments from the police; the courts; the legal and medical professions; motorists and other road users; the road safety lobby; and the trade and industry. There was general consensus on the need to improve and simplify the law and a majority supported evidential breath testing - although some voiced fears over the accuracy of the equipment. The special procedures for high-risk offenders were generally welcomed; but a division of opinion was reported on the issue of the removal of restrictions on the powers of the police to breath test. Not surprisingly, when the Transport Bill 1981 was presented police powers remained restricted.

The appearance of a Green Paper four years after Blennerhassett has been explained by three developments - the new Minister of Transport, Norman Fowler, was strongly in favour of implementing Blennerhassett; the size of the Conservative majority in Parliament obviated the possibility of defeat by a backbench revolt; and technical advances had cleared the way for reform of the law (Baggott 1990).[5] The mood seemed generally optimistic that the Blennerhassett recommendations would be introduced. This optimism was ill-founded. It was to be 1981 before legislation was enacted (Transport Acts 1981 and 1982), and May 1983 before the new provisions were brought into force. A seven-and-a-half-year wait.

Notes

1. Blennerhassett's 82 pages looked rather meagre when compared with the 200 plus pages of the Australian report; which contained a wealth of statistical, scientific and comparative data, together with an extensive index and bibliography and a draft Bill.

2. This would involve back-calculation, despite the Committee's earlier observation that 'no reliable method of back-calculation exists' (para.8.5).

3. There is some confusion of meaning on the term 'random testing'. As used by the Committee and others, it means police powers to test any person driving or attempting to drive - the requirement that there be a 'reasonable suspicion' of alcohol present in the driver's body being removed. This is also known as unfettered discretion. The term also has a more precise meaning related to the random stopping of drivers at say a static police check.

4. For some reseach evidence see Belson (1975); Southgate & Ekblom (1984); Moxon & Jones (1984); Smith & Gray (1985).

5. The Home Office Central Research Establishment in co-operation with the police 'carried out extensive field and laboratory trials to evaluate devices for possible use for evidential breath testing purposes' (Department of Transport 1979:4). For details of the operational and laboratory trials which were carried out see Birch (1980) and Isaacs et al. (1980).

6 The new law (1983-1992)

The Transport Act 1981

'Measures to improve road safety' were promised in the Government's legislative programme for the 1980-81 Parliamentary Session. They were contained in the Transport Bill 1981. Introducing the Bill in the Commons Norman Fowler, the Secretary of State for Transport, made it clear that the intention was to restore the effectiveness of the law as a deterrent to drink-driving. Judging the available penalties sufficient, the Transport Secretary considered that: 'The crucial question concerns the enforcement of the law, so we have taken steps to enable enforcement to be more efficient than it is at present' (*Parl.Debs.* (Commons) 996:860). The Bill aimed to: 'simplify (the law), clarify it, remove needless technicalities and thereby make it more difficult for the guilty to get off by means of silly technical defences. In addition (it will be made) easier for the police properly to administer and enforce the law' (*Parl.Debs.* (Commons) 996:939).

However, police testing powers were not to be widened. A threefold justification was advanced - other reforms contained in the Bill would improve the operation of the law; existing police powers were sufficient; and increased powers had the potential to damage police/public relations. The Secretary of State gave way several times on the point of increased police powers, but any prospect of amending the legislation in this direction appeared bleak as he finished with 'The onus on those who want random testing is to establish beyond all reasonable doubt that new powers are necessary. I am advising the

House that it is my view, and the view of the Government, that such new powers are not necessary' (Parl.Debs.(Commons) 996:862). The expected attempt in the Lords to introduce random testing was debated and withdrawn; and Commons backbench attempts to widen the discretionary powers of the police also failed. However, police powers were expanded in a separate Lords' amendment. The Bill had originally been drafted to reflect the case law established in *Morris v Beardmore*, which had the effect of giving defendants sanctuary in certain cases. Police objections prompted a Lords' amendment to allow the police entry in certain circumstances (see below) which survived a heated Commons debate. The Bill received the Royal Assent on 31 July 1981.

The Transport Act 1981 introduced substantial changes to road traffic law, practice and procedure. In particular, it substantially amended the existing offences under s.5 of the Road Traffic Act 1972 (the impairment offences) and wholly replaced the previous drink-drive provisions contained in ss.6-12 of the 1972 Act (the prescribed-level offences). The Act came into force on the 6 May 1983.

The new law

The drink-drive offences under the Road Traffic Act 1972, as amended by the Transport Acts 1981 and 1982, became:

* Driving or attempting to drive a motor vehicle while unfit through drink or drugs (s.5(1)).
* Being in charge of a motor vehicle while unfit to drive through drink or drugs (s.5(2)).
* Driving or attempting to drive a motor vehicle on a road or other public place after consuming so much alcohol that the proportion of it in the person's breath, blood or urine exceeds the prescribed limit (s.6(1)(a)).
* Being in charge of a motor vehicle on a road or other public place after consuming so much alcohol that the proportion of it in the person's breath, blood or urine exceeds the prescribed limit (s.6(1)(b).
* Without reasonable excuse, failing to supply a specimen for a breath test (s.7(4)).
* Without reasonable excuse, failing to supply specimens of breath, blood or urine for analysis (s.8(7)).

Although some of the new provisions were similar or identical to the existing law, there were six main changes:

Introduction of evidential breath testing Under the old law breath analysis had been used for roadside screening purposes only. If the breath test proved positive, a sample of blood or urine had to be provided for laboratory analysis and the results were used in court as evidence of the defendant's blood-alcohol concentration. Under the new law a positive screening test, or a refusal to take a screening test, was followed by arrest and the requirement to provide two samples of breath for evidential purposes - the lower of the two readings to be taken. The defendant's right to supply a sample of blood or urine was removed in most cases (but see below).

Abolition of the principle in Scott v Baker Conviction no longer depended on the police complying strictly with the procedural requirements for the screening breath test, which had been necessary for a *lawful arrest* under the old law. Section 8(1) of the Act entitled an officer to require specimens of breath, blood or urine 'in the course of an investigation'; and no mention was made of the arrest or its legality.

'Hip-flask defence' all but abolished The onus was now on the accused person seeking to take advantage of the defence to show that alcohol had been taken after the accident and before the request for, and administration of, an evidential breath test *and* that but for this alcohol the accused would have been below the limit; or, if the charge was brought under s.5, fit to drive at the time of the evidential tests.

Wider discretion to breath test The power to test still depended on the commission of a moving traffic offence, an accident, or suspicion of alcohol in the driver's body tissues, but was widened to include drivers who 'are or were' in charge of motor vehicles; and the suspicion no longer had to arise while the person was still driving or attempting to drive (s.7(1)). The latter meant that a driver could be stopped, for whatever reason, and if the officer then suspected that the presence of alcohol a request could be made for a sample of breath for screening purposes; but if there were no grounds for such a suspicion a valid request for a breath test could not be made.

Police powers of entry The police were given a power of entry in all cases where the suspected offence was one of driving, attempting to drive or being in charge of a motor vehicle when unfit through drink or drugs(s.5(6)); and in excess alcohol cases where there had been an accident involving injury, to arrest or to require a screening breath test; or if a breath test had proved positive or a person had failed to provide a breath test after having been requested to do so, to arrest - to any place where the constable suspected the driver to be and if need be could enter such a place by force (s.7(6)).

Introduction of 'high-risk' offenders provisions Special procedures for high-risk offenders were not introduced under the Act, but a modified version of the provisions recommended by Blennerhassett was announced by the Secretary of State, to be operative from the day the Act came into force. This would apply to any motorist twice convicted in ten years of a drink-drive offence where both offences showed a blood-alcohol level more than two-and-a-half times the legal limit. These offenders would only have their licence returned when they had been medically certified as fit to drive and thus satisfied the Secretary of State's Medical Adviser that they did not present a danger to the public.

Commentary on the new law

Despite Blennerhassett and the Government's consultative document favouring the introduction of a single drink-drive offence to simplify the law, both the impairment and excess alcohol offences were retained. But the latter was to be simplified with the introduction of evidential breath testing and the elimination of the loophole cases; although doubts over the new testing methods and procedures appeared to threaten a fresh wave of case law. Police powers were more clearly defined, but fell short of those recommended by Blennerhassett and others; and the high-risk offender provisions appeared weak when compared with the Blennerhassett proposals. As with previous drink-drive legislation the new law was an uneasy compromise which attempted to increase the effectiveness of the law without further alienating its critics. It can be considered under four heads - evidential breath testing; policing; the new law in the courts; and an evaluation of its effectiveness.

Evidential breath testing

The most controversial changes brought about by the Transport Acts were the introduction of evidential breath testing[1] and the removal of the defendant's right to supply a specimen of urine or blood for analysis. Many objections were raised, most of which reflected a lack of knowledge and subsequent mistrust of the scientific techniques to be employed.[2] Not surprisingly, the procedures were attacked on the grounds of accuracy - of the measurement of alcohol in the breath and the correlation of breath-alcohol to blood-alcohol levels. The old argument, that the same blood-alcohol level could produce different degrees of impairment in different drivers, was now joined by the contention that even if a maximum blood-alcohol level for all drivers was agreed, irrespective of any other evidence as to impairment, doubt existed that it could be accurately equated to a breath-alcohol level;[3] and, further, there were misgivings about the ability of the new machines to measure reliably breath-alcohol levels in the first place.

Contemporary scientific opinion did question the accuracy of the equipment as a measuring device (e.g. Feldman & Cohen 1983; Joye 1983), and there was apprehension concerning the practical application of the tests - on the one hand, the taking of a sample from the same orifice through which any alcohol was imbibed and the effective purging of the machine between tests; and on the other, the possibility of cheating the machine into giving a low reading by means such as hyperventilation and incomplete exhalation (Jones 1982; Strachen 1983). The Government's own research, which compared the results of two consecutive tests on each of a sample of suspected drivers, produced a difference of up to 20mg per 100ml in one in every 14 cases and a difference of up to 5mg per 100ml in 44 per cent of the sample (Department of Transport 1979). To allow 'for deviations in the operation of the device' the Government originally suggested a breath-alcohol level of 40 microgrammes (mcg) per 100ml as corresponding to the blood-alcohol level of 80mg per 100ml, but was convinced subsequently that this level was unrealistically high.

The breath-alcohol level was set at 35mcg of alcohol per 100ml of breath, a level said to be commensurate with 80mg of alcohol per 100ml of blood (Denney 1986). However, the Home Office advised the police not to prosecute below 40mcg of alcohol per 100ml of breath, equating with 92mg per 100ml[4] - the transition to breath, in its efforts not to go below the previous legal limit resulted in a significant increase in the legally permissible breath alcohol concentration. For the law's opponents this was not enough to compensate for claims of the test's flawed accuracy (e.g. Beaven 1985); while for the anti-drink-drive-lobby it represented a backward step by significantly raising the blood-alcohol level. Further, under the old law a driver had the right to provide a sample of either blood or urine for laboratory analysis, but under the new provisions this right was removed and - unless there was no machine available; the accused was unable to supply a sample of breath on medical grounds; or a medical practitioner had advised that the person might have been under the influence of drugs - replaced with the requirement to provide two samples of breath on an approved evidential breath testing machine.

In an attempt to ameliorate any sense of harshness which the new procedures and the removal of the motorists right to 'double check' them (by having a sample of blood or urine to take for private analysis) might cause, the new law provided that an evidential breath test reading of 50mcg per 100ml or less would give a driver the option of asking for a blood or urine sample to be taken for evidential purposes (the officer to specify which).

As expected, considerable difficulty arose when the Act came into force. Evidential testing immediately came under attack on the grounds of inaccuracy and unreliability - as part of 'an endeavour to find as many loopholes in the new statutory provisions as were found in the old' (Halnan & Spencer 1985). Even the Transport Minister, Lynda Chalker, conceded that the new machines were 'inherently less accurate than the previous blood test method' (*Checkpoint*, Radio 4, 17 August 1983). On this first point, the weight of criticism aimed against the evidential breath testing machines led the Government to introduce a monitoring programme for six months from 16 April 1984. Drivers were offered the opportunity to provide a sample of blood or urine in addition to the two evidential breath tests. The results of the tests were compared and a report was published in March 1985 which assessed the accuracy and reliability of the breath testing machines (Paton et al. 1985). The study, involving 12,000 breath tests, concluded that the machines accurately measured alcohol levels, although the Lion Intoximeter could overcompensate for acetone, resulting in an under-estimation of the alcohol level. To foster public confidence in the experiment Sir William Paton, Professor of Pharmacology at the University of Oxford, had been appointed to conduct an independent scrutiny of the monitoring arrangements and an assessment of the report which would flow from them. Sir William approved the monitoring arrangements and his main conclusion on the report was that the Intoximeter and Camic equipment and procedures were acceptable and did not place subjects unjustly in jeopardy; and that the system was weighted, if anything, too heavily *in favour* of the drinking motorist. Sir William drew attention to what he called 'unjustified non-prosecution' resulting from the policy of not prosecuting at levels below 40mcg per 100ml - the report found that four-fifths of those subjects who gave a lower breath result of 39mcg 'would have blood-levels not merely over the limit of 80mg, but over the prosecution limit of 87mg, with some of them considerably higher'.

The Government took the report as confirmation of the fundamental acceptability of the machines and their operating procedures. However, the non-statutory option of blood or urine for readings of 50mcg per 100ml or less, which had been continued after the six-month experimental period to await publication of the report, was continued. As Giles Shaw, Minister of State at the Home Office, put it: 'I think it is right to allow a little more time for public confidence to be re-established ... before withdrawing the non-statutory option ... But I am not convinced that there is a long-term case for retaining it and I intend to review the position in 12 months time with a view to withdrawing the non-statutory option' (*Parl.Debs.*(Commons) 25.6.85:342-3). In the event, the non-statutory option was maintained until January 1989, when the Home Secretary announced that it was to be discontinued.

Policing the new law

Despite the results of public opinion polls and changing police attitudes towards random testing, the powers of the police to administer a breath test were left basically unchanged. However, the courts confirmed that by virtue of s.7(1) of the 1981 Act suspicion of alcohol being present in the driver's body no longer had to arise while the person was still driving or attempting to drive - the police could exercise their general powers to stop motorists and if the suspicion of alcohol then arose could require a breath test (see below). In some police force areas systematic vehicle stops were introduced to check for the presence of alcohol, but the practice did not attract public support.[5] The police, accused of behaving in an underhand way and of exceeding their powers, largely abandoned systematic stops in the interests of good police/public relations.

The new law in the courts[6]

'Rather surprisingly the new drink/driving provisions are producing almost as many cases appearing in the reports as those generated by the original provisions first contained in the Road Safety Act 1967' (Halnan & Wallis 1987). This was not surprising as old habits die hard and drivers, with the financial resources needed to engage specialist advocates and expert witnesses, were as anxious as ever to avoid compulsory disqualification from driving. The new provisions came under attack on procedural technicalities, as had the old law; and the evidential breath-testing machines provided further opportunities for challenge - defence lawyers were encouraged to 'examine closely every angle of a breathalyser case, and in particular the procedure carried out by the operator of the machine' (Quinn 1984:358). However, the courts were unwilling (or unable?) to allow the generation of loopholes in the law which would admit technical defences (Fields & Heming 1986); resisted the many attempts to discredit the breath-test machines (Denney 1986); and attacked the 'thriving industry' devoted to getting motorists off drink-drive charges.[7]

By 1987 it seemed 'that every loophole for the drinking driver has been closed and lawyers could only be employed to mitigate or plead for special reasons to be found' (*Solicitors' Journal* 131:1072). Yet it took several House of Lords and Divisional Court decisions to arrive at this position and fresh attempts to discover novel defences continue (Watkins 1987). The case law developments to 1992 can be considered under five heads - loophole cases; failure to provide a specimen; machine challenges; random testing; and backtracking.

The loophole cases

While there were 'ingenious attempts to find new loopholes' (Samuels 1984), the courts appeared ready to apply the general law on exclusion of evidence as laid down in *Kuruma* and *Sang* (*supra*). A trio of cases (all before the Divisional Court) held that the police no longer had to prove a lawful arrest before evidence of analysis of excess alcohol could be admitted. The leading case was *Fox v Gwent Chief Constable* [1986] 1 AC 281. The defendant was the driver of a motor vehicle which was involved in an accident. No other person or vehicle was involved. The driver and his passenger left the vehicle and returned home. The police, who had no knowledge of the physical condition of either the driver or his passenger, went to the defendant's house. After receiving no reply to their knocking, the police officers entered the house through the closed but unlocked door and requested a breath test from the defendant, who refused. The defendant was arrested and taken to the police station, where he complied with a request to provide breath specimens, which proved positive. The defendant was charged with failing to provide a specimen of breath under s.7(4) of the 1972 Act and driving with excess alcohol contrary to s.6(1) of the Act. The justices convicted on both charges. The Divisional Court, upheld by the House of Lords, quashed the conviction under s.7(4), holding that at the time of the request the police were trespassers, but upheld the conviction for driving with excess alcohol. The House held that: 'A lawful arrest was no longer an essential prerequisite of a breath test ... (and) that it was well established that in general relevant evidence was admissible even though obtained illegally, though there might be a discretionary jurisdiction to exclude it if it had been obtained oppressively or through a trick' (281-2). The rule to be applied in drink-drive cases was thus to be much the same as for any other crime; and the courts appeared unwilling to admit the sort of technical and unmeritorious defences which had plagued the old law.

The principle in *Sang* was later modified s.78 of the Police and Criminal Evidence Act (1984) which came into force on 1 January 1986,[8] and provided that:

> the court may refuse to allow evidence on which the prosecution proposes to rely ... if it appears to the court that, having regard to all the circumstances, including the circumstances in which the evidence was

obtained, the admission of the evidence would have such an adverse effect on the fairness of the proceedings that the court ought not to admit it.

Cases have continued to come before the court which challenge police powers and procedures. A number of the most important are considered here.

Matto v DPP [1987] RTR 337   The police had trespassed and behaved oppressively and the initial breath test had not been given voluntarily. The Divisional Court held that the evidence (the subsequent positive breath test) should have been excluded because of the officer's illegality and *mala fides*. The difference between *Fox* and *Matto* seems to be that in the former case the officers acted wrongly but in good faith, and in the latter the officers acted deliberately wrongly and in bad faith.

DPP v Warren [1992] 3 WLR 884   The House of Lords overruled earlier decisions dealing with the procedure to be followed by the police when obtaining a blood or urine sample from a driver. Section 7(1) Road Traffic Act 1988 allows a constable to require a driver suspected of committing an offence under ss.3A, 4 or 5 to provide a specimen of breath, blood or urine. Under s.7(3) blood or urine can only be required at a police station or hospital and only at a police station if:

(a)   the constable has reasonable cause to believe that for a medical reason a specimen of breath cannot or should not be given; or

(b)   a breath analysis machine is not available or it is not practicable to use it; or

(c)   there is a suspicion on medical advice of driving under the influence of drugs.

Waren was arrested for driving with excess alcohol, but as the Intoximeter at the police station was not working the constable pursuant to s.7(3) asked Warren to provide an alternative sample. Previous cases had held that although the decision was that of the constable, the defendant had to be given the opportunity of specifying blood or urine and explaining his choice, to allow the constable to make an 'informed decision'. The House of Lords held that the constable does not have to give the driver the chance to express a preference. The House also clarified the procedures a constable must follow under s.7(3) and under s.8(2).[9]

R v Bolton Magistrates' Court Ex parte Scally [1991] RTR 84   A motorist who pleaded guilty to a drink-drive offence as his blood sample showed excess alcohol, received a Royal Pardon after it was discovered that the swab used to clean the skin before taking a blood sample was impregnated with alcohol. This opened the way for a large number of drivers, in the same circumstances, to attempt to get their convictions quoshed. Four such drivers applied to the Divisional Court (including a barrister (Scally) and a solicitor) and succeeded in having their convictions quoshed.

DPP v Cocoran [1992] RTR 289 The standard charge sheet used for some 20 years in cases of failing to provide breath, blood or urine samples was held to be defectively worded and legally invalid for duplicity. This decision opened the possibility of as many as 200,000 drivers being able to challenge their convictions. However, the view that 'it is very unlikely that such a defendant will succeed in court' (Light 1992) was confirmed in *Shaw v DPP* [1993] RTR 45 (and five other cases) which refused to follow the decision in *Cocoran*.

Failure to provide a specimen

Section 7(6) Road Traffic Act 1988 provides that it is an offence to fail to provide a specimen without reasonable excuse. It has been stated that: 'no excuse can be adjudged a reasonable one unless the person from whom the specimen is required is physically or mentally unable to provide it or the provision of such a specimen would entail a substantial risk to his health' (*R v Lennard* [1973] RTR 252[10]). A number of successful prosecution appeals from acquittals by magistrates have been heard where there has been no evidence of physical or mental impairment or any causal link between impairment and the failure to supply a specimen (e.g. *DPP v Ambrose* [1992] RTR 285). Cases have also been brought where drivers have claimed that a fear of AIDS has precluded them from providing a specimen. In *De Freitas v DPP* [1992] Crim LR 894 it was made clear that genuine fear can amount to a defence if classified as a mental condition amounting to a phobia; and in *DPP v Kinnersley* [1993] RTR 105, although not amounting to a defence, such a fear was held to amount to special reasons not to disqualify.

Machine challenges

Defence pleas alleging the improper operation of the breath-test machines came thick and fast.[11] They fell into three categories - failure to satiate the machine; major disparity between the two readings; and detection of acetone without any apparent medical justification (Beaven 1984; Dossett 1984). They all failed - as, eventually, did what became known as the 'Basingstoke defence', which relied on the interpretation of the machine print out as not a statement, as it was not easily intelligible to the defendant (*Gaimster v Marlow* [1984] 78 Cr App R 156).

However, a successful defence was mounted in *Howard v Hallett* [1984] RTR 535, where the operator of the machine mistakenly took only one sample. On realising the error, the machine was switched on again and the defendant asked for two more samples, the lower of which was given in evidence. The police admitted that the first reading had been the lowest of the three. It was held that only the evidence of the first and second specimens was admissible and the higher of those two readings was to be disregarded. The Divisional Court held that the statutory procedure in s.8 of the Act had to be complied with if the sample was to be admissible, and accordingly directed the defendant's acquittal. A decision which 'appears to have established a rigid approach to the exclusion of improperly obtained specimens, and some of the cases following it are reminiscent of the worst excesses of *Scott v Baker*' (Hirst 1990:149). Nevertheless, the consequence seems to be that irregularities before the administration of the breath-testing device can be ignored at the discretion of the court (under s.78 PACE - see above), but that the statutory criteria must be strictly adhered to once in front of the Intoximeter.

Another successful defence appeared in *Cracknell v Willis* [1987] 3 All ER 801. The House of Lords was called upon to consider the question of how far a motorist was entitled to challenge the reliability of the reading given by the evidential breath-test machine. The magistrates had refused to let the appellant adduce evidence of his consumption of alcohol prior to arrest, which, it was claimed, would show that the breath-test reading was false. However, the House unanimously held that a defendant could adduce evidence of the amount of alcohol which he had consumed in order to show that the approved breath-analysis machine was defective. Lord Griffiths put the rhetorical question of whether a teetotaller who had dined with two bishops, had refused a screening test, been arrested, thought better of it and given a sample of breath, which had proved positive could 'be convicted without the opportunity of calling the two bishops as witnesses to the fact that he had drunk nothing that evening?' Finding for the accused, Lord Griffiths urged caution when dealing with 'trial by machine' and expressed the view that if Parliament wished to provide for an irrebuttable presumption that the breath-testing machine was reliable, or that the presumption could only be challenged by a particular kind of evidence, then Parliament must take the responsibility of so deciding and spell out its intention in clear language.

Random testing

The random stopping of vehicles fell to be considered by the Divisional Court in *Chief Constable of Gwent v Dash* [1986] RTR 41. Vehicles were stopped by the police for no reason other than to give an officer experience of the breath-test procedure. The defendant's car was among those stopped. The constable noticed the smell of alcohol on the defendant's breath and subsequent specimens of breath proved positive. The justices convicted, but on appeal the Crown Court, quashing the conviction, held that the random stopping of vehicles amounted to malpractice, rendering the specimen of breath and subsequent procedure unlawful. However, the Divisional Court held that provided there was no malpractice, caprice or opprobrious behaviour on the part of the officers there was no restriction on the police stopping drivers for the purpose of ascertaining whether they had alcohol in their body. The random stopping of vehicles did not of itself amount to malpractice. But the police had no power to require breath tests at random.

Back calculations

In *Gumbley v Cunningham* [1989] AC 281 the defendant crashed his car, killing his brother, a front seat passenger, and suffering concussion. He was taken to hospital where, some four-and-a-half hours after the crash, he gave a blood sample, which was found to be under the limit (59mg). Gumbley claimed loss of memory as to the amount he had to drink. He was charged (*inter alia*) with driving with excess alcohol. The prosecution relied on the fact that since the 1981 Act the level of alcohol at the time of driving rather than at the time of the test is relevant and called two expert witnesses who testified that even using an hourly elimination rate of 6mg (15 was said to be the norm)[12] Gumbley would have been over the limit at the time of the crash. The decision was upheld in the Divisional Court and by the House of Lords; although the House echoed the words of Mr Justice Mann that the prosecution should not seek to rely on evidence of back calculation save where that evidence is easily understood and clearly persuasive of the presence of excess alcohol.

The case attracted much media attention which either applauded the fact that a driver could not escape liability in such cases, or warned that the practice was an erosion of civil liberties. A political row broke out, with the Transport Minister, Peter Bottomley, vigorously defending the conviction against complaints that the police were writing their own law, while Labour's legal spokesperson, Nicolas Brown, demanded a change in the law to prevent 'backtracking'. For while a driver should not escape liability because of a delay in taking a test (the prosecution position is obviously stronger if the driver's actions have caused the delay) the science of back calculation is open to some very strong scientific objections' (Walls & Brownlie 1985; Denney 1986a; Lewis 1987).

Evaluating the new law

The new law can be evaluated under four heads. First, its success in the courts; secondly, its operational effect on policing and trials; thirdly, its impact on levels of drink-driving; and fourthly, its influence on road casualty figures.

In the courts

A substantial number of cases on drink-driving continued to fill the Divisional Court, 'as advocates persist in seeking any possible weakness in evidence or procedure' (Halnan & Wallis 1989). Inevitably, one or two succeeded. But, as discussed above, the Act was in legal terms generally successful. The courts confirmed the abolition of the rule in *Scott v Baker*; the power of the police to stop vehicles at random to check if the driver had been drinking alcohol; and the use of backtracking by the prosecution. And challenges to the evidential breath testing equipment were mostly defeated. As Halnan et al. (1987) put it: 'the courts seem determined to try and prevent the creation of loopholes in the legislation'.

Operational efficiency

Policing The number of screening breath tests carried out by the police increased considerably following the introduction of the new law, rising from

207,000 in 1982 to 241,000 in 1983. However, the first full year of the new law saw the number of screening breath tests fall to 208,000, but this was an atypical year, due chiefly to the resource implications of policing the miner's strike. In 1985 the number of tests increased to 250,000 and continued to rise each year - in 1991 562,000 tests were carried out. The number of positive breath tests also showed a substantial increase, although as a percentage of tests carried out there has been a steady decline of positive tests, as would be expected if many more tests are carried out - the downside of which is, of course, that many more innocent people are being stopped and breath tested. In terms of increased police activity and the catching of drink-drivers the law achieved its aim. Whether increased police powers would further improve the effectiveness of the law is considered in Chapter 7.

Trial The elimination of most of the loophole cases allowed the courts to apply the law more confidently; so that drink-drive trials came to be noted for certainty of conviction rather than technical legal defences. The largest proportionate increase in findings of guilt among motoring offences between 1982 and 1983 was for drink-drive offences, which went up from 75,000 in 1982 to 98,000 in 1983 - an increase of just over 30 per cent. In 1984, the first full year of operation of the new law, the number of drivers convicted of drink-driving topped 100,000 for the first time, rising to a high of 119,000 in 1988. In 1991 there were some 113,200 convictions for drink-drive offences.

Level of drink-driving

The level of drink-driving is difficult to measure. Several sources of information can be utilised. First, the *Stats 19 accident report form* which is completed by the police after an accidents record whether any driver was required to provide a sample of breath, and if they were, the result of that test. These data indicate the level of drink-driving from the percentage of drivers who give positive tests, and the number of casualties in alcohol-related accidents - where one or more drivers failed a breath test. However, not all accidents are identified and of those which are, not all drivers are required to provide a specimen of breath. Further, a driver may not be tested because of serious injury or death. Secondly, casualties in accidents which occur between 10pm and 4am are traditionally associated with drink-driving. Thirdly, Coroners in England and Wales and Procurators Fiscal in Scotland supply data to the Transport and Road Research Laboratory concerning the blood-alcohol levels of those aged 16 and over who die within 12 hours of being injured in a road accident. And, fourthly, the number of positive breath tests recorded by the police and the number of convictions in the courts are used as indicators of drink-driving levels - these data depend to a large extent on police enforcement practices.

Available data are recognised to be of only limited accuracy and it is therefore not possible to reach any certain conclusions from them, but all suggest that levels of drink-driving have reduced over the past 10 years. Support for this view comes too from driver surveys which 'indicate a substantial reduction in the number of people who risk drinking and driving, possibly as much as 50 per cent between 1978 and 1986' (Sabey 1990). The role played by changes in legal policy in the generation of these reductions is unclear.

Casualty rates

Britain has seen a steady decline in road casualties since the mid-1960s, and in road deaths since the early 1970s (see Appendix 1 Table 4), despite the continued expansion of motor traffic (Appendix 1 Table 3). Ten-year figures illustrate this trend:

	1965	1975	1985	per cent change 75-85
Killed	7,952	6,366	5,165	-19
Seriously injured	97,865	77,122	70,989	-8
Slightly injured	292,120	241,462	241,379	-0
Total Casualties	397,937	324,950	317,524	-2

(Source: Department of Transport 1987)

Figures for 1991 are 4,568 deaths and 311,000 injuries, while 1993 is likely to see the number of death fall below 4,000. Declining casualty figures have been attributed to a number of factors, including improved vehicle safety standards, safer roads, improved medical facilities and fewer motor bikes and children. But what credit should be given to the drink-drive legislation for the reduction? Official sources lavished praise on the 1967 Act as a life-saving measure (see Chapter 4), but the reforms introduced in 1983 were overshadowed by the new seat belt provisions. The Department of Transport (1987:6) gave little credit to any decrease in drink-driving for saving lives:

Other measures may be mentioned but in rather more cautious terms, since our understanding of their effect - at least in the long term - is based on less certain, more circumstantial, evidence. These include: driver and rider training; legislation regulating road user behaviour (for example, on speed limits and drinking and driving); and education and publicity programmes.

This is not surprising, as estimating the number of alcohol-related deaths and injuries is in itself problematic. As Foster et al. (1988:1430) explain: 'in Britain the precise number and relative proportions of deaths among drivers, passengers, and pedestrians in road traffic accidents related to alcohol is not known'.

116

It is difficult to isolate causes and widely varying estimates have been advanced. Those campaigning against drink-driving tend to put the figure for deaths at some 1,800 per year (e.g. CADD) while the National Audit Office Report implicated drink-driving as a cause of 20 per cent of road deaths (NAO 1988) and Foster et al. (1988) calculated that as many as 23 per cent of total road deaths are attributable, at least in part, to alcohol. This would mean some 1000 (NAO) or 1,250 (Foster et al.) of the 5,052 people killed on the roads in 1988 died either wholly or partly as a result of drink-driving. What does seem to be agreed is that in line with other road casualties the number of alcohol-related deaths and injuries on the roads has declined steadily over the last ten years. As shown in this table produced by the Department of Transport:

Year	Fatal	Serious	Slight	Total
1979	1,790	9,100	21,600	32,490
1980	1,570	8,800	20,500	30,870
1981	1,540	8,100	19,200	28,840
1982	1,670	8,800	20,700	31,170
1983	1,200	7,500	18,700	27,400
1984	1,280	7,500	19,500	28,280
1985	1,130	7,500	19,500	28,130
1986	1,060	7,000	18,600	26,660
1987	980	6,400	17,300	24,680
1988	840	5,650	16,200	22,690
1989	870	5,325	16,400	22,595
1990	800	4,650	15,400	20,850
1991	700	4,205	13,950	18,855

(Source: Department of Transport 1989, 1992)

Broughton & Stark (1986) set out to examine the trends in alcohol-related casualties between 1979 and 1984; and sought to separate the impact of the new law from other factors. They found that 'In non-built-up areas, the legislation has led to a casualty reduction of 5-10 per cent among car occupants injured at the time of day when drink/driving is chiefly a problem. No such benefits have been found in built-up areas, and indeed the number of front seat passengers injured in these areas appears to have risen'.

It has proved difficult to assess the impact of the 1981 Act on casualty figures; but, while the effect of the provisions cannot be demonstrated as clearly as the initial gains attributed to the 1967 Act, it was according to Ross 'effective in reducing traffic casualties in the context of the Christmas Crusade' (Ross 1987, 1988). The continuing reduction in yearly casualty figures may owe something to the law, particularly any long-term deterrent effect; intensified policing; and other factors such as improved medical response and changing drinking patterns.

Summary

To link changes in police activity, numbers convicted, levels of drink-driving, and casualty figures directly with the introduction of the new provisions would be an obvious over-simplification, but increases in the first two of these and a decrease in the last two are changes which would indicate that the reforms were having the desired effect. The new provisions produced an increased rate of screening breath tests and convictions; largely overcame the problems faced by the courts in the loophole cases; and seem to have played some part in the declining drink-driving and road casualty figures - but there was no room for complacency. Road casualties remained unacceptably high and, despite the difficulties of establishing the nature and extent of the relationship between alcohol and road accidents, it was accepted that drink-driving was implicated in some of these casualties.

Pressure for reform

As has been seen, the 'new drink-drive law' is broadly based on a report published in 1976. Since then, and particularly during the second half of the 1980s, there have been significant developments in the drink-drive debate and various strategies aimed at further reductions in alcohol-related road casualties have been proposed. These range from wide-scale debates on alcohol policy and road safety to tactical 'preventative measures' (Sabey 1985) such as publicity, information and education to change attitudes; and rehabilitation programmes to reduce re-offending. By the end of the 1980s the stage seemed set for further reform of legal policy and the drink-driver, these developments are considered further in Chapter 7.

Notes

1. Two machines were approved for the purposes of evidential testing - the Intoximeter 3000 (adopted by 39 forces) and the Camic Breath Analyser (adopted by four constabularies - Northumbria, Durham, Cleveland and North Yorkshire).

2. See, for example, Quinn (1984); and the regular feature in the *New Law Journal*, 'The Microgrammes are Coming' (later called 'Microgrammes' and 'Microgramme Corner'), which, for example, questioned the effect on breath test results of recent vomiting/regurgitation (1983:219) and mouthwashes and breath fresheners/deodorisers (1983:118,712).

3. See further Gatt (1984:250) who questioned not only the accepted ratio between breath and blood of 2300:1, but also found that 'the temperature of the breath has a profound effect on the concentration of alcohol measured'.

4. To convert breath-alcohol readings in mcgs to blood-alcohol concentrations in mgs it is necessary to multiply by 2.3.

5. Questions were raised in Parliament and reports called for from the Chief Constable of Sussex (Roger Birch, whose high-profile approach to drink-driving had been apparent for some years - see, for example, Light 1986) who had been particularly pro-active in his policies.

6. For a detailed account of the provisions see Halnan & Wallis (1989).

7. Lord Justice Watkins reported in *The Guardian* (16 Febraury 1990).

8. See further Halnan & Wallis (1989); Hirst (1990); Tucker (1990).

9. Section 8(2) gives drivers with a lower breath specimen not exceeding 50mcgs/100mls an option to request it to be replaced by a blood or urine sample. But see also *DPP v Gordon* [1990] RTR 71; *Patterson v DPP* [1990] RTR 329; *Edge v DPP* [1993] RTR 65; *Meade v DPP* [1993] RTR 151.

10. See also *Grady v Pollard* [1988] RTR 316; *Nicholas v DPP* [1992] RTR 413.

11. Dr Paul Williams, Marketing Director, Lion Laboratories, was called as an expert witness on 90 occasions in 1984. Lion Laboratories published a book in 1987, which contained summaries of all relevant Divisional Court judgements and statements made by Dr Williams in evidence (price £51).

12. The Home Office report found 3.6 per cent of their sample to have an hourly elimination rate of between 2.3 and 4.6mg (Paton et al. 1985). However, of the 300 plus persons measured by the marketing director of Lion Laboratories the lowest rate was 12mg; more experienced drinkers were said to have higher elimination rates and for a rate as low as 6mg per hour the subject would be extremely young, or a teetotaller, or have a thick liver (Gold 1986).

7 Beyond the new law (1980-1992)

The new law, based on mid-1970s thinking and addressing chiefly technical procedural matters, provided mainly refinement rather than reform of legal policy and the drink-driver. Thus the pressure for reform, which had provided the impetus for the setting up of the Blennerhassett Committee in 1975 continued. This, coupled with expanded interest in alcohol policy and road safety, ensured that the drive for reform would intensify into the next decade, which saw a number of influential official and quasi-official investigations into both alcohol policy and road safety; the expansion of the Government's drink-drive publicity campaigns; and increased Parliamentary activity on alcohol-related issues. These together with a rapidly expanding research literature gave drink-driving a similarly high profile to that which it had attracted in the 1960s. This chapter considers these developments, their implications for legal policy and the practical proposals which emerged.

Alcohol policy

In 1981 the DHSS published *Drinking Sensibly*, to present 'a balanced overall picture of the Government's policies on the health and social issues relating to alcohol' (DHSS 1981:7). A year later the Alcohol Education and Research Council was set up to support research and education in the alcohol field, and in 1983 the recently established Addiction Research Centre based at the Universities of Hull and York won an ESRC contract for a five-year programme which aimed to 'identify the impediments (fiscal, political, structural and procedural) to the development of a coordinated national approach to the prevention of alcohol- and tobacco-related problems' and suggest ways to eliminate or reduce these problems (Addiction Research Centre 1988). The Centre published its findings in 1990 (Maynard & Tether 1990; Godfrey & Robinson 1990). In September 1987, an inter-departmental Ministerial Group on Alcohol Misuse, headed by the Leader of the Commons, John Wakeham, was announced by Douglas Hurd, the Home Secretary and John Moore, the Social Services Secretary, with a brief to conduct a systematic review of Government policy for combatting alcohol-related problems, including drink-driving.[1]

These initiatives reflected growing concern over alcohol-related problems. From them came support for the need to investigate the link between *per capita* consumption of alcohol and alcohol-related harm, including drink-driving.[2] Further support for consumption theory was to be found in a review of US research by Tether & Godfrey (1990:159) who contended that: 'If the level of drink-driving accidents is linked to the level of alcohol consumption, then policies which are designed to control that consumption may also affect the levels of drink-driving and associated harm. Indeed policies such as tax changes may be more effective than specific drink-driving measures'. As Dunbar (1985:3) and others have argued, a reduction in drink-driving needs countermeasures which fall into a wider framework of measures aimed against alcohol abuse generally - 'A national alcohol policy would be a strategic approach to drink-driving, with drinking and driving countermeasures being essentially tactical in nature'.

Road safety

A House of Commons Transport Committee on Road Safety reported in 1985. The report contained several recommendations on the law relating to drink-driving - which it saw as 'one of the most serious road safety problems in the country' (House of Commons 1985:81) - but it came out against the introduction of random breath testing (see below). A separate review of road safety by an Inter-departmental Working Group was commissioned by Ministers in 1983. Its report (Department of Transport 1987), which was accepted by the Government, suggested that the aim should be to reduce road casualties, by the year 2000, by a third. This was to be achieved by proposals designed to provide safer roads and safer vehicles, together with measures to change public attitudes to road safety, as 'there appear to be few new opportunities for legislation which would be acceptable and cost effective'. The working group concluded that there was no case for any change in drink-driving legislation 'in the immediate future'. This was not surprising as the working group had been instructed to take account of 'two key considerations' - that no increase in overall resources for road safety should be assumed, and that there should be a presumption against the imposition of new legislative controls on road users, except where unavoidable.

The National Audit Office Report on road safety, published in 1988, took a much more positive line on measures to combat drink-driving, which it saw as 'a major cause of road accidents costing at least £360 million and involving some 20 per cent of road deaths each year' (NAO 1988:3). Its recommendations are considered below. It was clear from these reports that road traffic law was considered an important factor in regulating road users' behaviour. It was also apparent that road traffic law, which had developed piecemeal over the years, needed to be updated, harmonised and simplified. A major review of road traffic law was long overdue. The Road Traffic Law Review was set up on 31 January 1985 by the Secretaries of State for Transport and the Home Department, with the agreement of the Secretary of State for Scotland.[3]

Road Traffic Law Review

The terms of reference of the Review were to consider improvements to road traffic law to simplify the law and make it more acceptable. Its report, published 12 April 1988 (Department of Transport/Home Office 1988), 'contained some imaginative, clear and highly pertinent proposals' (Tether & Godfrey 1990:150), which, along the lines of contemporary penological thinking, and in step with road safety campaigns, sought to give the serious offender who maimed or killed his or her just deserts and, by way of retesting and training provisions, to reduce the chances of re-offending. The Review contained 137 recommendations and advocated what Bottoms (1977) has termed a bifurcated approach - diversion of minor offenders from the criminal justice system and increased penalties 'for those motorists who pay no heed to laws designed for other road users' protection' of which 'the greatest public concern is about the extremely bad, especially drunken driver who kills'. This approach was well received, as in cases where motoring offenders had caused death or serious injury the law was generally perceived to be hopelessly inadequate (Spencer 1985; Wallis 1988). Seven 'major changes in the law' were proposed - reformulation of the law relating to 'very bad driving' (reckless, causing death); the possibility of conviction for a lesser charge than that brought; the introduction of a specific offence of 'bad driving' causing death when the driver was unfit through drink or drugs; increased penalties for failing to stop or report an accident (to bring the offence into line with penalties for drink-drive offences); obligatory disqualification for the redefined very bad driving offence; the sitting of an extended driving test for those disqualified for 12 months or more; and an experiment to enable courts to order drink-drivers to attend training courses.

For legal policy and the drink-driver the Review addressed several issues (Wesson 1988) - the most dramatic was the introduction of a 'separate, specific offence to deal with the driver who causes a fatal accident whilst driving badly (i.e. carelessly) and under the influence of drink or drugs' (23.7), carrying a maximum of five years imprisonment. The offence was intended to counter the perceived inadequacy of the existing law in cases where death is caused by a driver under the influence of alcohol. Further, the Review recommended the scrapping of insurance policies designed to protect motorists against the consequences of disqualification, the possibility of forfeiture of vehicles by the courts, the introduction of server training in licensing renewals[4], and the expansion of alcohol education schemes for first offenders.[5] However, on the general debates surrounding legal policy and the drink-driver - such as high-risk offenders, blood-alcohol limits and random breath testing - it said very little, but as pointed out in the introduction to the Review - 'we have not been invited to examine the *whole* of road traffic law, enforcement and sentencing'.

The Review was welcomed by both the popular and legal press and by interested organisations, including the motoring associations. However, the report adopted a narrow approach to motoring crime and concentrated on 'correcting' offenders, with any general deterrent message coming through tougher punishment rather than increasing the perceived and actual risk of apprehension. This led Spencer (1988:721) to conclude that 'the North Report is valuable in that it proposes many changes in road traffic law which would make it fairer and more rational than we have at present. But sadly, its impact on road safety is unlikely to be great'. This is a realistic assessment; an important opportunity for wholesale reform of the law had been lost. The limited nature of the report can, it seems, be explained by two main factors. First, its terms of reference and secondly, the influence of pressure groups such as CADD, government publicity and general media hype. These issues are discussed further in Chapter 8, their aim appears retributive rather than reductive. This focus is reflected in many of the recommendations of the report. However, such measures - for example, tougher penalties and forfeiture of vehicles - may produce important symbolic effects; as may the scrapping of 'chauffeur plan' insurance policies and the introduction of server responsibility. This is important in the context of the increased interest which has recently attracted to the symbolic significance of the law and its possible reductive effect beyond simple and general deterrence (see Chapter 8). Further, recent work by Riley (1991) has provided an insight into the operation of such educative and symbolic processes (see below).

The Transport Secretary, Paul Channon, announced that there would be a period of consultation, but that Ministers would report to the Commons before the summer recess. Early legislation was promised. A White Paper was published in February 1989 (Home Office 1989). The Road Traffic Act 1991, which came into force on 1 July 1992 gave effect to North's main recommendations, including the introduction of a new offence of 'causing death by careless driving while under the influence of drink or drugs' carrying a maximum penalty of five years imprisonment,[6] two years disqualification from driving and an unlimited fine (s.3); and gave statutory recognition to 'rehabilitation' courses for drink-drive offenders (ss.30,31).[7]

Publicity campaigns

Christmas drink-drive crackdowns by police forces and government publicity campaigns have been a 'tradition' since the Road Safety Act 1967. From 1979, to 1982 a series of high-profile radio and television 'don't drink and drive' campaigns was mounted to precede the introduction of the 1981 Act; and continued, albeit on a smaller budget, for the first year of the new law. The 1984 Christmas campaign proved controversial. It was launched under the slogan 'Stay low, or you might live to regret it'. The replacement of the traditional 'Don't Drink and Drive' slogan attracted strong criticism for sending the wrong message. The Government's justification was that it is not illegal to drink and drive and that the campaign was aimed specifically at young people (in the 16-19 age group), for whom, said Transport Minister, Lynda Chalker, a message of complete prohibition was a 'turn-off'. For Christmas 1985 the campaign targeted male drivers and motor cyclists under 35 years of age and the Department substituted the slogan 'Think you can drink and drive? Think again'. However, while the message seemed to be more acceptable, there was criticism that it had been designed with no evaluation of the 1984 campaign completed. The campaigns were also criticised for being mounted only over Christmas. In 1984 The Department of Transport, supported by the House of Commons Committee, had indicated that it was 'giving active consideration to developing a more wide ranging and continuous programme of education ... which would go beyond the confines of a single annual publicity campaign' (*Parl.Debs.*(Commons) 2:35). In 1986 ('European Road Safety Year') the Government intensified its propaganda campaign. An advertising agency was appointed with a brief to make drink-driving socially unacceptable; the Department of Transport published a free booklet, *The Facts About Drinking and Driving* (Transport and Road Research Laboratory 1986); and the first summer campaign was launched on 1 May. For Christmas 1986 the 'Don't Drink and Drive' slogan was resurrected, together with others of an unashamedly emotional nature such as 'If you drink and drive you're a menace to society' and 'What should you call people who slaughter 1,100 a year?'. The 1986 campaign was criticised as under-funded, and for excluding television commercials. In 1987 the Department trebled the campaign budget to £3.5 million and produced a series of highly emotive television commercials, which were run in June/July, October, and December - 'with the object of making drinking and driving socially unacceptable' (Department of Transport 1988:28). The Department used the slogan 'Drinking and driving wrecks lives'. The campaigns were launched by the Transport Secretary, Paul Channon, but clearly bore the mark of Roads and Traffic Minister, Peter Bottomley, (appointed in 1986), and the influence of the Campaign Against Drinking and Driving. For 1988 the campaigns remained as for 1987, with some new television commercials being made to supplement the previous ones. An interesting development was the assistance given to the 1988 campaign by the private sector - publicans, brewers, soft drink producers, clubs, supermarkets and off-licences.

These campaigns were crucially important for legal policy and the drink-driver. They sought to increase the deterrent effect of the law by increasing drivers' perceptions of the risk of being caught; attempted to change attitudes to drink-driving; were often accompanied by a police crackdown; and were used by the Department of Transport to resist legal reforms, particularly random testing. But were the campaigns effective? Opinions from the police, press and public varied. Each campaign was followed by the publication of lists of casualty and breath tests figures, both regional and national. Changes in the casualty and positive breath test rates compared with other years or times of the year were then used to assess the success or failure of the campaigns. The data used was often incomplete and other variables, especially changes in police practice, mostly ignored. There was no reliable evidence on the effectiveness of the campaigns in reducing drink-related road casualties and as one commentator put it: 'they are almost certainly not cost effective' (Raffle 1986). This did nothing to dissuade the Government from their use. The first reliable data were produced on the 1983 campaign; which for a number of reasons was particularly intensive. Dubbing it the 1983 'Christmas Crusade against Drinking and Driving' Ross (1987:476) concluded that 'The experience of the Christmas Crusade reinforces the expectation that deterrent interventions involving highly publicized campaigns increasing the certainty of punishment for illegal behaviour can be successful over a limited period of time'. This accords with the findings produced by Ross on the operation of the 1967 Act (Ross 1973) and the 'Cheshire Blitz' (Ross 1977). However, it cannot be used as evidence of the success of the 1983 publicity campaign as the novelty of the new law, a police crackdown and other newsworthy developments also contributed. An internal evaluation conducted after the 1985 campaign concluded: 'The campaign has high recognition, particularly among the prime target (young adult males). However, little change in accident levels was recorded'. Similarly, a Department of Transport internal paper suggested that its campaigns had little effect on public attitudes. This was followed by a Department of Transport report which concluded that the campaigns had failed to produce measurable results and that there was no clear link between the campaigns and the saving of lives (Department of Transport 1987). Even so, Parliamentary Questions on the campaigns met with optimistic replies. For example: 'Our research shows that our campaigns are making an impact. There is evidence of a long-term reduction in the amount of drinking and driving' (*Parl.Debs.*(Commons) 20.6.88:452). However, no such evidence appeared then to exist; though the work of Riley (1991) may now provide some support for such a view (see below).

Parliamentary activity

Parliamentary activity on drink-driving continued after the introduction of the new law. For the 1983/4 session it was mainly on the accuracy of the breath-testing devices, the Government evaluation of the non-statutory option to request a blood or urine sample; and the cost and effectiveness of the Government's drink-drive campaigns. The 1984/5 session saw interest in the non-statutory option continue, concern expressed over the controversial 'Stay Low' message of Christmas 1984 and the start of the Parliamentary campaign for the introduction of random breath testing. For 1985/6 concern over the cost and effectiveness of the Government campaigns (particularly that of summer 1986) was again much in evidence, together with penalties, the level of the blood-alcohol concentration and requests for statistics and more research. Prior to the 1986/7 session police powers had not been a major issue in the Commons. December 1986 saw the debate on policing the drink-drive laws hot up. To points on increased police powers the Government answered that existing powers were adequate; to requests for existing powers to be used more effectively, the Government replied that operational policy was a matter for individual chief officers of police; and to other points on the legal response, the Government countered that the North Report was awaited. For the 1987/8 session the major Parliamentary drink-drive issue was random breath testing. On 17 November 1987, Roland Boyes moved a ten-minute Bill - the Road Traffic (Random Breath Testing) Bill which proposed amendments to the Road Traffic Act 1972 to empower the police to carry out random breath tests at the roadside. The Bill got no further. The session also saw two unsuccessful attempts to lower the legal blood-alcohol limit for drivers from 80mg to 50mg per 100ml.[8] In the 1988/9 session virtually all of the existing road traffic provisions were replaced by three consolidating enactments - the Road Traffic Act 1988, the Road Traffic Offenders Act 1988 and the Road Traffic (Consequential Provisions Act) 1988 -which were brought into force on 5 May 1989. The campaign for random testing continued in 1988, with a private members Bill presented on 21 December by John Home Robertson - the Road Traffic (Breath Tests) Bill which sought to amend the Road Traffic Act 1988 to redefine the powers of the police to administer breath tests; to make further provisions for the deterrence and detection of alcohol; and for connected purposes. It got no further. The Road Traffic Act 1991, welcomed by the Transport Minister, Malcolm Rifkind, as an important contribution to the reduction of deaths and injuries on the roads, once again excluded random breath testing - which was blocked by a Government three line whip.

Research literature

By the late 1980s the road safety and alcohol lobbies had converged on drink-driving, which together with a rapidly expanding body of research, was to prove important in both promotional terms and the development of a wide range of drink-drive countermeasures. Preventative measures such as publicity, education and rehabilitation were often presented as a package (BMA 1988). For as Sabey (1986:43) put it: 'experience has shown that emphasis on particular actions carried to excess is not effective ... a coordinated combination of approaches is needed, with two objectives in mind: modifying the behaviour of present day road users and educating future generations of road users'. However, road traffic law remained the principal response to drink-driving; there were two main developments. First, attempts were being made to identify the drink-driver to develop categories of drink-driver - social, young, and problem (high-risk) - and specific responses for each group. Secondly, means of improving the deterrent effect of the law were still being sought.

Identifying the drink-driver

Effective policies need to identify the demographics and habits of those who drink and drive (Havard 1985; Clare & Bristow 1987). To this end the Transport and Road Research Laboratory has produced data drawn from driving licence records to provide an overview of the court processing of motoring offenders, including convicted drink-drivers (Broughton 1986) and data on drivers who have not been convicted of a drink-drive offence in the previous 10 years have been gathered by Clayton et al.(1984). These provide useful basic information on the drink-driver, which has been supplemented by data from Riley (1984) in his self-report study. However, it was not until the publication of two studies in 1988 that detailed information on the drink-driver in England and Wales was made available - one examined the alcohol intake of accident involved drivers, the other, the alcohol levels of drivers stopped at roadside surveys.

Accident involved drivers In conjunction with the Transport and Road Research Laboratory the Nottinghamshire police screened all drivers involved in accidents over a 12-month period. Of the 8,853 drivers sampled, 89 per cent were given a roadside screening test, of which 94 per cent were negative, 1.2 per cent had consumed some alcohol and 4.5 per cent were over 80mg per 100ml. Those over 80mg plus a random sample of those with negative results were selected for interview - a total of 1,043. It was found that one-third of those over the limit were aged between 20 and 24; 95 per cent were male; 50 per cent of accidents occurred between 10pm and 1am; 65 per cent occurred on Fridays, Saturdays, and Sundays; the drink most commonly consumed before an accident was beer (83 per cent); and the incidence of drink-driving was greatest in semi-skilled manual workers and the unemployed (Everest & Jones 1988).

Roadside surveys The Blennerhassett Committee had recommended roadside surveys to provide data on drinking levels of drivers actually on the road. The Transport and Road Research Laboratory conducted roadside surveys in Sussex and Warwickshire between the hours of 10pm and 3am on Thursday, Friday and Saturday nights for a period of eight weeks between April and June 1988 (Sabey et al. 1988). As well as providing information about their drinking behaviour, drivers were asked to volunteer a breath sample. Less than 2 per cent refused to take part and a further 1 per cent refused to provide a breath sample. Of the 2,600 drivers who agreed to take part and provided a breath sample 17.3 per cent had consumed some alcohol, 5.3 per cent were over half the legal limit, 1.7 per cent were over the limit and 0.2 per cent were more than twice the limit. Three-quarters of those over the limit had been drinking beer, cider or lager and public houses were the most likely drinking venue.

Categorizing the drink-driver

From the data provided by these surveys it has been argued that the drink-driver is not a single homogenous type, and that an effective policy needs to identify different types of drink-driver, devise suitable strategies for each and then target specific groups. Two basic classifications have been developed - by drinking habits and by experience (of both drinking and driving). Drinking habits ranged from the social to the problem drinker. Inexperience equated with youth.

By drinking habits Sabey (1986) developed a continuum of drinking habits linked to blood-alcohol concentration levels and postulated suitable responses. At one end is the 'social' drinker, with blood-alcohol concentrations from zero to 80mgs per 100mls, who is considered most likely to be deterred by the threat or experience of punishment and might be dissuaded from drink-driving by publicity and information. Next is the 'heavy drinker, with blood-alcohol concentrations over 80 and up to 200mgs, who would require counselling. The 'high-risk' drinker is said to be characterised by blood-alcohol concentrations of above 200mgs, also in need of counselling, while those at levels of 400mgs are termed 'alcoholics', in need of medical intervention. The implications of this model, if accurate, are apparent from Dunbar (1985:6):

> The overwhelming majority of drivers involved in serious and fatal crashes due to their own alcohol consumption have alcohol concentrations of 100mg or higher, usually much higher. Contrary to common opinion, the overwhelming bulk of accidents in which alcohol plays a role do not involve merely one or two drinks - far greater quantities of alcohol are involved. The legal limit of 80mg is rarely reached by normal social drinking.

Those at the far end of the spectrum - the problem drinkers or 'alcoholics' are, due to their dependence on alcohol, unlikely to be deterred from drink-driving by criminal law sanctions. However, they may choose not to drive. If they do drive legal policy is designed to catch them and remove their driver's licence, which of course is of itself no guarantee that they will not continue to drive; but at present, unless offenders come within the high-risk category, they will have their driving licence returned automatically at the end of the period of disqualification.

High-risk offenders In pre-breathalyser days scientific opinion was keen to stress that it was not just the drunken, but also the drink-driver who was a danger on the road. From the late 1960s, with the introduction of blood-alcohol testing and the recording of blood-alcohol levels by Coroners, it became apparent that drivers who were found to be over the limit fell largely between 100mg and 200mg (Keen 1968); problem drinkers were 'disproportionately represented among drinking and driving offenders' (Dunbar 1986); and those involved in fatal accidents were likely to have high blood-alcohol concentrations and a history of heavy drinking (Crompton 1982).[9] It was also claimed that chronic alcoholics or problem drinkers rather than occasional drinkers were the cause of road accidents (Birrell 1970). These findings led to a call for special attention to be paid to what came to be called 'high-risk offenders' - alcohol-dependent drivers unable to separate their drinking from their driving (Havard 1978). Blennerhassett recommended the introduction of 'special procedures' for this group, but the Government rejected the Committee's proposals as it was unable to work out a practical way in which magistrates' courts, with such an offender before them, could establish whether the defendant's problem was 'cured' or whether he or she was likely to offend again (Department of Transport 1979:47-51).[10] Also, the Department of Transport has stated that there is 'a practical constraint on the number of cases that the DVLC and the Medical Advisory Branch can handle'; and there was considerable opposition to the proposals from the DVLC itself which feared increased work at a time when the Government was committed to reducing civil service personnel (Baggott 1988).

Consequently, much weaker provisions were introduced - any motorists twice convicted in ten years of a drink-drive offence, where both offences showed the blood-alcohol level to be more than two-and-a-half times the legal limit, would have their licences returned to them only when they had been medically certified as fit to drive and thus satisfied the Secretary of State's Medical Adviser that they did not present a danger to the public. (Blennerhassett had proposed defining the high-risk offender as someone convicted twice in 10 years *or* over 200mg.) It was estimated that this would involve some 300 drivers each year. The driver was to be invited to attend for interview and medical examination and could be referred to a local hospital for a blood sample to be analysed. The results of the interview and any blood analysis would determine the Secretary of State's decision on whether to refuse the issue of a licence - borderline cases were to be referred to a psychiatrist specialising in alcoholism (Halnan 1985; Taylor 1986).

The 'risk' level is generally considered to have been set too high and the 10-year period too long (e.g. Steele 1984; BMA 1988). A lower level of 150mg has been suggested which would involve a far higher number of drivers. For example, in 1981 about 56 per cent of the 57,000 convictions involved blood-alcohol levels above 150mg; of these, some 3,000 drivers per year would have qualified for the high-risk procedures. In 1984 the Government expressed itself willing to consider a lower threshold 'in the light of experience' with the existing provisions; and the Wakeham Committee in 1988 recommended to the Department of Transport that it should consider 'as a matter of urgency' whether the high-risk procedure should be extended to any driver with two or more drink-driving convictions. The Department accepted the suggestion and proposals were announced at the end of 1988 to extend the provisions to those who have been disqualified at two-and-a-half times or more over the legal limit; have been disqualified for failing to provide a specimen; or have had any two drink-driving disqualifications within a 10-year period. It was estimated that this would involve some 40,000 drivers a year - legislation was expected in 1990. The original provisions have yet to be evaluated and the extended provisions wait to be introduced. Dunbar (1986:69) posits two reasons for this reluctance to act on the high-risk offender. First, an inability on the part of the treatment procedures and centres to cope with the numbers involved; and, secondly, 'a resistance to accept the consequences of a public health approach to alcohol problems' as 'greater numbers of people are likely to be found whose problems are the legitimate targets of intervention'.

Work carried out by the Tayside Safe Driving project has added a further dimension to the danger posed by the high-risk offender. As Dunbar et al. (1985:827) put it: 'problem drinking, as distinct from driving under the influence of alcohol is ... an important factor in traffic safety'. The Tayside study found that among older drink-drivers accident risk was affected not only by their being under the influence of alcohol, but by a combination of factors including chronic alcohol-induced deterioration. A high proportion of such drivers were found to be from professional and managerial groups - the types most likely to evade arrest for drink-driving as they would be of respectable appearance driving well-maintained vehicles (Dunbar 1985). Additionally, Dunbar (1987) criticises the high-risk offender scheme on the basis of research findings 'from a number of European countries' for being too centralised (regional administration is suggested) and conservative ('all drinking drivers over the age of 30 should be screened') and for being too late (Dunbar proposes intervention at conviction rather than before a licence is renewed).

By experience The 1980s saw a general increase in concern over young people and drinking (e.g. BMA 1986; Home Office 1987) and the British Crime Survey found that figures for drink-driving in the 16 to 30 age group were much higher than the average at one in three men (overall one in five) and one in seven women (overall one in eleven) (Riley 1984). Further, the accident risk level for young and inexperienced drivers has been shown to be higher than for older more experienced drivers (Havard 1986; Everest & Jones 1987). Similar findings in other countries have led to the introduction of special measures for young people (Benjamin 1987). For example, in the US the legal age for driving has been raised to 21 and in Australia learner drivers and first year licence holders are subject to lower blood-alcohol concentration limits (zero or 20 where the limit is 50 and 20 or 50 where the limit is 80).

Other data from domestic studies include - those aged 20-24 have the highest rate of failing breath tests; 39 per cent of drivers aged 20-24 who are killed in road accidents have blood-alcohol concentrations over the legal limit; 32 per cent of drink-drive convictions fall in the under 25 age group; 21 is the peak age for drink-drive convictions; and the chances of conviction have been calculated at 0.4 per cent (Home Office 1987). Analysis of the drinking and driving habits of those in the 17-29 age group led the Home Office report to conclude that 'there appears to be a very considerable drinking and driving problem involving beer-drinking young men'.

Studies carried out by the Transport and Road Research Laboratory produced similar results - those most at risk of drink-driving have been found to be male, semi-skilled or unemployed in the 20-24 age group (Everest & Jones 1988; Sabey et al. 1988), as has later Home Office research conducted by Riley (1991). Consequently, special measures have been proposed for young offenders, which include the introduction of a lower blood-alcohol concentration limit, improved education, and better enforcement; as well as the possibilities for prevention offered by raising the minimum drinking age.[11]

Deterrence

Deterrence is the central aim for legal policy and the drink-driver. As an individual deterrent, Shapiro & Votey (1984) found that an actual arrest experience reduces the probability that a person will drink and drive again (see also Homel 1988). However, the general deterrent effect is widely assumed to be weak.

Ross (1973) postulated a strong but short-lived general deterrent effect for the 1967 Act. He also examined Scandinavian drink-drive laws, often cited as examples of effective deterrent measures, and claimed (Ross 1975, 1978, 1981, 1984, 1984a, 1988a) them to be ineffective - the 'Scandinavian Myth' as Ross termed it. His findings were doubted by Zimring (1978) and challenged by Snortum (1984, 1984a, 1988; Snortum et al. 1986); in particular, for Ross's narrow focus on 'simple deterrence', ignoring the wider role of law in society (see Chapter 8).

However, there is general agreement that the drink-drive law has had weak deterrent effect. Why should this be? Some claim that the penalties are too low;[12] or the level of enforcement is too low (Riley 1985 estimates the chances of apprehension as 1 in 250); or both - and then go on to argue that the level of either or both should be raised. Whether this approach would prove effective is debatable, but it is interesting to note that even among those who feel that it would be, often it is considered not to be practical politics because public attitudes towards drink-driving are thought to be such as not to permit it.

Penalties and sentencing

The Criminal Law Act 1977 made drink-drive offences triable only summarily and increased the maximum sentence to imprisonment for six months and a fine of £1000. The Transport Act 1981 did not increase the penalties, but in 1984 the Home Secretary, under powers conferred by s.143 of the Magistrates' Courts Act 1980, increased the level of fines to keep pace with inflation, increasing the maximum fine for drink-drive offences to £2000. Further increases in the available penalties were introduced by the Road Traffic Act 1991. As with other offences the history of the sentencing of drink-drive offenders is littered with charges both of excessive leniency and excessive severity, although for drink-driving, allegations of leniency far exceed those of severity. Also, there are allegations of disparity in the sentencing of motoring cases, including drink-driving (Hood 1972; RoSPA 1984; Department of Transport/Home Office 1988); despite the fact that the sentencing process in these cases has for some time relied on the Magistrates' Association *Guidelines* and Unit Fines. In the majority of simple drink-drive cases disqualification from driving and a fine are handed down; other measures available to the courts, such as prison, probation and community service orders, are rarely used. Further, disqualification is mandatory.

Aside from pressure for increased punishment for drink-drivers who maim and kill, the available penalties and current sentencing practice in drink-drive cases seem generally accepted as sufficient. Some argue for increased penalties as a method of improving the deterrent effect of the law, but the available research does not support the contention that harsher penalties are the key to boosting deterrence (Hilton 1984; Ross 1984; Glad 1985). Rather 'it may be that it is easier to manipulate the fear of legal consequences, and hence general

131

deterrence, by changing the perceived probability of being caught' (Farrington 1978:69).

Enforcement

It has been demonstrated, as with other offence types, that the *perceived* risk of apprehension is at least as and probably more important than the severity of the punishment. So that despite high hopes when the breathalyser was introduced in 1967, and its initial success in reducing the incidence of drink-driving, its effect quite quickly decayed - perhaps its effect was short lived as drivers came to accept the higher risk of being caught or came to see that the risk was not as high as they had feared.

Guppy (1984), from a study in two English towns, arrived at a mean value for perceived likelihood by drivers of the chance of being stopped by the police when over the limit of 1 in 190 and of being charged with a drink-driving offence of 1 in 355. A considerable degree of overestimation; as the probability of being stopped and breath tested when over the limit was found to be between 1 in 650 and 1 in 1,600 in one of the towns studied and between 1 in 2,850 and 1 in 5,910 in the other.

An extension of police powers, and in particular the introduction of random breath testing (RBT), has been suggested as a means of increasing the deterrent effect of the law, by raising both the actual and perceived chances of drink-drivers being caught.

Police powers and random breath testing

The debate on police testing powers intensified after the coming into force of the 1981 Act to become the central issue for legal policy and the drink-driver. Three models can be considered -'limited discretion'; 'unfettered discretion'; and 'random breath testing'.

Limited discretion

Existing powers give the police a discretion to test drivers who have been involved in an accident or are suspected of the commission of a moving traffic offence, or of having alcohol in the body. The first two of these are relatively straightforward and the third has been clarified by the decision in *Dash v Chief Constable of Gwent* [1986], where it was held that the police can stop vehicles under their general powers (s.163 Road Traffic Act 1988) and if they reasonably suspect that a driver has consumed alcohol request a breath test - driver demeanour, smell of alcohol or a positive answer to the question 'have you consumed any alcohol?' being the usual grounds for raising the suspicion of alcohol being present in the driver's body.

132

Unfettered discretion

'Unfettered discretion' would give the police power to test any driver in any circumstance without the need to provide a reason of the sort required under present discretionary powers. The Blennerhassett Committee recommended unfettered powers for the police, because of the definitional problems which it saw inherent in any attempt to limit police powers. Unfettered discretion, the Committee felt, was 'central and fundamental to the reforms which we propose'. There was much resistance to the proposal, coming among others from the police, and the recommendation was not implemented. The police now favour this option, but it has been resisted by most other groups and commentators on the grounds that it would be too wide, an encroachment on civil liberties and open to bias, discrimination and abuse.

Random breath testing

At the time of Blennerhassett the term RBT was used interchangeably with unfettered discretion - the police could stop any motorists at random and carry out a breath test. However, RBT has since come to have a more technical meaning. RBT (sometimes referred to as 'static RBT') combines an intensive police presence with widespread publicity. Road blocks are set up on a pre-determined stretch of road and a random sample, say one in five, of the drivers of vehicles passing through is tested. All types of vehicle are stopped, including public service and goods vehicles. The aim of RBT is general deterrence. It is a long-term measure designed not to catch more drink-drivers (existing powers would be retained for that purpose), but to deter more drivers by increasing their perception of the chances of being caught (Dunbar 1987). As RBT is intended to deter rather than catch drink-drivers, the lower the rate of positive test results the better the system is working - 'the ideal result of random breath testing would be total deterrence - and hence a detection rate of zero' (BMA 1988:57).

Comparative evidence A good deal of comparative literature exists to inform the RBT debate (e.g. Dunbar et al. 1987; Kearns et al. 1987; Vingilis & Vingilis 1987; Homel 1988; Breakspere 1990), which has been utilised extensively by those seeking to secure the introduction of RBT in England and Wales (see below). Broadly, it has been claimed that the introduction of RBT has been followed by significant reductions in road casualties; and that its introduction has neither adversely affected police/public relations nor become a drain on police resources. However, data from available studies is rather more complex than such simple assertions would have us believe. An overview of comparative RBT literature has been carried out by Riley (1991). As might be expected the literature reveals that the way in which RBT powers are exercised by the police differs between jurisdictions, as does the volume of publicity and media attention. Data from Australia suggest that the extent of police enforcement and the amount of publicity and media attention are crucial to the effectiveness of RBT. This is supported by more detailed data from Finland which lead Riley (ibid.,37-8) to conclude that:

It seems likely that the long-term benefits of RBT in Finland depend on the high level of police enforcement activity, which has been maintained and even increased since the measure was first introduced, and sustained media attention to drink-drive issues which are regularly covered in peak-time TV and radio programmes.

This accords with data gathered by Ross and others on the effectiveness of current domestic legal policy following the Road Safety Act 1967. Riley suggests that overall the evidence from other jurisdictions which have introduced RBT shows that: 'Low levels of enforcement with RBT, even if well publicised, produce only marginal and transitory effects. High levels of enforcement and sustained media attention seem necessary to achieve substantial long-term reductions in accidents and fatalities' (ibid.,38).

It may be, therefore, that increased enforcement practices by the police under existing powers, coupled with sustained high-level media attention could produce similar results to a rigorously implemented RBT policy. However, it is still possible that a fully integrated programme of RBT would be superior to a fully developed policy based on current police powers. Further arguments in the RBT debate are considered below.

The move towards RBT By the end of 1988 there was said to be 'a growing body of Parliamentary opinion for random breath testing', and the results of public opinion surveys strongly supported it,[13] but the Government continued to resist its introduction. In Parliamentary debates three main objections to RBT have been raised. First, that RBT adversely impinges upon civil liberties; secondly, that it would be a drain on police resources; and thirdly, that RBT could damage police/public relations, by allowing the police to treat a person as a suspect where no suspicion exists.

The civil liberties implications of RBT did alienate organisations such as *Liberty* (NCCL) but in 1988 *Liberty* reviewed its policy and accepted that RBT offered positive gains in the reduction of drink-drive casualties, which outweighed its disadvantages for civil liberties; indeed, it was claimed, that if properly carried out RBT could actually reduce discrimination in the application of the drink-drive laws, supplementing police discretion with an objectively chosen sample of drivers for testing. However, *Liberty* continues to oppose unfettered police discretion which is open to abuse against certain groups (e.g. black and young people) and to leniency against others (e.g. well-to-do middle-aged women) (McElree 1990). There is, of course, still a risk of discrimination in the siting of the RBT checks - some form of monitoring would be necessary to ensure that particular locations were not being constantly singled out for attention.

The second objection, that the introduction of RBT would be a drain on police resources, can probably be dismissed in the light of comparative experience. Drawing on the available studies, particularly Dunbar et al. (1987), Riley (1991:38) concludes that 'Using modern equipment which allows individual drivers to be given an initial breath test in about 30 seconds, the necessary resources could be made available without a massive increase in the number of officers deployed or in the hours worked'. Even if increased police resources were to be deployed Riley estimates that a properly implemented RBT programme would, as it has done in New South Wales, provide resource savings in health and welfare of such a magnitude as 'to represent a highly cost-effective initiative'.

The third objection, that RBT could adversely affect police/public relations is, of course, of particular concern to the police themselves; and is, as we have seen throughout the post-war development of legal policy in relation to the drink-driver, one which has attracted considerable attention. However, public opinion surveys show majority support for RBT; and evidence from New South Wales shows that support for RBT actually increased after its introduction (Cashmore 1985). Also, by using existing general powers to stop motorists, the police have found themselves open to the charge that they have introduced 'random testing through the back door', and can be accused of abusing or exceeding their powers (Joslin 1990); which has obvious ramifications for police/public relations.

Another factor which militated against the introduction of RBT was the police argument that they had sufficient powers and all that was needed was for the Government to make the exact nature of these powers clear to the public. However, according to the Traffic Committee Chairman of the Association of Chief Police Officers (ACPO), since July 1988 the police have accepted the need for increased powers (Joslin 1990) - albeit unfettered discretion rather than RBT. And two years earlier, ACPO in its evidence to the House of Commons Transport Committee had expressed the view that:

> The only way that the drinking driver can be dissuaded from his dangerous habit is to increase the likelihood of his being caught ... the police must be given unfettered discretionary power to test the sobriety of any driver or person in charge of a motor vehicle on a road.

But the Committee gave preference to the evidence given by the Transport Secretary, Nicolas Ridley, that the police had sufficient powers and that unfettered discretion would be 'intolerable', and would meet with public hostility. The Committee felt that existing powers were under-used and that adequate resources were necessary to allow the police to fully utilise these powers. It is a pity that RBT of the 'static' type - 'a collective, formal, standardised roadside breathalyser exercise applied to either all or a disciplined sample of drivers using a road at the chosen time, and under a senior police officer's control' (Barker 1990) - was not then sufficiently developed to put before the Committee.

The National Audit Office Review (1988) considered RBT and reported on its success in other countries, but the Government continued to argue that RBT was not needed, that existing laws were sufficient and that public awareness campaigns are effective. In answer to a Parliamentary Question on what response he had made on the NAO recommendation that further consideration be given to random breath testing junior transport minister, Peter Bottomley, replied 'none' (*Parl.Debs.*(Commons) 6.7.88:598). Resistance seems to have come mainly from the Home Office which considered existing powers to strike the right balance between enforcement and freedom of the individual.

As mentioned above, the 1987/8 and 1988/9 Parliamentary Sessions saw the campaign for RBT gather momentum. By the spring of 1988 the Government had announced that RBT was 'not ruled out' and many groups and individuals had given the campaign their backing. In particular, a group chaired by Roland Boyes had met on several occasions at the House of Commons. It was comprised of representatives of the BMA, the Royal College of Psychiatrists, Friends of the Earth, CADD (Campaign Against Drinking and Driving), the Parliamentary Advisory Committee on Transport Safety, Alcohol Concern and Action on Alcohol Abuse - all of which were committed to RBT. The crucial missing voice was that of the ACPO - a change of policy had been signalled, but a public statement was still awaited.

Unfortunately, when it came ACPO rejected RBT calling instead for the police to be given unfettered discretion, arguing that it was necessary to target areas and individuals to maximise the efficient use of resources and to maintain public support - which they felt might be adversely affected by mass road blocks and roadside testing (Josling 1990).

By 1988 support for extended police powers was considerable. An unpublished consultation exercise carried out by the Home Office in 1989 showed some 3,000 of the 3,400 or so individuals and organisations responding to be in favour of increased powers for the police.[14] However, despite further attempts, police powers remain unchanged.

Options for legal policy

The 1980s saw the emergence of a wide variety of responses to drink-driving throughout the Western world, with access to overseas initiatives made widely available through regular international conferences and a rapidly expanding comparative literature. This has allowed comparisons of the effectiveness of drink-drive countermeasures to be made between jurisdictions. How does the response in England and Wales compare with developments in other countries? For Ross (1988) England and Wales has an excellent record on drink-drive countermeasures, while for others, this country has been complacent 'and is becoming relatively more so year by year as we fall behind other nations' initiatives' (Dunbar 1985:7).

What are these initiatives and why have they not been introduced here? In 1985 an umbrella organisation - Action on Drinking and Driving (ADD) - was formed, to bring together individuals and organisations interested in drink-driving and to formulate a manifesto for reform. Looking to the manifesto, and to other sources, the consensus for reform seems to be:

* high visibility roadside random testing to increase the deterrent effect of the law;
* intensified discretionary breath tests to apprehend more offenders;

* redefined high-risk offender procedure to include any driver convicted twice within a ten-year period or once with a blood-alcohol concentration exceeding 150mg per 100ml;
* improved identification scheme for problem drinkers;
* treatment programmes for convicted problem drinkers;
* a lower blood-alcohol concentration limit of 50mg per 100ml;
* lower blood-alcohol concentrations for young and provisional licence holders;
* immediate suspension of driving licence on giving a positive breath test;
* increased severity of sentences, particularly where drivers have caused death or injury.

The move for reform

Reforms contained in the Transport Act 1981 were based on mid-1970s thinking, and were outdated before they were brought into force. Pressure for action on alcohol problems, road casualties and drink-driving continued unabated. The drive for reform was intensified by increased interest in health and fitness among an influential strata of society, which highlighted the health risks associated with alcohol; a growing green lobby, which stressed the environmental dangers of the motor vehicle; and the emergence of pressure groups committed to the 'fight against the drink-driver'. A central figure in the drink-drive debates from 1986 to 1991 was Peter Bottomley, Minister for Roads and Traffic, whose influence is apparent in many of the major debates in the second half of the 1980s.[15]

Further, there was an upsurge of interest from a wide variety of individuals and organisations including a well-developed research and policy community concerned with alcohol issues. These included national bodies such as Alcohol Concern, Action on Alcohol Abuse, The Institute of Alcohol Studies, and the BMA; industry and commerce, particularly brewers, insurance companies, and taxi and bus firms; and statutory and voluntary agencies such as alcohol advisory centres, the probation service, and local health authorities.

Conferences and seminars mushroomed while many initiatives were developed and proposed. For example, successful campaigns against chauffeur insurance schemes and the licensing of petrol stations to sell alcohol were mounted; there was a proliferation of non- and low-alcohol drinks; schemes such as 'Wheel Watch', designated driver, and free bus services were promoted; various engineering options were proposed - from ignition immobilisers and automatic lights flashing in cars driven by drink-drivers to wide white lines painted on roads to steer drunks more safely home (Ross 1985); motor insurance policies exclusive to non-drinkers (Ansvar, Pearl 'Drive-Wise'); server training for bar staff and/or host liability; the lowering of the permitted blood-alcohol concentration to 50 or zero; medical examinations, alcohol education and driving test resits prior to the return of a suspended driving licence; automatic gaol sentences, vehicle confiscation and longer periods of disqualification; compulsory car stickers for convicted drivers; newspaper and television advertisements listing the names of convicted drivers; 'good citizen' badges and rewards for reporting drink-drivers ('the new bounty hunters'); and even privatised random breath testing. These developments gained momentum through the 1980s and a peak of interest in alcohol-related issues was reached in the last years of the decade, which, together with extensive media coverage, generated what the reformers understandably interpreted as the optimum conditions for a massive attack on drink-driving. It never came.

Despite all the rhetoric, legal policy remains much the same as it was in 1967. The provisions of the Transport Act 1981 helped to make the processing of cases less problematic and there have been significant increases in screening breath test and conviction rates; but options for legal policy, likely to increase its effectiveness, have not been introduced, despite the development of the necessary political climate. Chapter 8 offers some thoughts as to why this should be.

Notes

1. Members were drawn from the Departments of Health, Social Security, Transport, Trade and Industry, Education and Science and Employment; the Home Office; the Treasury; the Ministry of Agriculture, Fisheries and Food; and the Scottish and Welsh Offices.

2. Of the factors which determine how a society drinks, price, availability and advertising are clearly identifiable and controllable (Office of Health Economics 1981). See further Hauge (1988).

3. Membership was four civil servants (two from each Department), R.E. Allsop, Professor of Transport Studies, University College, London and Dr Peter North, Principal, Jesus College, Oxford, who chaired the group.

4. For a recent study of alcohol-server training schemes see O'Brien & Light (1993).

5. Based on a scheme pioneered by Hampshire Probation Service (see further Martin 1986). The findings from an evaluation funded by the Department of Transport and the Alcohol Education Research Council are still awaited, despite the study being completed in 1991.

6. The Government has announced its intention to double the maximum penalty to ten years by an amendment to the Criminal Justice Bill then passing through Parliament (29 June 1993).

7. The Road Traffic Act 1991 inserted new ss.34A-C in the Road Traffic Offenders Act 1988 which provide for possible reduced disqualification for drivers who attend alcohol rehabilitation courses approved by the Secretary of State, subject to a number of conditions which must be fulfilled. The Department of Transport issued a press release on 3 December 1992 containing details of approved courses.

8.   In the Road Traffic (Blood Alcohol Concentration Limit) Bill, a second ten-minute Bill, introduced by Roland Boyes in March 1988 (*Parl.Debs.*(Commons) 16.3.88:1115-7); and in an amendment to the Criminal Justice Bill 1988 (new clause 83) moved by Ann Taylor, which failed by 139 votes to 281 (*Parl.Debs.*(Commons) 28.6.88:220-44).

9.   About one-third of drivers and one-quarter of motorcycle riders killed have blood-alcohol concentrations over the legal limit; more than half have levels more than twice the limit; and more than one-third levels over 200mg per 100ml (Sabey 1986).

10.   For a rather technical account of identifying offenders 'who are at high risk of being alcohol dependent' see Dunbar et al. (1983, 1985, 1985a); Hagart (1985).

11.   In the US States that failed to raise the minimum legal drinking age to 21 years by October 1986 were threatened with the loss of federal highway construction funds - see further Vingilis & De Genova (1984); Asch & Levy (1987); Coate & Grossman (1987, 1988); DuMouchel et al. (1987).

12.   See, for example, the views of MADD (Mothers Against Drunk Driving) in the US and CADD (Campaign Against Drinking and Driving) in the UK. Such groups propose harsher punishment in the interests of deterrence, but appear equally motivated on retributive grounds. This sentiment is widely demonstrated (not just among members of these groups) in cases where a drink-driver has been involved in an accident which has caused death or serious injury.

13.   Of those sampled 77 per cent (National Opinion Polls for the Institute of Alcohol Studies 1987); 73 per cent (Marplan 1987 for Drink Wisely North West); 72% (Consumers Association 1987); 80 per cent (Marplan 1988 for Drink Wisely North West) and 93 per cent (*The Independent*, 7 December 1988) were said to support the introduction of RBT.

14.   One group whose views are little known is traffic police officers. A small survey of 45 traffic officers was carried out at Bristol Polytechnic in 1991. Of the 43 replies, 77 per cent replied yes to the question 'would you welcome a change in the law to be given the power for RBT of the static type?'; and 76 per cent believed 'the introduction of such powers would deter more people from drink-driving'.

15.   Attracting a great deal of press attention - most supporting his hard line approach, much critical of his opposition to RBT and some hostile. For example, Auberon Waugh, writing in *The Spectator* in 1988, concluded that Bottomley 'is obviously insane or at any rate mentally deranged'

8 The failure of reform

Drink-driving contributes to the number of road deaths and injuries; and the criminal law is invoked as one of a number of tactical countermeasures. While the law cannot solve a social/public health problem it is generally agreed that it can be utilised to reduce the incidence of drink-driving and some of the casualties which flow from it.

A strategic approach to drink-driving would require radical official action on alcohol and/or transport policy. Successive governments have fought shy of formulating an effective alcohol or transport policy. This is not surprising. It would take a suicidal cabinet to push through measures designed to restrict or deprive the citizen of his (usually) or her freedom to drink and to use personal transport; but something had to be done or at least be seen to be done about the damage caused to society by alcohol consumption and road transport. Action against the drink-driver fitted the bill. There was sufficient evidence to link alcohol with road accidents; and, despite reluctance to condemn the drink-driver, in the event of a fatal accident the socially acceptable drink-driver became transformed into the 'killer drunk'. Also, the *drunken* driver attracted widespread condemnation.

This approach diverted attention away from larger issues associated with alcohol consumption and transport policy and allowed people to maintain freedom of choice on how they drank and travelled - the only limitation was that the two should not be combined. Yet even this was not an absolute prohibition, as drink-driving was only proscribed above a specified blood-alcohol concentration; and while most people had little idea of how this translated into actual alcohol consumption, they quickly realised that unless they were drunk or caused an accident they were likely to attract neither social disapprobation nor police attention. These factors have played an important part in contemporary legal policy and the drink-driver.

The development of legal policy

As has been seen, the history of legal policy and the drink-driver has been characterised by long periods of inattention, interspersed with several periods of intense activity. These 'hot spots' are apparent at the end of the 1920s (Chapter 1), in the 1960s (Chapter 3), at the end of the 1970s (Chapter 5) and in the late 1980s (Chapter 7). Each has been followed by reform of the law: the Road Traffic Act 1930 (Chapter 2); the Road Safety Act 1967 (Chapter 4); the Transport Act 1981 (Chapter 6); and the Road Traffic Act 1991.

By the 1960s a general consensus had emerged, founded on the scientific and technical developments of the previous 30 years, for the need to initiate effective countermeasures to drink-driving; and the 1967 Act sought to implement fully the proposed reforms which had been developed (in the event all were enacted save for increased police testing powers). During the 1970s this consensus began to dissipate; the result was that reforms suggested in this period were only partly implemented and then after a seven-year wait. This process continued during the 1980s and despite a quite extraordinary amount of propaganda and several well-formulated policies for reform the only significant change in the law was the introduction of a new offence of causing death under the 1991 Act.

Despite arguments that drink-drive provisions are more readily accepted today than in 1967, when the breathalyser made its compulsory debut, the reforming success of the 1967 Act has not been repeated; indeed reform seems to have become less easy since the 1967 Act. It is not that the law is now in optimum condition - that it needed further development was recognised by the architects of the 1967 Act, who thought that further reforms would come with increased familiarity and acceptance over the years. But this has not been the case. Five arguments will be advanced which attempt to offer some explanation. First, the drink-drive provisions have not been as effective as they might have been, due to a concentration on simple deterrence; secondly, attempts to manipulate public attitudes to drink-driving may have backfired; thirdly, the literature and state of knowledge on drink-driving, at first sight complete and consistent, is inconclusive and contradictory in several crucial respects; fourthly, the drink-driver is not a 'suitable enemy'; and fifthly, measures such as RBT and lower blood-alcohol concentrations would widen the net of the criminal justice system unacceptably.

Beyond simple deterrence

Investigation of the effectiveness of the criminal law as a method of controlling the drink-driver has tended to concentrate on simple deterrence theory. And, though there is little doubt that over the past few years there has been a change in attitude on the part of some drivers who no longer 'take the risk'(Snortum & Berger 1986), and that this number could be increased with better enforcement procedures, in order to make any substantial and sustainable reduction it is necessary to move public opinion against drink-driving. The law can help to make this shift and will itself benefit as the criminal law works best when it reinforces what is generally accepted as right behaviour. The literature on this aspect of the law is tentative. For the purposes of exposition it will be examined under three heads - indirect effects, informal sanctions and instrumental expressive effect - which are not discrete, but interact and overlap.

Indirect effects Light (1988) has argued that one reason why the criminal law has not succeeded as well as many had hoped in suppressing drink-driving is that convictions for the offence are not thought to be sufficiently stigmatic - while many people regard the drink-driver as not being on the right side of the law, they nevertheless do not regard him or her as a 'criminal'. It is not only the formal punishment which is of relevance to the deterrent effect of any criminal prohibition; other less direct consequences of a conviction (such as stigma and job loss) being of equal and in some cases greater importance. An obvious example is the case of the teacher or bank manager convicted of a minor shop-lifting offence - whilst the offence in itself is relatively trivial and the punishment, likely to be an affordable fine, would cause little hardship, the indirect effects would be keenly felt.

In the case of a conviction for drink-driving these indirect effects are minimal (although a job may be lost through disqualification from holding a driving licence); and, in particular, little stigma attaches to such a conviction.[1] It can be argued that such side effects are an undesirable feature of the criminal process, as they in effect lead to a person being punished twice. And this may well be true. But what is being pointed out here is that the way in which the indirect effects on those with a drink-drive conviction differ from those which surround conviction for other offences has an important *symbolic* effect.

Informal sanctions Informal sanctions, as Pasternoster et al. (1983) and others have termed them, also need to be considered. Stigma is attached to being convicted or even apprehended for a criminal offence, but it can also attach to the commission of a criminal act for which the offender is not apprehended. This 'disapproval of significant others' will obviously vary for different offences and between social groups and situations. It is clear that for some offences, for example, the sexual abuse of children, the disapproval felt by those who know of the offence is in almost all cases very high, and that the subsequent criminal processing of a known offender will *in itself* not give rise to a higher level of disapproval. So that a person would generally not be able to engage in this behaviour without a high level of censure from those around him or her. It is equally clear that the act of drink-driving is for many something that can be engaged in without much censure from those present at the time. However, censure may increase if an offender is caught and successfully prosecuted.

It would be interesting to know whether, for drink-driving, the stigma of the act is more, less, or equal to the stigma of a conviction for the offence. This would give us some idea of the strength or weakness of the 'informal sanctions' which are operating.

However, how can we be sure that censure and stigma will not lead to deviance amplification rather than deviance reduction? Labelling theorists did not address the question of how censure may operate in these opposing directions. However, Braithwaite has taken these ideas further and has examined the effects of what he terms 'shaming'. He suggests that shaming as opposed to 'non-shaming' is essential for there to be any crime reductive effect. Further, Braithwaite (1989:4) submits that for deviance reduction shaming alone is not enough, it must be 'reintegrative shaming' rather than 'disintegrative shaming' for:

> Contrary to the claims of some labelling theorists, potent shaming directed at offenders is the essential necessary condition for low crime rates. Yet shaming can be counterproductive if it is disintegrative rather than reintegrative. Shaming is counterproductive when it pushes offenders into the clutches of criminal subcultures: shaming controls crime when it is at the same time powerful and bounded by ceremonies to reintegrate the offender back into the community of respectable citizens.

Braithwaite, however, seems unclear as to which type of shaming attaches to drink-driving or whether shaming can attach to drink-driving at all - for he observes that 'recent years in some Western societies have seen more effective shaming aimed at certain kinds of offences' including drunk driving, but then continues that:

> Use of alcohol, tobacco and marijuana cannot be controlled in Western societies because it attracts little or no shame. Similarly, drunk driving is beyond control and does not attract the shame one would expect in proportion to the harm it does because most adults, who have themselves engaged in the offense, suffer discomfort in construing the behavior shameful. (p.166)

This apparent inconsistency may well arise from the attempt to conflate attitudes to drink-driving in 'Western societies', as differences exist between countries (Snortum et al. 1986). And Braithwaite may also be pointing out that shaming for drink-driving has increased, but is still not at a level which its propensity for harm deserves.

Instrumental expressive effect Little attention has been paid to the function of the criminal sanction which has been referred to as long-term deterrence (Cross 1981) or denunciation/expressive (Walker 1980), but is perhaps better termed 'instrumental expressive'. Here the sanction acts in a symbolic way to define conduct which society will not tolerate (expressive) and to build up a climate of opinion against it, thus reducing its incidence (instrumental). So that society's expression of intolerance towards a particular form of conduct serves not only retributive purposes, but also works towards suppression of the conduct. As

Andenaes (1977:51) has put it: 'from the legislator's perspective, creating moral inhibitions is of greater value than mere deterrence, because the former may work even when a person need not fear detection and punishment'.

This function of the law, as a moral rather than a fear manipulator, and hence different from deterrence, has been expounded by Williams & Hawkins (1986:559) who ask us 'to head the admonitions of Andenaes (1974) and Gibbs (1975) that legal sanctions can prevent crime through mechanisms other than general deterrence' *some* of which are dependent upon perception:

> It could be argued that the perceived certainty of legal sanctions strengthens one's belief that other condemn the act. This belief may in turn reduce criminal involvement. In other words, because individuals perceive a high likelihood of arrest, they may also perceive that their close associates will strongly disapprove of their involvement in criminal activity, which prevents them from engaging in crime. While this sequence would not be indicative of a deterrent effect (as usually defined), it would show that the legal sanctions play a significant role in the crime control process by maintaining the social disapproval of crime.

The law thus deters if a potential offender avoids an act for fear of the punishment, but can also moralise, educate and habituate so that a potential offender avoids an act because it is thought of as not the right thing to do. As Walker (1991:21) puts it: 'it is possible to credit penalties with other useful effects on the public: educating it, or at least satisfying it'.

It is exceptionally difficult (perhaps even impossible) to measure the relative effects of 'moral compliance, private self-interest and exposure to the law' (Shapiro & Votey 1986) with any accuracy. And in the absence of any evidence to the contrary it was for some time commonly assumed that any instrumental expressive effect generated by the drink-drive laws was, as with their deterrent value, weak; indeed it was sometimes claimed by parts of the reform lobby that the operation of the drink-drive laws actually reinforced the notion that drink-driving was not a 'real crime'.

However, Berger and Snortum (1986:139) produced findings 'consistent with the view of Andenaes that general deterrence should be more broadly construed to include the moral component as well as the fear component of the law' and Snortum et al. (1986) in a comparative analysis of compliance with the drink-drive laws in Norway and the US concluded that their 'findings tend to support Andenaes' theory of *general prevention*'; while recent evidence from England and Wales (Riley 1991) supports the suggestion that legal policy can produce such an educative or instrumental expressive effect.

In 1986 Riley conducted a national survey in which '1,700 drivers were interviewed about their beliefs, attitudes and behaviour towards drinking and driving'. The sample was split into three groups - those in areas where enforcement policy by the police was high, those where it was low, and those where it was 'normal'. As might be expected, there was less drink-driving in the 'high-enforcement' areas. This could be taken as evidence of a raising of the perception of drivers that they would be caught, leading to increased deterrence;

144

but interviews with drivers did not support such a supposition: for although drivers reported a reduction in drink-driving behaviour, they did not have an increased perception of the chances of being caught; rather:

Drivers in the high-enforcement areas were, on average, less likely to say that driving and drinking were necessary to their social lives, more likely to anticipate disapproval from family and friends, more likely to recognise the accident risks of driving after drinking and were less likely to report effects of alcohol on mood. But there were no area differences in the main risk-related factor discriminating drink-drivers from other drivers: the increased risk of being stopped by the police after drinking. (Riley 1991:31)

It is interesting to compare these findings with those produced by the Road Research Laboratory survey discussed in Chapter 4, which was conducted among motorists and non-motorists before and after the publicity campaign which accompanied the passing of the Road Safety Act 1967. The study found that although drivers' behaviour had been favourably affected, attitudes to drink driving 'have hardly changed'. In other words, changes in behaviour had been produced by deterrence only, which may well explain its short-lived effect . For longer lasting results there was a need to change attitudes. The importance of the educative effect of the law, particularly in the form of rigorous enforcement and media support, although then still to be fully articulated, was nevertheless apparent in the report which concluded that 'the evidence of increased knowledge of the law from the survey suggests that the extent to which the law is enforced is likely to be important' (Sheppard 1968:37). As Riley (1991) was later to confirm: 'High levels of enforcement had their effect through reinforcing social pressures against drink-driving and increasing awareness of greater accident risk for alcohol impaired drivers'.

What is significant about Riley's work is not only that increased policing, with its attendant publicity and media attention, produced a decrease in drink-driving behaviour through, it seems, a general educative effect, but that it did not point to increased enforcement raising the general deterrent effect of the law. The importance of publicity and media attention has been pointed out by Ross in his studies of deterrence and English drink-drive initiatives, such as the Road Safety Act 1967 (Ross 1977); the 'Cheshire Blitz', which only produced a deterrent effect when 'the press "discovered" and negatively commented on the "blitz" (Ross 1977); and 'the ability of publicised enforcement to produce deterrent results as demonstrated by the "Christmas Crusade" of December 1983' (Ross 1988:68). Further, Ross (1988a) cites Canadian research (Mercer 1984, 1984a; Vingilis et al. 1981) 'as evidence that a successful blitz requires quantum increases in both enforcement and publicity'. Could it be that the examples given by Ross arise not from deterrence, but from a general educative or instrumental expressive effect?

Additional evidence is available from similar observations concerning the success of RBT in Australia (Sutton 1986; Cashmore 1985; Carseldine 1985; Arthurson 1985; Homel 1986), 'where police activity was supported with the investment of millions of dollars in advertising, along with free coverage

145

generated by intense media interest (Ross 1988:74). Homel (1988:270) explains that success has differed in various states according to the means of implementation. For example, 'RBT in New South Wales has achieved a permanent deterrent effect through a combination of extensive publicity and continued, visible, and intensive enforcement'.

Publicity and media attention disseminate information on changes in legal policy to potential offenders and may also serve to increase perceptions of the chances of being caught, prosecuted and punished; but Riley's work provides support for the idea that legal policy has also a general educative or instrumental expressive function and better helps to explain the way in which 'deterrence' has worked in the past. For as Snortum (1988) has put it: 'Deterrence of Alcohol-impaired Driving' is 'An Effect in Search of a Cause': that cause, or at least part of it, may now have been uncovered and further work is needed to explore more fully the deterrent and educative effects.

Summary The law thus has a wider role than simple deterrence and the failure of faith in the criminal justice system's ability to give substantial long-term returns, in the form of reduced casualty rates, judged on narrow scientific studies as advanced by Ross (1973, 1984) must be balanced against the law's far-reaching use as an indicator of acceptable and unacceptable behaviour (Vingilis 1987). This is important for the present discussion, as the seemingly limited and uncertain returns promised by changes in the law, when judged merely on simple deterrence, may be outweighed by other considerations such as resource implications (Department of Transport 1987) and the wrath of the right-wing libertarians. Yet a recognition of the wider 'educative' potential of the law could, in the balance of gains and losses, answer both the resource and the civil liberties objections to more rigorous enforcement.

Public attitudes

Road traffic law appears to be widely perceived as different from the general criminal law. In everyday thinking and language the terms 'crime' and 'criminal' are applied to conduct in which the predominant elements are blatant dishonesty, deliberate violence, cruelty, depravity or contempt for human life and welfare. (Department of Transport/Home Office 1988:2.15)

As has been seen, attempts to change public attitudes towards motoring crime have been apparent since the second world war; with the target for these efforts changing in the 1960s from the 'road hog' to the drink-driver. Official campaigns on drink-driving have been run since the introduction of the 1967 Act and the first of these were fairly benign public education messages (e.g. 'Think before you drink before you drive'; 'Don't drink and drive - you know it makes sense'), which moved on to threats concerning the legal consequences of drink-driving (mainly loss of driving licence), and then settled down to a combination of both. However, from 1986 the Department of Transport adopted the approach being pursued in some other quarters and embarked on a series of heart-rending campaigns based not on education or legal threats, but on

146

shocking, insulting and shaming the drink-driver. This has provoked something of a backlash from those bold enough to speak out and instilled in many others a sense of fear and confusion. This can perhaps be understood in the light of Braithwaite's work discussed above, as the shaming being utilised is clearly of a disintegrative rather than a reintegrative nature.

Affronting the drink-driver In 1980 Her Majesty's Chief Inspector of Constabulary reported that 'The person who drives whilst under the influence of drink is now recognised by people generally as one of the most serious threats to life and limb. This anti-social behaviour brings untold misery to innocent victims and their families' (HMCIC 1980:35). This statement was quite typical of *informed* opinion on drink-driving at the time. The scientific evidence linking alcohol and traffic casualties had become well known and presented an apparently unambiguous target for those committed to reducing road casualties - it was thought that if the drinking of alcohol before driving could be eliminated a significant proportion of road casualties could be avoided. But, over the next few years, this brand of strong yet rational approach to the need to convince the public of the dangers of drink-driving was left behind, and in its place came invective and abuse. For example, RoSPA for its 1985 Christmas Campaign had this to say:

'Although he may look like the man next door, the drunk driver is a potential killer armed with alcohol and a high calibre ton of metal. Only when the community at large regards the drunk driver in the same way as a man armed with a gun will we see any improvements in attitudes towards drink-driving'.

Such statements from the director of a road safety organisation might be expected, but when in 1986 the junior Transport Minister, Peter Bottomley, suggested that 'drunken drivers should be likened to muggers and should receive mandatory gaol sentences', and referred to the 'drunken driver as public enemy number one', things seemed to be getting a little out of perspective. Government drink-drive campaigns adopted a similar approach from 1986 with the slogan 'What should you call people who slaughter 1,100 a year?' and 'If you drink and drive you're a menace to society'. (Plans to use posters branding drink-drivers as murderers had to be abandoned by the Transport Minister, after objections from the Home Office.) This approach was intensified for the 1987 campaign with the message that 'Drinking and driving wrecks lives' and a series of television commercials (e.g. featuring a mother whose daughter would never leave hospital). The following years saw the harrowing television commercials continued (e.g. the sad school room with the empty desk). The 1992 Christmas campaign was particularly poorly received, and as the Chairman of the ACPO traffic committee put it: 'the video produced by the Department of Transport was extremely hard-hitting. It is difficult to visualise how much further one could go in terms of publicity' (*Alcohol Concern* 8:7). For summer 1993 more of the same is promised with a £1.6 million campaign of 'hard-hitting television commercials').

The emergence of this strategy, intended by the Department of Transport (1988): 'to dramatise the consequences of drunken driving', can be ascribed to various factors. It seems clear that it owed something to sustained campaigning by organisations such as CADD and that it built on the alcohol/road casualty consensus which emerged after the introduction of the 1967 Act. It was also very much the product of Peter Bottomley, who seemed convinced that publicity campaigns were the best response to drink-driving, and employed marketing teams who put their creative talents into overdrive in the interests of road safety and lucrative government contracts. But in the absence of any reliable evaluation their effectiveness remains largely unknown. Despite this the campaigns continue - the latest thought harrowing enough to be limited to transmission after the nine o'clock watershed.

In defence of the drink-driver On 24 December 1988 an article appeared in *The Guardian* headed 'In defence of the safe drinking driver'. The author expressed a not uncommon view that: 'A large number of drivers - those who have never had accidents - are fed up being branded along with the irresponsible, mostly young, drinkers who cannot handle themselves, much less their cars, after a minimal amount of alcohol'. This sentiment identifies a major problem with the emotional tirade against drink-driving in that it appears to castigate the ingestion of alcohol in however small an amount before driving. This then chastises a significant proportion of the population. For many people do combine drinking and driving on some occasions. And some break the law. Perhaps they are rightly castigated and should not mix drinking with driving, but are they responsible for killing '1,100 a year', are they 'public enemy number one'? This might alienate a section of society which resents the insults directed, in their opinion, unfairly against them; others might be confused about how much alcohol is needed to transform them into a 'killer drunk' (see further below); or simply dismiss the whole message as being too extreme for credence. And are metaphors about 'loaded guns' really very useful? The President of the National Licensed Victuallers' Association had this to say at a drink-drive conference:

> Now I know it will go against everything that many people here today stand for when I say that some drivers - and that goes for some of my customers - feel they are able to take a drink (and I stress *a drink*) and still drive safely. In doing that they have not broken the law and they are not criminals. Yet, morally, public opinion in this country casts anyone who takes a drink and drives as a social outcast or, worse, a homicidal maniac. (Jones 1990:36)

The hint of a backlash was apparent from the mid-1980s. But to question the campaign against the drink-driver was considered heretical. Auberon Waugh wrote in the *Spectator* (14 July 1984:6):

> One of the least pleasing aspects of the British press is its extraordinarily sanctimonious attitude towards allegedly 'drunken' drivers ... For some reason the press has decided to give these unfortunate 'drunk' drivers the

treatment usually reserved for sadistic child murderers, pederasts generally and certain kinds of drug pusher.

He was dismissed (probably correctly) as a reactionary eccentric. But the relentless and harrowing bombardment against drink-driving, which seemed to have developed a purpose of its own, lost touch with general public opinion - for as Packer (1968:144) has put it - 'Armed robbery and drunken driving are not likely to be placed on a par, even if the latter is likely to result in a greater number of deaths'.

Little work has been done to ascertain the effects of the moral crusade against drink-driving and its possible backlash; but what seems to have happened is that while many drivers may publicly hold strong views against drink-driving, privately they may feel otherwise - 'public opinion polls are notorious for discovering that people are in favour of righteousness and against sin' (Adams 1985). For example, in a survey conducted into magistrates' attitudes towards drink-driving, one respondent ranked a drink-driving offence as much more serious than an offence of stealing from a shop. However, when asked later in the interview whether she would resign if convicted of a drink-drive offence she answered no, but said she would resign if convicted of theft from a shop (Light 1993).

A confused literature

Developments in legal policy and the drink-driver have to a large extent flowed from advances in and dissemination of research and scientific knowledge (e.g. Drew et al. 1959; Dale 1964). As Zimring (1988:384) has put it:

> The facts and figures of social scientists have been building blocks for changes in policy on a transnational basis throughout much of the Western world. A scholarly community long involved in this study of the relationship between alcohol and traffic safety has now generated a worldwide market for its wares.

A massive literature has been developed which has over the years been used to present a rational and coherent case for reform. However, as the criminal justice response to the drink-driver has become more efficient, gaps and contradictions in the literature have become apparent. As Gusfield (1988:112-3) comments:

> Since the late 1930s, and especially since the 1960s, DUI (driving under the influence) has been the object of thousands of studies, many aimed at evaluating the effects of official controls or countermeasures. Despite all this sound and fury, the significance is only slightly more than in Shakespeare's time. Our knowledge is meagre, incomplete, and often misleading.

149

These issues have been raised throughout the development of legal policy and the drink-driver, but their importance has increased as other aspects of the subject are made clearer and more certain. Three issues, fundamental to responses to drink-driving, remain problematic - alcohol as a *cause* of road casualties; setting the permitted blood-alcohol concentration; and driver knowledge of blood-alcohol level.

Challenging the 'malevolence assumption' Establishing the causal link between alcohol and traffic casualties has been central to the study of drink-driving; but 'we still have only the murkiest idea of the role alcohol plays in traffic fatalities' (Ross 1986:663). However, as Jacobs (1989:27) points out: 'since drunk driving has become a prominent American social problem, the measure of its importance has been the number and percentage of traffic fatalities and casualties attributable to drunk drivers'. We should not be surprised therefore that much of the research and public discussion on drink-driving has begun to suffer from what Collins & Hamilton (1982) termed the 'malevolence assumption' - the inference of causality whenever alcohol is associated with an unwelcome event. As Gusfield (1988:129) has put it:

> It is highly important to recognise the "malevolence assumption" in much of the literature, both academic and popular, about DUI (driving under the influence). This is the assumption that the fault of the accident is attributable to the driver, and only to one of the drivers, and, if alcohol was present in one of the drivers, his or her driving was responsible for the accident.

Other factors such as inattention, fatigue, sickness, excessive speed, weather and road conditions, age and condition of car, deterioration of reaction and sight due to age, and the use of other drugs (both legal and illegal) may be ignored. Casual use of over-simplified single cause explanations, especially by the reform lobby, has led to a questioning of the role of alcohol in road accidents. Gusfield (1988:130) again: 'yet, whatever research may show concerning alcohol use and accident risk, we must place this knowledge in context. Automobile deaths result from a number of considerations, one of which is DUI'.

Incorrectly ascribing the cause of some traffic accidents solely to alcohol has at least three unwelcome consequences. It diverts attention away from other contributing or causal factors; leads to a questioning of the reliability of the drink-driving literature generally; and adds fuel to the policy of 'affronting the drinking driver'.

The campaigning bodies, particularly CADD, have been instrumental in promulgating a simple causal nexus between alcohol and traffic accidents. So the number of accidents caused by alcohol becomes exaggerated and every drink-driver becomes a potential killer. This matches experience in the US, which some years before Britain saw the emergence of drink-drive pressure groups (MADD, SADD and RID). For 'Part of the answer lies in the passionate lobbying by the families of the accident victims. Those people understandably perceive all drunk driving as extremely dangerous, although the chances of

150

causing a death has been estimated at one in every 330,000 miles of impaired driving' (Ross 1986:664).

Given free-reign in their use of inflated drink-drive casualty statistics, these groups have, in effect, been allowed to hijack the road safety and alcohol policy issues and reduce them both to a highly emotional campaign of questionable efficiency aimed against the convergence of one aspect of alcohol problems and traffic danger, the drink-driver. For: 'To the survivors, all drunk drivers are surrogates for the one who killed a relative ... (and) ... because nobody wants to defend drunk driving or oppose grieving mothers, there has been virtually no opposition to organisations like MADD' (Ross 1986:664).

Rational debate on the drink-driving issue has been allowed to take second place to emotively retributive clamourings; the result has been much rhetoric but little change in legal policy.

Setting the limit The Licensing Act 1872 and the Criminal Justice Act 1925 provided for the criminal offence of drunk in charge of a carriage (motor vehicle). In recognition of the evidence which suggested that the drinking as well as the drunken driver was a danger on the roads the Road Traffic Act 1930 introduced the offence of 'incapable' driving. However, courts and juries confused this with 'drunk and incapable' and the drinking driver escaped conviction. Consequently, the Road Traffic Act 1962 legislated for the 'impaired driver'; but on many occasions the drinking driver still escaped conviction. The Road Safety Act introduced the objectively proved 'excess alcohol' offence, which the 1981 Act made easier to operate - drivers a court might not consider to be 'drunk' but who were shown to have a blood-alcohol concentration above the limit of 80mg/100ml could be found guilty of an offence. But at what level should the blood-alcohol concentration be set? The calculations are determined on averages. So that a person with a very low tolerance to alcohol who might feel quite incapable of driving could still be below the limit while another person may be capable of driving but be above the limit. The limit was set at 80mg as a result of the research carried out by Drew et al. (1959) which suggested that above that level very few people would be unimpaired. The lower limit of 50mg, favoured by many, would, said Drew, produce too many false positives. Some suggest a zero limit.[2] There is disagreement about where the level should be set and how impairment differs between individuals at any given level. Further problems are caused by the suggestion that it is not the average drink-driver, but the excessive drink-driver who is responsible for most alcohol-related crashes. Other evidence, as yet unpublished, produced by the Cranfield Institute of Technology has concluded from clinical trials that up to a blood-alcohol concentration of 30mg per 100ml driving performance shows an improvement.[3] The literature is in urgent need of refurbishment. It is necessary to establish whether it is the social drinker, of whatever age, who is a danger on the road, or just the problem drinker, the drunken driver, and the inexperienced drink-driver.

Keeping to the limit For drink-driving the line between criminal and non-criminal behaviour is unclear. The blood-alcohol concentration has been set at 80mg, but how is a driver to know whether that limit has been reached? It is like trying to keep within a speed limit in a vehicle with no speedometer. As one Member put it (*Parl. Debs.* (Commons) 931:307):

> One remarkable thing about drinking and driving cases is that nobody - no hon. Member, for example - in having two, three or maybe four drinks can know whether he is breaking the law. That has always struck me as a regrettable and dangerous part of the law. Also, there has over the years been almost a veil of secrecy surrounding the acquisition and use of the breathalyser. (Sir J. Langford-Holt)

The answer to the question 'how can I be sure that I have not drunk over the limit?' is usually 'by not drinking at all before driving'. But a justifiable response is that 'the law does not say that I cannot drink at all before driving'.

Factors relevant to the amount of alcohol needed to reach the limit have already been discussed, but how is a driver to calculate when he or she has reached 80mg? Two methods are available - information for self-estimates and machines for self-testing. The problem with information is that it can only give a rough guide for self-estimation. Consequently, in the interests of safety, public advice tends to lead people to believe that they can drink three to five units before reaching 80mg (Wood 1986), but scientific evidence suggests that much higher levels of alcohol consumption are necessary (Roscoe 1988).

In a study of men who admitted to driving after drinking less than half knew how much alcohol it would take to put them over the limit. Most guessed that the limit was lower than it actually was and believed that they were regularly breaking the law. This led Clayton (1986) to speculate that such drivers reinforce the social acceptability of drink-driving as they are less likely to condemn others, believing that they could equally well be caught. So the person who says 'I only had two glasses of wine' is believed, often sympathetically.

Why should drivers not have access to machines similar to those used by the police? Should all cars have a 'drinkometer' next to the speedometer - not as an immobiliser, but for information? Or, more economically, should breath-test machines be available in drinking establishments? The introduction of such machines has been strongly resisted in this country - arguments used against them include possible unreliability, that they encourage people to drink up to the limit, that blood-alcohol concentration levels may still be rising, and that the machines may be abused by people using them for drinking games. However, a six-month evaluation of 30 coin-operated machines in drinking establishments in New South Wales produced positive results - the machines received a lot of use, especially from high-risk (young male) groups; there was considerable educative value, of relating drinking to blood-alcohol concentrations; a third of those who registered over the limit refrained from driving; and there was a low level of deliberate misuse (Mackiewicz 1988).[4] Methods of self-estimation, even if reliable, have certain drawbacks but they may have a useful part to play in the regulation of drink-driving, for drivers' lack of knowledge of alcohol intake in relation to blood-alcohol concentration renders the law uncertain and alienates unnecessarily many drivers from supporting reform.

'Suitable enemies'

Attempts to change public attitudes towards motoring crime, especially drink-drive offences have been noted above. Yet while it seems clear from public opinion surveys that attitudes towards drink-driving appear to have hardened over the last 20 years it is less clear whether attitudes genuinely have changed and why, if they have, the law has failed to respond. Various public opinion polls have shown that those in favour of tougher measures for drink-drivers rose from some 40 per cent in 1970 (Gallup 1976) to some 85 per cent in 1980 (Mori Poll 1980); the North Report noting 'a lack of recent knowledge on public attitudes to road traffic offences' (para.1.14) commissioned a survey which showed that in terms of relative seriousness the public seem to rank drink-drive offences, even when there is no accident, above both shoplifting and burgling an empty dwelling house (Brook (1987); and a recent study of magistrates' attitudes to the offence supported these findings so far as shoplifting was concerned. A sample of 33 magistrates asked to rank driving with excess alcohol where no accident had been caused against theft from a shop, value £50, gave the following responses - ten thought the drink-drive offence to be 'much more serious', ten 'more serious', four 'same/about the same', five 'less serious', and one much less serious (Light 1993). And a study by Corbett and Simon (1991) which sought to measure 'police and public perceptions of the seriousness of traffic offences' concluded that for both groups drink-drive offences were rated as the most serious of the offences considered. If these results are accurate, it suggests that the law now lags behind changes in public opinion (although as mentioned above, public statements may differ from private feelings).

Why does this ambivalence continue and why does the law not respond to the expressed changes in public attitudes? It may be that the drink-driver is not what Christie (1984) has termed a 'suitable enemy', in that he or she does not attract fear and abhorrence in the same way as say a mugger or drug dealer does, and the offence is one with which a wide variety of people can identify, unlike mugging and drug dealing. Bottoms (1977), in his essay on 'the renaissance of dangerousness', considered the exclusion of the persistent drink-drive offender from official discourse on 'dangerous' offending and quoted with qualified approval Mathiesen (1974:77-8) when he said:

> In our society, acts dangerous to human beings are increasingly being committed. Largely, however, these acts are committed by individuals and classes with considerable power in society ... Punishment, in our age imprisonment, is largely used against petty thieves and other relatively harmless individuals.

Bottoms went on to point to the 'dominant positivism of the two committees' as a possible reason for the omission of some offence types as 'positivism has typically been prepared to rest content with existing societal definitions of antisocial action, and not look critically beyond them'. This might also provide clues for the generation of what Cohen (1973) termed 'folk devils' and 'moral panics' and the exclusion of certain forms of harmful conduct from the process. Further, for decisive action to be precipitated, it seems to be necessary to be able to identify a reasonably small group of offenders, who can be singled out as being somehow different from the population generally; for drink-driving this does not seem to be possible (despite attempts to categorise certain groups such as high-risk and young offenders). The number of drink-drive offences is large and assumed to be attributable to a wide cross-section of society; and it is also thought to be an offence which most people have at some time or will in the future commit. However, Jacobs (1989:42) challenges what he terms the 'myth of universal offending':

> There are many myths about drunk driving. One of the most common is that it is a crime that practically everyone commits. Perhaps all that is meant by such an assertion is that on some occasion over a lifetime a high percentage of Americans have driven a vehicle after having imbibed enough beverage alcohol to perceive some effects. Even if a high percentage of people on a small number of occasions over the course of a lifetime have driven while intoxicated, this would not make drunk driving a crime that everyone commits, at least if the assertion implies that drunk driving is a regular or customary behaviour.

Nevertheless, drink-driving is widespread and its commission is within the realms of possibility for a far greater number of people than many other types of crime.

Widening the net

The present legal limit and restricted police powers mean that for many drivers, so long as they maintain their vehicle in good condition and drive carefully, they can drink and drive either within the law or with very little chance of being caught. If the limit was lowered many more criminals would be created and if the police were to be given wider powers, while deterring more, they may also apprehend those who do not usually end up in the criminal justice system. A fully effective response to drink-driving would widen the net of the criminal justice system considerably and catch those who traditionally do not find themselves subject to the criminal process.

There would be ramifications for all aspects of the criminal justice system if a large section of the population was to be criminalized in this way. And this could be one reason why the introduction of RBT has been resisted. For as Peter Bottomley put it: 'RBT is no more than a slight diversion which would not catch the worst drink-drivers and would affect only the 'social and silly drinker'.

Targeting the criminal sanction Refusal to implement reforms likely to increase the chances of apprehension for all drink-drivers, even the 'respectable classes' driving with care in well-maintained vehicles, left open the question of how the law could be further developed. Research and ironically the reform lobby provided an answer, the problem of drink-driving could be re-defined. As alcohol-related accidents show drivers to have high blood-alcohol concentrations or to be young, male, aggressive drivers also likely to engage in dangerous or high-speed driving, attention, it was said, should be focused on these and the 'ordinary drinking driver' left to 'fumble along slowly trying to negotiate their trip'. The police were ready to respond:

> If reliable research, as is currently being carried out by the Transport and Road Research Laboratory, produces the profile of the drink-driver as an individual in a certain age group, driving certain types of car, at certain times of day and in certain locations, it makes sense for the police to target these people (Joslin 1990:25).

While it may indeed make sense, it also ensures that the criminal justice system retains its staple diet of young working class males. And as Gusfield (1988:135) has put it:

> Perhaps the saliency given to youth as the central actors in the DUI drama is a means of achieving compromise between the organisational and political concerns of the courts and the police, on one hand, and the demands of the citizens movements on the other. Young people have achieved a status as a separate group in American life, a source of both concern and fear, a new form of the dangerous class in America. Further, they are also a relatively weak political group.

It seems that the same can be said for England and Wales.

Policy and prospects

Motorised road transport has brought tremendous advances to society, but at an awful cost. We seem virtually to have surrendered the environment to the motor car and accept a toll of deaths and injuries which would be unacceptable in any other context. Having said that it must be noted that Britain has one of the best safety records of any industrialised Western nation and despite a huge increase in the number of motor vehicles, road casualties have declined significantly, in absolute as well as relative terms. For example, in 1966, the year before the introduction of the breathalyser, there were 13.3 million vehicles licensed on our roads and 7,985 road deaths; by 1991 the number of vehicles had risen to 24.5 million while road deaths fell to 4,568. But the scale of the tragedy remains staggering.

Legal policy can never be a complete answer to the problem of road casualties, although it is clear throughout the history of legal policy and the drink-driver that the law can have some effect in reducing traffic deaths and injuries. So too can other measures such as publicity, education, and engineering, but the answer to road casualties lies in transport policy, the answer to alcohol problems in

155

alcohol policy. By the end of the century the number of vehicles using the roads will have increased dramatically with alcohol consumption forecast to remain at its present level, which leave no room for complacency. Yet the need to formulate a rational alcohol policy has never been fully accepted by either the public or the Government. In strategic terms, the alcohol reform lobby has failed. The social and economic pressures against them were too great and they have been marginalised as 'killjoy' abstainers and interfering do-gooders. A similar fate seems to have befallen the road traffic lobby. Rather than directing attention at transport issues and alcohol policy the focus is on the deviant minority. And as Ross (1986:664) has put it:

> To interpret social problems solely in terms of individual irresponsibility is in tune with our times. The automobile and liquor industries are delighted to blame accidents on the abuse of their products by a small fraction of consumers, and to join in public relations campaigns to discourage such abuse. How painless that is compared with making safer cars or admitting that alcohol is a dangerous drug.

Nevertheless, substantial gains have been made in relation to drink-driving, most significantly in the area of legal policy; which has developed over a period of 100 years and is now a reasonably well-organised response, in criminal law terms, to the problem. Originally concerned with drunken drivers, attempts were made to define and punish the drink-driver; then in 1967 legal policy directed its efforts towards securing convictions and improving deterrence. The last of these has now assumed prime importance and has met with limited success (albeit much of it short-lived). However, for many it appears that the convenience of private transport in their social lives, much of which involves alcohol, still outweighs the deterrent effect of the law.[5] In the balance of gains and losses the chances of being caught appear to be crucial, as do efforts to promote the educative or instrumental expressive function of the law. Yet, in the 1980s, the legal response stopped short of reforms which would have refined the effectiveness of the law in deterring, catching and educating more drink-drivers. Some possible explanations have been offered in this last chapter - first, the drink-drive provisions have not been as effective as they might have been, due to a concentration on simple deterrence; secondly, attempts to manipulate public attitudes to drink-driving may have backfired; thirdly, the literature and state of knowledge on drink-driving is inconclusive and contradictory in several crucial respects; fourthly, the drink-driver is not a 'suitable enemy'; and fifthly, measures such as RBT and lower blood-alcohol concentrations would widen the net of the criminal justice system unacceptably.

The underlying rationale of legal policy and the drink-driver appears to have remained rooted in the notion that drink-driving is not a 'real crime', the 'there but for the grace of God go I' syndrome and perhaps even a realisation that the criminal law can never solve what is in origin a public health and transportation problem. For many, the attractions of private transport and the pervasive position of alcohol as societies 'favourite drug' lead them to accept the risks inherent in drink-driving in return for automotive and social 'freedom'. It is then only special categories of drink-driver for whom the criminal sanction must be refined - the young and the high-risk offenders. For the rest care and moderation are claimed to be sufficient.

Notes

1. Clayton et al. (1984) found that 'except among teetotallers there was little social stigma associated with driving after drinking'.

2. At a conference organised by the *Publican* magazine and the Institute of Innkeeping (14.9.87) the Director of Operations, Whitbread Inns (South East) said the licensed trade would vigorously oppose a zero limit - it could, he said, result in the closing of some 10,000 public houses putting 50,000 people out of work.

3. Personal communication 20 May 1991 (Guppy A.). But this effect may be due to extra nervousness on the part of the subjects as they are under observation.

4. The siting of breath-test machines in drinking establishments may also have an effect on 'pub culture', by providing a physical reminder of the drink-drive law and disapproval from other customers of an intended drink-driver may invoke the sort of reintegrative shaming postulated by Braithwaite and discussed above.

5. Corbett & Simon (1991) in their study of 'rational choice' explanations for committing traffic offences list convenience and laziness as categories of explanation peculiar to drink-drive (and parking) offences.

APPENDIX 1 TABLE 1

Motor Vehicles in Use (Great Britain) 1904-1925

Year	Total Vehicles	Cars
1904	-	8,465
1905	-	15,895
1906	-	23,192
1907	-	32,451
1908	-	40,902
1909	-	48,109
1910	143,877	53,196
1911	192,877	72,106
1912	245,235	88,265
1913	305,662	105,734
1914	388,860	132,015
1915	406,821	139,245
1916	427,974	141,621
1917	341,122	110,435
1918	229,428	77,707
1919	330,518	109,715
1920	650,148	186,801
1921	845,799	242,500
1922	952,432	314,769
1923	1,105,388	383,525
1924	1,299,629	473,528
1925	1,509,627	579,901

Source: Plowden (1971)

APPENDIX 1 TABLE 2

Street Accidents (Great Britain) 1909-1928

Year	Fatal	Non-fatal	Total
1909	1,070	27,161	28,231
1910	1,241	30,191	31,432
1911	1,449	32,679	34,128
1912	1,664	35,741	37,405
1913	1,962	41,290	43,252
1914	2,220	57,626	59,846
1915	2,849	58,457	61,306
1916	2,678	49,980	52,658
1917	2,295	41,759	44,054
1918	2,094	34,591	36,685
1919	2,488	47,262	49,750
1920	2,704	53,734	56,438
1921	2,678	59,943	62,621
1922	2,768	67,491	70,259
1923	2,979	80,122	83,101
1924	3,631	94,584	98,251
1925	3,971	111,502	115,473
1926	4,803	119,484	124,287
1927	5,195	128,748	133,943
1928	5,978	141,604	147,582

Note: Each accident causing death or personal injury is counted as one accident only, irrespective of the number of persons killed or injured thereby. An accident in which more than one vehicle is involved is also counted as one accident only. Cases in which only the driver or rider is killed or injured are included.

Source: Home Office (1929)

APPENDIX 1 TABLE 3

Motor Vehicles with Current Licences (Great Britain) 1926-1991 (millions)

Year	Current Licences	Year	Current Licences
1926	1.7	1960	9.4
1927	1.9	1961	10.0
1928	2.0	1962	10.6
1929	2.2	1963	11.4
1930	2.3	1964	12.4
1931	2.2	1965	12.9
1932	2.2	1966	13.3
1933	2.3	1967	14.1
1934	2.4	1968	14.4
1935	2.6	1969	14.8
1936	2.8	1970	15.0
1937	2.9	1971	15.5
1938	3.1	1972	16.1
1939	3.1	1973	17.0
1940	2.3	1974	17.3
1941	2.5	1975	17.5
1942	1.8	1976	17.8
1943	1.5	1977	-
1944	1.6	1978	17.8
1945	2.6	1979	18.6
1946	3.1	1980	19.2
1947	3.5	1981	19.4
1948	3.7	1982	19.8
1949	4.1	1983	20.2
1950	4.4	1984	20.7
1951	4.7	1985	21.2
1952	5.0	1986	21.7
1953	5.3	1987	22.2
1954	5.8	1988	23.3
1955	6.5	1989	24.2
1956	7.0	1990	24.7
1957	7.5	1991	24.5
1958	8.0		
1959	8.7		

Source: Department of Transport (1992)

APPENDIX 1 TABLE 4

Casualties from Road Accidents (Great Britain) 1926-1991

Year	Killed	Injured	Year	Killed	Injured
1926	4,886	139,000	1960	6,970	348,000
1927	5,329	154,000	1961	6,908	350,000
1928	6,138	171,000	1962	6,709	342,000
1929	6,696	178,000	1963	6,922	356,000
1930	7,305	185,000	1964	7,820	385,000
1931	6,691	209,000	1965	7,952	398,000
1932	6,667	213,000	1966	7,985	392,000
1933	7,202	224,000	1967	7,319	370,000
1934	7,343	239,000	1968	6,810	349,000
1935	6,502	228,000	1969	7,365	353,000
1936	6,561	234,000	1970	7,499	363,000
1937	6,633	233,000	1971	7,699	352,000
1938	6,648	233,000	1972	7,763	360,000
1939	8,272	-	1973	7,406	354,000
1940	8,609	-	1974	6,876	325,000
1941	9,169	-	1975	6,366	325,000
1942	6,926	148,000	1976	6,570,	340,000
1943	5,796	123,000	1977	6,614	348,000
1944	6,416	131,000	1978	6,813	350,000
1945	5,256	138,000	1979	6,352	334,000
1946	5,062	163,000	1980	6,010	329,000
1947	4,881	166,000	1981	5,846	325,000
1948	4,513	153,000	1982	5,934	334,000
1949	4,773	177,000	1983	5,445	309,000
1950	5,012	201,000	1984	5,599	324,000
1951	5,250	216,000	1985	5,165	318,000
1952	4,706	208,000	1986	5,382	321,000
1953	5,090	227,000	1987	5,125	311,000
1954	5,010	238,000	1988	5,052	322,000
1955	5,526	268,000	1989	5,373	342,000
1956	5,367	268,000	1990	5,217	341,000
1957	5,550	274,000	1991	4,568	311,000
1958	5,970	300,000			
1959	6,520	333,000			

Source: Department of Transport (1992)

APPENDIX 1 TABLE 5

Incidence of Drink-Drive Offences Prosecuted and Convicted (England & Wales) 1929-1991

Year	Total Offences(a)	Offences Prosecuted(b)		Findings of Guilt	
		Total	% of (a)	Total	% of (b)
1929	1,730	1,724	99.6	1,232	71.4
1930	1,789	1,786	99.7	1,265	70.8
1931	2,130	2,127	99.9	n/a	n/a
1932	1,952	1,948	99.8	1,456	74.7
1933	2,064	2,059	99.8	1,595	77.3
1934	2,267	2,265	99.9	1,781	78.6
1935	2,478	2,471	99.7	1,966	79.6
1936	2,849	2,848	99.9	2,374	83.4
1937	3,040	3,036	99.9	2,475	81.5
1938	2,870	2,864	99.8	2,325	81.2

1939 - 1945 figures not published

Year	Total Offences(a)	Total	% of (a)	Total	% of (b)
1946	2,088	2,087	99.9	1,635	78.3
1947	2,091	2,090	99.9	1,656	79.2
1948	1,827	1,822	99.7	1,423	78.1
1949	2,134	2,131	99.9	1,682	78.9
1950	2,817	2,816	99.9	2,261	80.3
1951	3,378	3,378	100	2,652	78.5
1952	3,150	3,150	100	2,349	74.5
1953	3,258	3,257	99.9	2,490	76.5
1954	3,609	3,608	99.9	3,012	83.4
1955	3,869	3,867	99.9	3,311	86.1
1956	4,458	4,456	99.9	3,795	85.1
1957	4,656	4,654	99.9	3,942	84.7
1958	5,073	5,066	99.8	4,284	84.6
1959	5,720	5,715	99.9	5,029	88.0
1960	6,807	6,806	99.9	5,525	81.1
1961	7,547	7,545	99.9	6,170	81.8
1962	8,482	8,478	99.9	6,642	78.3
1963	9,280	9,276	99.9	7,394	79.7
1964	9,531	9,269	99.9	8,255	78.6
1965	10,504	10,500	99.9	9,116	78.6
1966	11,329	11,327	99.9	9,859	87.0
1967	11,951	11,950	99.9	10,406	87.1
1968	22,757	22,746	99.9	20,957	92.0
1969	29,434	29,427	99.9	26,392	89.7

162

1970	31,847	31,834	99.9	29,069	93.0
1971	46,039	46,028	99.9	42,259	91.8
1972	55,605	55,590	99.9	51,395	92.3
1973	57,758	57,715	99.9	55,347	95.9
1974	66,774	66,727	99.9	62,184	93.2
1975	70,394	70,332	99.9	65,200	92.7
1976	63,193	63,098	99.9	57,618	91.3
1977	*	58,699	-	53,000	90.3
1978	*	64,816	-	58,000	89.5
1979	*	75,000	-	67,000	89.3
1980	*	*	-	78,000	-
1981	*	*	-	71,000	-
1982	*	*	-	75,000	-
1983	*	*	-	98,000	-
1984	*	*	-	101,000	-
1985	*	121,200	-	107,000	88.28
1986	*	121,200	-	107,000	88.28
1987	*	130,500	-	115,000	88.1
1988	*	135,800	-	119,000	87.6
1989	*	129,500	-	114,300	88.3
1990	*	128,000	-	113,200	88.4
1991	*	119,000	-	103,800	87.2

* Data not given

Sources: *Offences Relating to Motor Vehicles*, Home Office Returns 1929-1976; Command Papers 1977-1979; *Offences Relating to Motor Vehicles*, Home Office Statistical Bulletins 1980-1992.

APPENDIX 1 TABLE 6

Committals for Trial for Drink-Drive Offences as a Percentage of Total Prosecutions (England & Wales) 1929-1978*

Year	Total Prosecutions	Committals	%
1929	1,724	96	5.5
1930	1,786	163	9.1
1931	2,127	136	6.3
1932	1,948	133	6.8
1933	2,059	128	6.2
1934	2,265	138	6.1
1935	2,471	134	5.4
1936	2,848	175	6.1
1937	3,036	166	5.5
1938	2,864	156	5.4

1939 to 1945 figures not published

Year	Total Prosecutions	Committals	%
1946	2,087	123	5.9
1947	2,090	216	10.3
1948	1,822	176	9.6
1949	2,131	199	9.3
1950	2,816	260	9.2
1951	3,378	413	12.2
1952	3,150	474	15.0
1953	3,257	437	13.4
1954	3,608	486	13.5
1955	3,867	476	12.3
1956	4,456	570	12.8
1957	4,654	609	13.0
1958	5,066	731	12.6
1959	5,715	718	12.6
1960	6,806	908	13.3
1961	7,545	971	12.9
1962	8,478	1,353	15.9
1963	9,276	1,367	14.7
1964	9,269	1,629	17.6
1965	10,500	1,744	16.6
1966	11,327	1,802	15.9
1967	11,950	1,700	14.2
1968	22,746	842	3.7
1969	29,427	1,464	4.9

1970	31,834	1,502	4.7
1971	46,028	2,282	4.9
1972	55,590	2,614	4.7
1973	57,715	3,241	5.6
1974	66,727	3,374	5.0
1975	70,332	3,333	4.7
1976	63,098	2,942	4.6
1977	58,699	2,954	5.0
1978	64,816	2,450	3.8

* Criminal Law Act 1977 removed the option of trial by jury

Source: *Offences Relating to Motor Vehicles*, Home Office Returns 1929-1976; Command Papers 1977-1978.

APPENDIX 1 TABLE 7

Comparison of Higher and Magistrates' Courts Conviction Rates for Drink-Drive Offences (England & Wales) 1953-1978*

| Year | Higher Courts | | | Magistrates' Courts | | |
| | Offences | Findings of Guilt | | Offences | Findings of Guilt | |
		Total	%		Total	%
1953	437	200	45.7	2,820	2,490	88.2
1954	486	206	42.4	3,122	2,806	89.8
1955	476	243	51.0	3,391	3,068	90.4
1956	570	254	44.6	3,886	3,541	91.1
1957	609	247	40.6	4,045	3,695	91.3
1958	731	371	50.8	4,335	3,913	90.2
1959	718	394	54.9	4,997	4,635	92.7
1960	908	525	57.8	5,898	5,525	93.6
1961	971	528	54.3	6,574	6,170	93.8
1962	1,353	675	49.8	7,122	6,642	93.2
1963	1,367	771	56.4	7,909	7,394	93.4
1964	1,629	892	54.7	7,640	7,363	96.3
1965	1,744	1,017	58.3	8,756	8,099	92.4
1966	1,802	1,012	56.1	9,525	8,847	92.8
1967	1,700	946	55.6	10,250	9,460	92.2
1968	842	598	71.0	21,904	20,399	93.1
1969	1,464	751	51.2	27,963	25,641	91.6
1970	1,502	1,098	73.1	30,332	27,872	91.8
1971	2,282	1,617	70.8	43,746	40,700	93.0
1972	2,614	1,813	69.3	52,976	49,502	93.4
1974	3,374	2,917	86.5	63,353	59,267	93.6
1975	3,333	2,737	82.1	66,999	62,463	93.2
1976	2,942	2,336	79.4	60,156	55,282	91.9
1977**	2,954	2,202	74.5	55,795	50,733	90.9
1978	2,450	1,970	80.4	62,366	55,850	89.6

* Data not recorded pre-1953
** Criminal Law Act 1977 removed jury trial (1979 only 180 committals)

Sources: *Offences Relating to Motor Vehicles*, Home Office Returns 1953-1976; Command Papers 1977-1978.

APPENDIX 1 TABLE 8

Findings of Guilt for Drink-Drive Offences Per Million Vehicles with Current Licence 1929-1991*

Year	Current Vehicle Licences (million)	Findings of Guilt Total	Per Million
1929	2.2	1,232	560
1930	2.3	1,265	550
1931	2.2	n/a	n/a
1932	2.2	1,456	661
1933	2.3	1,595	693
1934	2.4	1,781	742
1935	2.6	1,966	756
1936	2.8	2,374	847
1937	2.9	2,475	853
1938	3.1	2,325	750

1939 to 1945 court figures not available

Year	Current Vehicle Licences (million)	Findings of Guilt Total	Per Million
1946	3.1	1,636	527
1947	3.5	1,656	534
1948	3.7	1,423	384
1949	4.1	1,682	410
1950	4.4	2,261	513
1951	4.7	2,652	564
1952	5.0	2,349	469
1953	5.3	2,490	469
1954	5.8	3,012	519
1955	6.5	3,311	509
1956	7.0	3,795	542
1957	7.5	3,942	525
1958	8.0	4,284	535
1959	8.7	5,029	578
1960	9.4	5,525	587
1961	10.0	6,170	617
1962	10.6	6,642	626
1963	11.4	7,394	648
1964	12.4	8,255	665
1965	12.9	9,116	706
1966	13.3	9,859	741
1967	14.1	10,406	738
1968	14.4	20,957	1,455
1969	14.8	26,392	1,783

1970	15.0	29,069	1,937
1971	15.5	42,259	2,726
1972	16.1	51,315	3,187
1973	17.0	55,347	3,255
1974	17.3	65,184	3,767
1975	17.5	65,200	3,725
1976	17.8	57,618	3,237
1977	17.8	53,035	2,977
1978	17.8	57,820	3,258
1979	18.6	67,000**	3,602
1980	19.2	78,000	4,062
1981	19.4	71,000	3,659
1982	19.8	75,000	3,787
1983	20.2	98,000	4,851
1984	20.7	101,000	4,879
1985	21.2	107,000	5,047
1986	21.7	107,000	4,930
1987	22.2	115,000	5,180
1988	23.3	119,000	5,107
1989	24.2	114,300	4,723
1990	24.7	113,200	4,583
1991	24.5	103,800	4,237

* Vehicles licensed for Great Britain, convictions for England & Wales
(so that absolute rates cannot be trusted, but trends should be valid)

** From 1979 data only available to the nearest thousand

Sources: Department of Transport (1992) *Offences Relating to Motor Vehicles*; Home Office Returns 1929-1976; Command Papers 1977-1979; Home Office Statistical Bulletins 1980-1992.

Sentences of Immediate Imprisonment as a Percentage of Findings of Guilt for Drink-Drive Offences (England & Wales) 1929-1991

Year	Findings of Guilt	Prison Sentences Passed*	
		Total	%
1929	1,232	75	6.1
1930	1,265	56	4.4
1931	n/a	49	-
1932	1,456	37	2.5
1933	1,595	43	2.7
1934	1,781	87	4.9
1935	1,966	104	5.3
1936	2,374	116	4.9
1937	2,475	141	5.7
1938	2,325	115	4.9

1939 to 1945 figures not available

Year	Findings of Guilt	Total	%
1946	1,635	68	4.2
1947	1,656	81	4.9
1948	1,423	48	3.4
1949	1,682	54	3.2
1950	2,261	87	3.8
1951	2,652	223	8.4
1952	2,349	233	9.9
1953	2,490	189	7.6
1954	3,012	177	5.9
1955	3,311	209	6.3
1956	3,795	210	5.5
1957	3,942	182	4.6
1958	4,284	180	4.2
1959	5,029	209	4.2
1960	5,525	293	5.3
1961	6,170	231	3.7
1962	6,642	238	3.6
1963	7,394	224	3.0
1964	8,255	216	2.6
1965	9,116	218	2.4
1966	9,859	290	2.9
1967	10,406	276	2.7
1968	20,957	308	1.4
1969	26,392	340	1.3

1970	29,069	447	1.5
1971	42,259	513	1.2
1972	51,315	653	1.3
1973	55,347	767	1.4
1974	62,184	797	1.3
1975	65,200	861	1.6
1976	57,618	915	1.6
1977	53,035	1,100	2.0
1978	57,820	1,200	2.0
1979	67,000**	1,300	2.0
1980	78,000	1,400	2.0
1981	71,000	1,500	2.0
1982	75,000	1,600	2.0
1983	98,000	1,900	2.0
1984	101,000	2,600	3.0
1985	107,000	2,800	3.0
1986	107,000	2,800	3.0
1987	115,000	3,400	3.0
1988	119,000	3,800	3.0
1989	114,300	3,900	3.4
1990	113,200	3,800	3.4
1991	103,800	4,300	4.1

* Includes partly suspended; borstal training; youth custody; detention centre; YOI

** From 1979 data only available to the nearest thousand

Sources: *Offences Relating to Motor Vehicles*, Home Office Returns 1929-1976; Command Papers 1977-1979; Home Office Statistical Reports 1980-92.

APPENDIX 1   TABLE 10

Roadside Screening Breath Tests
(England & Wales) 1968-1991

Year	Number Required	Positive (%)	Negative (%)	Refused (%)
1968	51,000	51	42	8
1969	59,000	54	40	6
1970	73,000	54	40	6
1971	97,000	58	36	6
1972	120,000	58	36	6
1973	132,000	58	35	6
1974	124,000	56	37	7
1975	134,000	53	40	8
1976	134,000	43	49	9
1977	131,000	41	50	9
1978	142,000	42	49	10
1979	164,000	42	48	9
1980	180,000	41	50	9
1981	177,000	37	54	8
1982	207,000	35	57	8
1983	241,000	33	59	7
1984	208,000	35	58	7
1985	250,000	32	62	6
1986	303,000	28	68	5
1987	400,000	25	71	4
1988	443,000	23	74	4
1989	541,000	18	79	3
1990	597,000	16	82	2
1991	562,000	15	83	2

Sources: *Offences Relating to Motor Vehicles* 1968-1976; Command Papers 1977-1979; Department of Transport 1992.

Bibliography

Adams, J. (1985) *Risk and Freedom: the Record of Road Safety Regulation,* London, Transport Publishing Project.

Addiction Research Centre (1988) *Alcohol Policies: Responsibilities and Relationships in British Government,* Hull, ARC.

Alker-Tripp, H. (1936) The Traffic Problem, *The Police Journal, IX,* 74-97.

Allsop, R.E. (1965) Drinking Drivers, *New Society,* 30 December, 12-3.

Andenaes, J. (1974) *Punishment and Deterrence,* Lansing, University of Michigan Press.

Andenaes, J. (1977) The Moral or Educative Influence of Criminal Law, in Tapp, L.J. & Levine, F.J. (eds) *Law, Justice, and the Individual in Society: Psychological and Legal Issues,* New York, Holt Rinehart & Winston.

Andenaes, J. (1984) Drinking-and-Driving Laws in Scandinavia, in Victorin, A. (ed) *Scandinavian Studies in Law, 28,* 12-23.

Andenaes, J. (1988) The Scandinavian Experience, in Laurence, M.D., Snortum, J.R. & Zimring, F.E. (eds)(1988) *Social Control of the Drinking Driver,* Chicago, University of Chicago Press.

Anderson, L.S., Chiricos, G.T. & Waldo, G.P. (1977) Formal and Informal Sanctions: A Comparison of Deterrent Effects, *Social Problems, 25,* 1, 103-14.

Andreasson, R. & Bonnichsen, R. (1966) The Frequency of Drunken Driving in Sweden During a Period When the Supply of Alcoholic Drink was Restricted, in University of Indiana (ed) *Alcohol and Traffic Safety,* Indiana, University of Indiana.

172

Andreasson, R. & Handel, K. (1963) Report of the Working Party (v) on the Prevention of Accidents Due to Alcohol in Havard, J.D.J (ed)(1963) *Alcohol and Road Traffic (Proceedings of the Third International Conference)*, London, BMA.

Anon (1907) *Lancet, 1,* 1031.

Anon (1951) Quarterly Commentary - The King's Highway, *The Police Journal, XXIV*, 1-4.

Anon (1957) Drinking and Driving, *The Magistrate, 13*, 132-3.

Anon (1961) Chemical Tests for Intoxication - I & II, [1961] *Crim LR*, 5-19; 77-86.

Anon (1964) Drink, Driver, and Doctor - Recent Controversies, [1964] *Crim.L.R.*, 429-34.

Anon (1965) Police/Public Relations, *Police Review, LXXII*, 764.

Anon (1966) Alcohol and Traffic Safety [1966] *Crim.L.R.*, 69-74.

Anon (1968) Legalism v Justice, *The Magistrate, 24,* 78.

Anon (1974) Drivers who Refuse a Blood Test, *BMJ, 2,* 620-1.

Anon (1975) Sentencing the Drinking Driver - In Theory and Practice, *JPN, 139*, 60-2.

Anon (1976) Blennerhassett: Drinking and Driving, *JPN, 140, 245-6*.

Anon (1976a) Drinking and Driving: Procedures or Penalties? *JLS, 21,* 388-90.

Anon (1976b) Drinking Drivers and the Law, *BMJ*, 1103-4.

Anon (1978) Sentencing in Drink/Driving Cases, *JPN, 142*, 188-9.

Anon (1984) The Basingstoke Breathalyser - Theory v. The Real World, *JPN, 148*, 3-5.

Anthony, E. (1968) Sexual Perversions and the Law, *JPN, 132*, 315.

Archer, H.E. (1954) Recognition of Intoxication, [1954] *Crim LR*, 443-7.

Arthurson, R.M. (1985) *Evaluation of Random Breath Testing*, Sydney, Traffic Authority of New South Wales.

Asch, P. & Levy, D.T. (1987) Does the Minimum Drinking Age Affect Traffic Fatalities?, *Journal of Policy Analysis and Management, 6*, 2, 180-92.

Australian Law Reform Commission (1976) *Alcohol, Drugs and Driving*, Canberra, Australian Government Publishing Service.

Automobile Association (1968) Breath Tests a Year Later, *Drive*, Autumn, 1968, 113-9.

Automobile Association (1976) *Attitudes to the Police* - A Survey of Motorists, Basingstoke, AA.

Baggott, R. (1988) Drinking and Driving, *Teaching Politics, 17*, 66-85.

Baggott, R. (1990) *Alcohol, Politics and Social Policy*, Aldershot, Gower.

Barker, A. (ed)(1990) *Report of the Drink-Drive Conference*, Colchester, University of Essex.

Barker, T. (ed)(1987) *The Economic and Social Effects of the Spread of Motor Vehicles*, London, MacMillan.

Beaven, A. (1983) Querying the Intoximeter, *The Law Society's Gazette*, 2835-6.

Beaven, A. (1984) Querying the Intoximeter Again, *The Law Society's Gazzette*, 563-4.

Beaven, A. (1985) Intoximeter Malfunction, *Road Traffic Law Bulletin, 2,* 4, 25/30.

Beddard, R. (1974) Towards a European Traffic Law, [1974] *Crim LR,* 574-80.

Beirness, D.J. (1987) Self-Estimates of Blood Alcohol Concentrations in Drinking Driving Context, *Drug and Alcohol Dependence, 19,* 79-90.

Belson, A. (1975) *The Police and the Public,* London, Harper & Row.

Bendix (1959) The Case for a Traffic Corps, *Police Review, LXVII,* 272.

Benjamin, T. (ed)(1987) *Young Drivers Impaired by Alcohol and Other Drugs,* London, Royal Society of Medical Services.

Benyan, J. & Bourn, C. (1986) *The Police,* Oxford, Pergamon.

Berger, D.E. & Snortum, J.R. (1985) Alcohol Beverage Preference of Drinking Driving Violators, *Journal of Studies on Alcohol, 46,* 3, 232-9.

Berger, D.E. & Snortum, J.R. (1986) A Structural Model of Drinking and Driving: Alcohol Consumption, Social Norms and Moral Commitments, *Criminology, 24,* 1, 139-53.

Berridge, V. (1990) Prevention and Social Hygiene, *British Journal of Addiction, 85,* 1005-16.

Beyleveld, D. (1979a) Identifying, Explaining and Predicting Deterrence, *BJ Crim, 19,* 205-24.

Beyleveld, D. (1979b) Deterrence Research as a Basis for Deterrence Policy, *Howard Journal, 18,* 135-49.

Birch, D.J. (1985) Drink/Driving and Unlawful Arrest: Is the Boot on the Other Foot? *Crim LR,* 84-91.

Birch, R. (1980) The Involvement of Police in the Evaluation of Substantive Breath Measuring Instruments, in Goldberg (1980) *Alcohol, Drugs and Traffic Safety,* Stockholm, Almqvist & Wiskell.

Birch, R. (1985) paper presented to Action on Alcohol Abuse Policy Forum Deterring the Drinking Driver - Time to Think Again, 29 May 1985, Bristol.

Birrell, J.H.W. (1970) A preliminary note on the drinking driver in Australia, *Med Sci Law, 10,* 38-41.

Bloom, H. (1969) The Breathalyser Crack-Up, *New Law Journal,* 1001-2.

Bloom, H. (1969a) The Breathalyser Breaths Again, *New Law Journal,* 1147-8.

Blose, J.O. & Holder, H.D. (1987) Liquor by the Drink and Alcohol Related Traffic Crashes: a Natural Experiment Using Time Series Analysis, *Journal of Studies on Alcohol, 48,* 1, 52-60.

BMA (1927) *Report of a Committee on Tests for Drunkenness,* London, BMA.

BMA (1927a) Tests for Drunkenness, *Supplement to BMJ,* 19 February 1927.

BMA (1935) The Relation of Alcohol to Road Accidents, Report by BMA Committee, *BMJ Supplement (Alcohol and Road Accidents),* 27 July 1935.

BMA (1954) *Recognition of Intoxication,* London, BMA.

BMA (1958) *Recognition of Intoxication,* London, BMA.

BMA (1960) *The Relation of Alcohol to Road Accidents,* London, BMA.

BMA (1965) *The Drinking Driver,* London, BMA.

BMA (1974) *Alcohol, Drugs and Driving: a Supplement to the 'Drinking Driver',* London, BMA.

BMA (1986) Young People and Alcohol, London, BMA.

BMA (1988) *The Drinking Driver,* London, BMA.

BMJ (1980) Drinking and Driving: the leisurely approach, *BMJ*, 6208, 135-6.

Boney, G. (1971) *The Road Safety Act 1967*, London, Butterworths.

Borkenstein, R.F. (1963) Handling the Drinking Driver, in Havard, J.D.J. (ed) (1963) *Alcohol and Road Traffic (Proceedings of the Third International Conference)*, London, BMA.

Borkenstein, R.F. (1975) Problems of Enforcement, Adjudication and Sanctioning, in Israelstam & Lambert (eds)(1975) *Alcohol, Drugs and Traffic Safety*, Toronto, Addiction Research Foundation of Toronto.

Borkenstein, R.F. (1987) An Historical Survey of Alcohol, Drugs and Traffic Safety: Research Highlights, in Noordzij, P.C. & Roszbach, R. (eds) *Alcohol, Drugs and Traffic Safety*, T86, Amsterdam, Excerpta Medica.

Borkenstein, R.F. & Smith, H.W. (1961) The Breathalyser and its Applications, *Med Sci Law, 2*, 13-22.

Bottoms, A.E. (1973) Review of *Sentencing The Motoring Offender*, *British Journal of Criminology, 13*, 296-7.

Bottoms, A.E. (1977) Reflections on the Renaissance of Dangerousness, *Howard Journal, 16*, 70-96.

Bowden, K.M. (1966) Driving Under the Influence of Alcohol, *Journal of Forensic Medicine, 13*, 2, 44-67.

Braithwaite, J. (1989) *Crime, Shame and Re-Integration*, Cambridge, Cambridge University Press.

Breakspere, R. (1990) Policies Against Drink-Driving: Some Australian and American Experience, in Barker, A. (ed)(1990) *Report of the Drink-Drive Conference*, Colchester, University of Essex.

Bretten, G.R. (1977) *Special Reasons*, London, Shaw.

Brewers Society (1984) *UK Statistical Handbook 1983*, London, Brewing Publications.

Briggs, A. (1960) *They Saw It Happen: 1897-1940*, Oxford, Basil Blackwell.

Brogden, M., Jefferson, T. & Walklate, S. (1988) *Introducing Police Work*, London, Unwin Hyman.

Brook, L. (1987) *Attitudes to Road Traffic Law*, Contractor Report 59, Crowthorne, Transport and Road Research Laboratory.

Broughton, J. (1986) *Analysis of Motoring Offence Details from DVLC Driving Licence Records*, Research Report 77, Crowthorne, Transport and Road Research Laboratory.

Broughton, J. & Stark, D.C. (1986) *The Effect of the 1983 Changes to the Law Relating to Drinking and Driving*, Research Report 89, Crowthorne, Transport and Road Research Laboratory.

Buikhuisen, W. & Jongman, R.W. (1970) A Legalistic Classification of Juvenile Delinquency, *BJ Crim, 10*, 109.

Butler, S. (1983) *Acquittal Rates*, Research & Planning Unit Paper 16, London, HMSO.

Calvert-Boyanowsky, J. & Boyanowski, E.O. (1980) *Tavern Breath Testing as an Alcohol Counter Measure*, Technical Report, Ottawa, Ontario, Ministry of Transport.

Camps, F.E. (1960) Tests for Intoxication and Their Application, *The Solicitors' Journal, 104*, 5-6.

175

Carr, B.R., Goldberg, H. & Farber, C.M.L. (1974) The Canadian Breathalyser Legislation: An Inferential Evaluation, in Israelstam, S. & Lambert, S. (ed) (1975) *Alcohol, Drugs and Traffic Safety*, Toronto, Addiction Research Foundation of Toronto.

Carseldine, D. (1985) *Surveys of Knowledge, Attitudes, Beliefs, and Reported Behaviours of Drivers - on the Topic of Drink-Driving and Random Breath Testing*, Sydney, Traffic Authority of New South Wales.

Cashmore, J. (1985) *The Impact of Random Breath testing in New South Wales*, Sydney, New South Wales Bureau of Crime Statistics and Research.

Cassel, H. & Havers, M. (1956) The Road Traffic Act 1956 - Changes in offences, [1956] *Crim LR*, 673-7.

Castle, B. (1984) *The Castle Diaries 1964-70*, London, Weidenfeld & Nicolson.

Chambers, L.W., Roberts, R.S. & Voelker, C.C. (1974) The Epidemiology of Traffic Accidents and the Effect of the 1969 Breathalyser Law in Canada, in Israelstam, S. & Lambert, S. (ed)(1975) *Alcohol, Drugs and Traffic Safety*, Toronto, Addiction Research Foundation of Toronto.

Ched, G. (1968) The Hazards of a Pin-Prick, *New Scientist*, 1968, 577-9.

Christian Economic and Social Research Foundation (1959) *Drunken-Driving and Drunk-in-Charge*, London, C.E.& S.R.F.

Christian Economic and Social Research Foundation (1975) *Recidivism Among Drunken Motorists: England & Wales 1964 to 1973*, London, C.E.& S.R.F.

Christie, N. (1984) opening address, Howard League Annual Conference, Oxford, September 1984.

Clare, A. & Bristow, M. (1987) Drinking Drivers: the Need for Research and Rehabilitation, *BMJ, 295*, 1432-3.

Clayton, A.B. (1986) Attitudes Towards Drinking and Driving: their Role in the Effectiveness of Counter-measures, *Alcohol, Drugs and Driving, 2,* 1.

Clayton, A.B., McCarthy, P.E. & Breen, J.M. (1984) *Drinking and Driving Habits, Attitudes, and Behaviour of Male Motorists*, Report SR 816, Crowthorne, Transport and Road Research Laboratory.

Coase, B.G. (1981) Breath Tests and the Trespassing Police Officer, *JPN, 145*, 145-6.

Coate, D. & Grossman, M. (1987) Change in Alcohol Beverage Prices and Legal Drinking Ages, *Alcohol Health and Research World,* Fall, 22-5.

Coate, D. & Grossman, M. (1988) Effects of Alcohol Beverage Prices and Legal Drinking Ages on Youth Alcohol Use, *Journal of Law and Economics, 31*, 145-71.

Codling, P.J. & Samson, P. (1974) *Blood-alcohol in Road Fatalities before and after the Road Safety Act 1967*, Crowthorne, Transport and Road Research Laboratory.

Cohen, J., Dearnaley, E.J. & Hansel, C.E.M. (1958) The Risk Taken in Driving Under the Influence of Alcohol, *BMJ, 1*, 1438-42.

Cohen, J. & Preston, B. (1968) *Causes and Prevention of Road Accidents*, London, Faber and Faber.

Cohen, S. (1973) *Folk Devils and Moral Panics*, London, Paladin.

Collins, J. (1982) Alcohol Careers and Criminal Careers, in Collins, J.J. (ed) (1982) *Drinking and Crime*, London, Tavistock.

176

Committee of Advertising Practice (1988) *The British Code of Advertising Practice*, London, C.A.P.

Connor, L.J. (1976) The Significance of the Decision in'Fox', *JPN, 150,* 136-7.

Connor, L.J. (1983) Drinking and Driving - Powers of Arrest on Private Premises, *JPN, 147,* 711-3.

Consumers Association (1986) Motoring Laws on the Move, *Which*, July 1986, 296-8.

Cooke, C. (1987) On the Campaign Trail, *Alcohol Concern, 3,* 3, 10-1.

Cook, J. (1987) The Drunk Driver - A Probation Service Initiative, *Road Traffic Law Bulletin, 4,* 41-2.

Cook, M. M. (1935) The Motorist and the Law, *The Police Journal, 8,* 350-62.

Corbett, C. & Simon, F. (1991) 'Decisions to Break and Adhere to Rules of the Road Viewed from the Rational Choice Perspective', paper presented to the 1991 British Criminology Conference - to be published by the Transport and Road Research Laboratory.

Corbett, C. & Simon, F. (1991a) Police and Public Perceptions of the Seriousness of Traffic Offences, *BJ Crim, 31,* 2, 153-64.

Cornish, W. R. (1968) *The Jury*, London, Allen Lane.

CPRS (1982) *Alcohol Policies in the UK*, Stockholm, Sociologiska Institutionen.

Cressey, D. (1974) Law, Order and the Motorist, in Hood, R. (ed) *Crime, Criminology and Public Policy: Essays in Honour of Sir Leon Radzinowicz*, London, Heinemann.

Critchley, T.A. (1967) *A History of the Police in England & Wales 900-1966*, London, Constable.

Crichton-Browne, J. (1927) Presidential Address, The True Temperance Society, unpublished.

Crompton, R. (1982) Alcohol and Fatal Road Traffic Accidents, *Med Sci Law, 22,* 189-94.

Cross, R. (1981) *The English Sentencing System*, London, Butterworths.

Dale, A. (ed)(1964) *The Role of the Drinking Driver in Traffic Accidents*, Department of Police Administration, Indiana University.

Davies, D.L. (1962) Normal Drinking in Recorded Alcohol Addicts, *Quarterly Journal of Studies on Alcohol*, 94-104.

Davies, M.R.R. (1955) Influence of Drink Offences in Road Traffic Law, [1955] *Crim LR*, 349-58.

Davies, P. & Walsh, D. (1983) *Alcohol Problems & Alcohol Control in Europe*, London, Croom Helm.

Denney, R.C. (1970) *The Truth About Breath Tests*, London, Nelson.

Denney, R.C. (1976) Breathing New Life into Britain's Breath Test Laws, *Chemistry & Industry, 15,* 424-5.

Denney, R.C. (1986) *Alcohol and Accidents*, Wilmslow, Sigma.

Denney, R.C. (1986a) The Use of Breath and Blood Alcohol Values in Evaluating Hip Flask' Defences, *New Law Journal, 136,* 923-4.

Denney, R.C. (1989) The Importance of the Roadside Screening Test, *New Law Journal*, 52-3;56.

Department of the Environment (1969) *Driving*, (3rd ed) (1979); reprinted (1981) London, HMSO.

Department of the Environment (1971) *Road Accidents 1969*, London, HMSO.
Department of the Environment (1972) *Road Accidents 1970*, London, HMSO.
Department of the Environment (1973) *Road Accidents in GB 1971*, London, HMSO.
Department of the Environment (1974) *Road Accidents in GB 1972*, London, HMSO.
Department of the Environment (1975) *Road Accidents in GB 1973*, London, HMSO.
Department of the Environment (1976) *Drinking and Driving* (the Blennerhassett Report) London, HMSO.
Department of the Environment (1976a) *Road Accidents in GB 1974*, London, HMSO.
Department of Transport (1979) *Consultative Document on Drinking and Driving*, London, HMSO.
Department of Transport (1980) *The Costs of Alcohol Misuse*, London, HMSO.
Department of Transport (1985) *Road Accidents Great Britain 1984*, London, HMSO.
Department of Transport (1986) *Road Accidents Great Britain 1985*, London, HMSO.
Department of Transport (1987) *Road Accidents Great Britain 1986*, London, HMSO.
Department of Transport (1987) *Road Safety: The Next Steps*, London, HMSO.
Department of Transport (1989) *Road Accidents Great Britain 1988*, London, HMSO.
Department of Transport (1989a) *Roads for Prosperity*, London, HMSO.
Department of Transport (1992) *Road Accidents Great Britain 1991*, London, HMSO.
Department of Transport/Home Office (1988) *Road Traffic Law Review Report* (North Report), London, HMSO.
Department of Health and Social Security (1981) *Drinking Sensibly*, London, HMSO.
Dix, M.C. & Lazel, A.D. (1983) *Road Users and the Police*, Oxford, OUP.
Doherty, F. (1966) Review of *Criminal on the Road*, *BJ Crim*, 6, 88.
Dossett, J.A. (1984) The Significance of a Difference between Two Successive Readings on the Lion Intoximeter 3000, *The Law Society's Gazette*, 2840-1.
Drew, G.C., Colquhoun, W.P. & Long, H.A. (1958) Effect of Small Doses of Alcohol on a Skill Resembling Driving, *BMJ*, 2, 993.
Drew, C., Colquhoun, W.P. & Long, H.A. (1959) *Effect of Small Doses of Alcohol on a Skill Resembling Driving*, Medical Research Council Memorandum No. 38, London, HMSO.
Dubowski, K.M. (1976) Breath Alcohol Analysis: Uses, Methods and Some Forensic Problems; Review and Opinion, *Journal of Forensic Science, 21*, 9-41.
DuMuchel, W., Williams, A.F. & Zador, P. (1987) Raising the Alcohol Purchasing Age: its Effects on Fatal Motor Vehicle Crashes in Twenty-six States, *Journal of Legal Studies, 16*, 1, 249-66.

Dunbar, J.A. (1985) *A Quiet Massacre: A Review of Drinking and Driving in the United Kingdom*, London, The Institute of Alcohol Studies.

Dunbar, J.A. (1986) What Do We Know About the High Risk Offender? in *Drinking and Driving - 10 Years on from Blennerhassett*, London, Institute of Alcohol Studies.

Dunbar, J.A. (1987) What We Can Learn from Other Countries, *Drinking and Driving: Controlling the Massacre*, London, Institute of Alcohol Studies, unpublished.

Dunbar, J.A., Martin, B.T., Devgun, M.S., Hagart, J. & Ogston, S.A. (1983) Problem Drinking Among Drunk Drivers, *BMJ, 286*, 1319-21.

Dunbar, J.A., Ogston, S.A., Ritchie, A., Devgun, M.S., Hagart, J. & Martin, B.T. (1985) Are Problem Drinkers Dangerous Drivers? *BMJ, 290*, 827-30.

Dunbar, J.A., Ogston, S.A., Devgun, M.A., Hagart, J., Ritchie, A. & Martin, B.T. (1985a) Problem Drinkers Among Drunk Drivers - their Problems and the Problems they Cause, *The Police Surgeon, 27*, 22-39.

Dunbar, J.A., Pentula, A. & Pikkarainen, J. (1987) Drinking and Driving: Success of Random Breath Testing in Finland, *BMJ, 295*, 101-3.

Dunbar, J.A., Pentula, A. & Pikkarainen, J. (1987a) Drinking and Driving: choosing the legal limits, *BMJ, 295*, 1458-60.

Easton, S.M. (1991) Bodily Samples and the Privilege Against Self-Incrimination, *Crim LR*, 18-28.

Ebor' (1964) The Breathalyser, *Police Review, LXXII*, 340.

Edwards, K.B. (1964) Evidence of Unfitness to Drive, *The Law Journal, 114*, 422-3.

E.G.B.T. (1954) Drunk in Charge, *The Solicitors' Journal, 98*, 275-6.

Elliott, D.W. & Street, H. (1968) *Road Accidents*, Harmondsworth, Penguin.

Elmes, F. (1959) Police and Public, *Police Review, LXVII*, 572.

Emmins, C.J. (1981) *A Practical Approach to Criminal Procedure*, London, Blackwell.

Everest, J.T. & Jones, W. (1987) Patterns of Accidents and Injuries Associated with Young Road Users, in Benjamin (ed)(1987) *Young Drivers Impaired by Alcohol and Other Drugs,* London, Royal Society of Medical Services.

Everest, J.T. & Jones, W. (1988) *The Drink/Driving Characteristics of Accident Involved Drivers Riders*, Research Report 149, Crowthorne, Transport and Road Research Laboratory.

Farmer, D.J. (1984) *Crime Control: The Use and Misuse of Police Resources*, New York, Plenum.

Farrington, D.P. (1978) The Effectiveness of Sentences, *JPN, 142*, 68-71.

Federal Office of Road Safety (1990) *Road Crash Statistics,* Canberra, FORS.

Feldman, J. & Cohen, H. (1983) The Questionable Accuracy of Breathalysers, *Trial, 19*, 54-9.

Fields, P.J.T. & Heming, D.C. (1986) Air on the Intoximeter, *The Solicitors' Journal, 130*, 438-9.

Firth, J.B. (1955) Aspects of Forensic Science, [1955] *Crim LR*, 282-9.

Fitzgerald, P.J. (1966) Review of *Criminal on the Road, LQR, 82*, 121-4.

Fitzgerald, P.J. & Pole, K.F.M. (1969) The Road Safety Act 1967, *New Law Journal*, 9 January 1969, 43-44; 16 January 1969, 61-63.

Flanagan, N.G., Lochridge, G.K., Henry, J.G., Hadlow, A.J. & Hamer, P.A. (1979) Blood Alcohol and Social Drinking, *Med Sci Law, 19*, 3, 180-5.

Flanagan, N.G. et al. (1983) The Effects of Low Doses of Alcohol on Driving Performance, *Med Sci Law, 23*, 3, 203-8.

Foon, A.E. (1987) Evaluation of a Single Drink-Driving Programme, *British Journal of Addiction, 82*, 189-92.

Ford, P. & Ford, G. (1957) *A Breviate of Parliamentary Papers 1900-1916*, Oxford, Basil Blackwell.

Ford, P. & Ford, G. (1969) *A Breviate of Parliamentary Papers 1917-1939*, Shannon, IUP.

Ford, P. & Ford, G. (1969) *Select List of British Parliamentary Papers 1833-1899*, Shannon, IUP.

Ford, P. & Ford, G. (eds)(1972) *Checklist of British Parliamentary Papers in the Irish University Press 1000 - Volume Series 1801-1899*, Shannon, IUP.

Foreman-Peck, J. (1987) Death on the Roads: Changing National Responses to Motor Accidents; in Barker, T. (ed)(1987) *The Economic and Social Effects of the Spread of Motor Vehicles*, London, Macmillan.

Forrester, G. (1981) Hip Flask Goodbye? *JPN, 145*, 723-6.

Foster, G.R., Dunbar, J.A. & Fernando, G.C.A. (1988) Contribution of Alcohol to Deaths in Road Traffic Accidents in Tayside, 1982-6, *BMJ, 296*, 1430-2.

Gallup, G.H. (1977) *The Gallup International Opinion Polls: G.B. 1937-75*, London, Random House.

Gatt, J.A. (1984) The Effect of Temperature and Blood: Breath Ratio on the Interpretation of Breath Alcohol Results, *New Law Journal*, 249-51.

Geller, E.S. & Lehman, G.R. (1988) Drinking Driving Intervention Strategies: A Person-Situation-Behaviour Framework in Laurence, M.D., Snortum, J.R. & Zimring, F.E. (eds)(1988) *Social Control of the Drinking Driver*, Chicago, University of Chicago Press.

Gibbs, J.P. (1975) *Crime, Punishment and Deterrence*, New York, Elsevier.

Glad, A. (1985) *Drunken Driving in Norway*, Oslo, Institute of Transport Economics.

Glover, H.A. (1977) Drinking and Driving - Recent Developments, *JPN, 141*, 169-71.

Godfrey, C. & Robinson, D. (eds)(1990) *Manipulating Consumption: information, law and voluntary control,* Aldershot, Avebury/Gower.

Gold, S. (1983) Microgrammes Are Here, *New Law Journal*, 432-3.

Gold, S. (1986) Microgumbley, *New Law Journal*, 650-1.

Goldberg, L. & Havard, J.D.J. (1968) *Research on the Effects of Alcohol and Drugs on Drivers' Behaviour*, Paris, Organisation for Economic Co-operation and Development.

Goodhart, A.L. (1963) Blood Tests and the Offence of Driving When Unfit Through Drink, in Howard (ed)(1963) *Alcohol and Road Traffic*, London, BMA.

Goodhart, A.L. (1970) The Road Safety Act 1967, *LQR, 86*, 27-32.

Goodhart, A.L. (1973) *LQR, 89*, 354, 161-5.

Gott, J. (1961) Drink and the Driver, *Police Journal, 34*, 133-4.

Gott, J. (1963) As others see us ..., *Police Journal, 36*, 226-7.

Gregory, P.G.M. (1968) *The Plight of the Motorist*, London, Conservative Political Centre.

G.S.W. (1963) Drink, Drugs and Driving - I and II, *The Solicitors' Journal, 107*, 283-4; 304-5.

Guppy, A. (1984) Perceived and Real Likelihood of the Detection of Drinking and Driving, PhD thesis, Cranfield Institute of Technology, unpublished.

Gusfield, J.R. (1981) *The Culture of Public Problems: Drinking-Driving and the Symbolic Order*, Chicago, University of Chicago Press.

Gusfield, J.R. (1985) Social and Cultural Contexts of the Drinking-Driving Event, *Journal of Studies on Alcohol, Supplement No 10*, 70-7.

Gusfield, J.R. (1988) The Control of Drinking Driving in the United States: a period in transition? in Laurence, M.D., Snortum, J.R. & Zimring, F.E. (eds) (1988) *Social Control of the Drinking Driver*, Chicago, University of Chicago Press.

Haddon, W. & Bradess, V.A. (1959) Alcohol in the Single Vehicle Fatal Accident, *Journal of the American Medical Association, 169*, 14, 1587-93.

Hagart, J., Dunbar, J.A., Devgun, M.S., Ogston, S., Martin, B. & Ritchie, A. (1985) Alcohol Screening Tests, *Police Surgeon, 28*, 15-28.

Hails, F. G. (1965) The Drinking Driver Analysed (i) and (ii), *The Law Journal, 115*, 329-31; 347-48.

Halnan, P. (1973) *Wilkinson's Road Traffic Offences* (7th ed), London, Oyez.

Halnan, P. (1975) *Wilkinson's Road Traffic Offences* (8th ed), London, Oyez.

Halnan, P. (1977) *Wilkinson's Road Traffic Offences* (9th ed), London, Oyez.

Halnan, P. (1984) *Drink Driving: The New Law*, London, Oyez Longman.

Halnan, P. (1985) Problem Drinkers, *The Magistrate, 41*, 9, 130-1.

Halnan, P. & Spencer, J. (1980) *Wilkinson's Road Traffic Offences* (10th ed), London, Oyez.

Halnan, P. & Spencer, J. (1982) *Wilkinson's Road Traffic Offences* (11th ed), London, Oyez.

Halnan, P. & Spencer, J. (1985) *Wilkinson's Road Traffic Offences* (12th ed), London, Oyez.

Halnan, P. & Wallis, P. (1987) *Wilkinson's Road Traffic Offences* (13th ed), London, Longman.

Halnan, P. & Wallis, P. (1989) *Wilkinson's Road Traffic Offences* (14th ed), London, Longman.

Halnan, P., Wallis, P., Spencer, J., McKittrick, N. & Niekirk, P. (1988) *Wilkinson's Road Traffic Offences,* 2nd cumulative supplement to the 13th edition, London, Longman.

Hamilton, C.J. & Collins, J.J. (1982) The Role of Alcohol in Wife Beating and Child Abuse: A Review of the Literature, in Collins, J.J. (ed)(1982) *Drinking and Crime*, London, Tavistock.

Harper, R. (1981) Drinking and Driving in 1980: a Good Year? *The Solicitors' Journal, 125,* 507-9.

Harrison, B. (1971) *Drink and the Victorians: the Temperance Question in England 1815-1872*, London, Faber & Faber.

Harrison, L. (1987) Data Note - 7 Drinking and Driving in Great Britain, *British Journal of Addiction*, *82*, 203-8.

Hauge, R. (1988) The Effects of Changes in Availability of Alcoholic Beverages, in Laurence, M.D., Snortum, J.R. & Zimring, F.E. (eds)(1988) *Social Control of the Drinking Driver*, Chicago, University of Chicago Press.

Havard, J.D.J. (1960) The Drinking Driver and the Law, [1960] *Crim LR*, 152-9.

Havard, J.D.J. (1962) Alcohol and Road Accidents, *The Practitioner, 188*, 498-507.

Havard, J.D.J. (ed)(1963) *Alcohol and Road Traffic* (Proceedings of the Third International Conference), London, BMA.

Havard, J.D.J. (1963a) Recent Developments in Alcohol and Road Traffic, *British Journal of Addiction,* 55-64.

Havard, J.D.J. (1964) Road Accidents and the Drinking Driver, *New Scientist, 398*, 24-6.

Havard, J.D.J. (1967) The Road Safety Bill Part I - A Medical View, [1967] *Crim LR*, 151-62.

Havard, J.D.J. (1975) Cross-National Comparisons of Drinking Driving Laws, in Israelstam & Lambert (eds)(1975) *Alcohol, Drugs and Traffic Safety*, Toronto, Addiction Research Foundation of Toronto.

Havard, J.D.J (1978) Alcohol and the Driver, *BMJ, 1*, 1595-7.

Havard, J.D.J. (1983) Changes in the Law on Drinking and Driving, *BMJ, 286*, 1455-6.

Havard, J.D.J. (1985) The Background to Existing Legislation, *Drinking and Driving: Ten Years on From Blennerhassett*, London, Institute of Alcohol Studies.

Havard, J.D.J (1986) Drunken Driving Among the Young, *BMJ, 293*, 774.

Hawkins, G. (1971) Punishment and Deterrence: The Educative, Moralizing and Habituative Effects, in Grupp, S.E. (ed) *Theories of Punishment*, London, Indiana University Press.

Heath, C. (1955) Comparative Enforcement in Great Britain, in *Proceedings of the Second International Conference on Alcohol and Road Traffic*, Toronto, University of Toronto.

Heather, N. & Robertson, I. (1985) *Problem Drinking: The New Approach*, London, Penguin.

Heather, N. & Robertson, I. (1986) Is alcoholism a disease? *New Society*, 21.2.86, 318-20.

Her Majesty's Chief Inspector of Constabulary (HMCIC)
-     (1960) *Annual Report for 1958-59*, London, HMSO.
-     (1964) *Annual Report for 1963*, London, HMSO.
-     (1965) *Annual Report for 1964*, London, HMSO.
-     (1968) *Annual Report for 1967*, London, HMSO.
-     (1969) *Annual Report for 1968*, London, HMSO.
-     (1977) *Annual Report for 1976*, London, HMSO.
-     (1978) *Annual Report for 1977*, London, HMSO.
-     (1979) *Annual Report for 1978*, London, HMSO.
-     (1982) *Annual Report for 1981*, London, HMSO.

Heydon, J.D. (1980) Entrapment and Unfairly Obtained Evidence in the House of Lords, *Crim LR*, 129-35.

Hilton, M.E. (1984) The Impact of Recent Changes in California Drinking-Driving Laws on Fatal Accident Levels During the First Post Intervention Year: An interrupted time series analysis, *Law & Society Review, 18*, 605-27.

Hirsh, B. (1965) Under the Influence of Drink, *Police Review*, 20 August, 700-1.

Hirst, M. (1990) Incorrect Procedures in Drink-Driving Cases, *Crim LR*, 143-52.

Homel, R. (1986) *Australia's Experience with Random Breath Testing*, paper presented at the University of New Mexico, Albuquerque.

Homel, R. (1988) *Policing and Punishing the Drinking Driver*, London, Springer-Verlag.

Homel, R. (1990) Drinking and Driving: Australia, in Alberta Solicitor General (ed) *Effective Strategies to Combat Drinking and Driving*, Alberta, Solicitor General.

Home Office (1928) *Return of Street Accidents Caused by Vehicles and Horses, 1927*, London, HMSO.

Home Office (1929) *Royal Commission on Transport, First Report, The Control of Traffic on Roads*, Cmnd. 3365, London, HMSO.

Home Office (1929a) *Minutes of Evidence Taken Before the Royal Commission on Transport*, HMSO, London.

Home Office (1975) *Report of the Committee on the Distribution of Criminal Business*, London, HMSO.

Home Office (1984) *Offences Relating to Motor Vehicles*, Croyden, Home Office, 24/84.

Home Office (1987) *Report of the Working Group on Young People and Alcohol*, Home Office Standing Conference on Crime Prevention, London, Home Office.

Home Office (1989) *The Road User and the Law*, London, HMSO.

Home Office (1989a) *Offences Relating to Motor Vehicles, England and Wales 1988*, Croydon, Home Office Statistical Unit.

Hood, R. (1972) *Sentencing the Motoring Offender*, London, Heinemann.

Hood, R. (1976) Review of *Deviant Drivers, BJ Crim, 16*, 97-8.

Hough, M. & Mayhew, P. (1983) *The British Crime Survey: first report*, Home Office Research Study no.76, London, HMSO.

House of Commons (1985) *First Report from the Transport Committee, Session 1984-5, Road Safety*, vol.1 Report and Minutes of Proceedings, vol.2&3 Minutes of Evidence, London, HMSO.

Hunt, L. (1982) *Alcohol Related Problems*, London, Heinemann.

Illing, H.A. (1962) Review of Middendorf, W. (1960) *Soziologie Des Verbrechens BJ Crim, 2*, 405.

Isaacs, M.J., Emerson, V.J., Fuller, N.A. & Holleyhead, R. (1980) Breath/blood ratios obtained in trials of three breath alcohol testing instruments, in Goldberg (ed)(1980) *Alcohol, Drugs and Traffic Safety*, Stockholm, Almqvist & Wiskell.

Israelstam, S. & Lambert, S. (eds)(1975) *Alcohol, Drugs, and Traffic Safety*, proceedings of the Sixth International Conference, Toronto, Addiction Research Foundation of Toronto.

Jacobs, J.B. (1988) *Researching and Conceptualizing Drunk Driving: An Invitation to Criminologist and Criminal Law Scholors*, New York, Centre for Research in Crime and Justice.

Jacobs, J.B. (1988a) The Law and Criminology of Drunk Driving, in Tonry, M. & Morris, N. (eds) *Crime and Justice A Review of Research Volume 10*, Chicago, University of Chicago Press.

Jacobs, J.B. (1989) *Drunk Driving: An American Dilemma*, Chicago, University of Chicago Press.

Jackson, R.M. (1964) *The Machinery of Justice in England*, 4th ed., Cambridge University Press.

Jeffcoate, G.O. (1958) An examination of reports of fatal accidents in three police districts from the point of view of the effect of alcohol, *British Journal of Addiction, 54,* 2, 81-103.

Jones, A.W. (1982) How Breathing Techniques Influence the Results of Breath Alcohol Analysis, *Med Sci Law, 22,* 275.

Jones, R. (1990) The View of the Licensed Trade, in Barker, A. (ed) *Report of the Drink-Drive Conference*, Colchester, University of Essex.

Jones, W. & Everest, J.T. (1987) *The Incidence of Alcohol in Road Accidents and Motoring Offences*, Digest of Research Report 125, Crowthorne, Transport and Road Research Laboratory.

Joslin, P. (1990) The Police View, in Barker, A. (ed)(1990) *Report of the Drink-Drive Conference*, Colchester, University of Essex.

Joye, R.I. (1983) Drunk Driving, *Trial, 19,* 60-6.

J.T.M. (1963) Drink and Driving, *The Magistrate, 19,* 64-5; 84-5.

Kearns, I., Vazey, B., Carseldine, D. & Arthurson, R. (1987) An Overview of the Random Breath Testing Trial in New South Wales, in Noordzij, P.C. & Roszbach, R. (eds) *Alcohol, Drugs and Traffic Safety*, T86, Amsterdam, Excerpta Medica.

Keen, R.I. (1968) Blood Alcohol Levels: A survey of Four Months in Manchester, *Med Sci Law, 8,* 150-2.

Kenny, P. (1972) Special Reasons and Special Offenders, *Crim LR,* 217-20.

Kidner, D.H. (1981) Consistency in Sentencing, *The Magistrate, 37,* 29-31.

Kier, D. & Morgan, B. (1955) *Golden Milestone: 50 Years of the AA*, London, Automobile Association.

Kivikink, R., Schell, B. & Steinke, G. (1986) A Study of Perceived Drinking-Driving Behaviour Changes Following Media Campaigns and Police Spot Checks in Two Canadian Cities, *Canadian Journal of Criminology, 28,* 3, 263-78.

Latham, D. & Halnan, P. (1979) *Drink/Driving Offences*, London, Oyez.

Laurence, M.D., Snortum, J.R. & Zimring, F.E. (eds)(1988) *Social Control of the Drinking Driver*, Chicago, University of Chicago Press.

Lasok, D. (1962) The Problem of Criminal Responsibility of Drunken Drivers, *Solicitor Quarterly, 1,* 47-59.

Ledermann, S. (1956) *Alcool, alcoolisme, alcoolisation*, Paris, Institute d'Etudes Demographiques.

Lee, L. (1959) *Cider with Rosie*, London, Hogarth Press.

Leeming, J.J. (1969) *Road Accidents - Prevent or Punish?*, London, Cassell.

Lewis, D.E. (1986) The General Deterrent Effect of Longer Sentences, *BJ Crim,* *26*, 47-62.

Lewis, K.O. (1987) Back Calculation of Blood Alcohol Concentration, *BMJ, 295,* 800-1.

Light, R.A. (1986) Deterring the Drinking Driver-Time to Think Again, *JPN,* *150*, 41, 649-51.

Light, R.A. (1988) Drinking, Driving, and the Legal Profession, *Howard Journal, 27,* 3, 188-97.

Light, R.A. (1992) Miscarriage or Technicality? *The Law Society's Gazette*, 37, 25.

Light, R.A. (1993) Magistrates' Attitudes to Drinking and Driving, in preparation.

Lloyd George, D. (1934) *War Memoirs of the David Lloyd George*, London, Odhams Press.

McCormack, E. W. (1937) Conflicting Medical Testimony in Cases of Drunkenness, *JPN, 101*, 196-7.

McElree, F. (1990) Random Breath Testing and Civil Liberties - The View of the National Council for Civil Liberties, in Barker, A. (1990) *Report of the Drink-Drive Conference*, Colchester, University of Essex.

McKittrick, N.A. (1987) Another Watershed in Drink/Driving Offences, *JPN, 151*, 832-4.

MacMillan, J. (1975) *Deviant Drivers*, Farnborough, Saxon House.

Mackiewicz, G. (1988) *The Efficiency and Educative Value of Coin Operated Breath Testers*, Melbourne, Road Traffic Authority.

Magistrates' Association (1975) *Suggestions for Assessing Penalties for Main Motoring Offences*, 5th ed., London, Magistrates' Association.

Magistrates' Association (1978) *Suggestions for Assessing Penalties for Main Motoring Offences*, 6th ed., London, Magistrates' Association.

Mandelbaum, D. G. (1967) Alcohol and Culture, *Current Anthropology, 6,* 3, 281.

Mannheim, H. (1950) *Social Aspects of Crime Between the Wars*, London, Allen & Unwin.

Marples, E. (1963) Opening Address, in Havard (ed)(1983) *Alcohol and Road Traffic*, London, BMA.

Martin, P.H. (1990) The Government's Approach, in Barker, A. (ed)(1990) *Report of the Drink-Drive Conference*, Colchester, University of Essex.

Martin, J.P. (1986) A Course for Drivers Convicted of Drink/Driving, *JPN, 150*, 182-4.

Martin, J.P. & Bradely, J. (1964) Design of a Study of the Cost of Crime, *BJCrim, 4*, 591.

Mason, J.K. (1984) Section 10 Defence to Charges of Driving with Excess Alcohol, *Solicitors' Journal, 32*, 539-42.

Masterman, C.F.G. (1910) *The Condition of England*, London, Methueun.

Maynard, A. (1989) The Costs of Addictions and the Costs of Control, in Robinson, D., Maynard, A. & Chester, R. (eds) *Controlling Legal Addictions*, London, Macmillan.

Maynard, A. & Jones, A. (1987) *Economic Aspects of Addiction Control Policies,* York, Centre for Health Studies Addiction Research Centre, University of York.

Maynard, A. & Tether, P. (eds)(1990) *Preventing Alcohol and Tobacco Problems,* Avebury/Gower, Aldershot.

Mercer, G.W. (1984a) *Drinking-Driving Police Blitz Activity, Media Coverage and Alcohol Related Traffic Accident Reduction,* Victoria, British Columbia, Ministry of Attorney General.

Mercer, G.W. (1984b) *An Evaluation of the April-May 1984 Drinking-Driving Roadcheck, Enforcement and Media Blitz,* Victoria, British Columbia, Ministry of Attorney General.

Messer, C. (1969) Road Safety Act Appeals, *The Magistrate, 25,* 99-100.

Messer, C. (1970) The Breathalyser - how to put it right, *The Magistrate, 26,* 34.

M.H.L. (1952) The Arrest of the Drunken Driver, *The Solicitor's Journal, 96,* 703-5.

Middendorff, W. (1968) Is There a Relationship Between Traffic Offences and Common Crimes?, *International Criminal Police Review, 214,* 4-13.

Ministry of Transport (1946) *Road Accidents,* London, HMSO.

Ministry of Transport (1953) *Sense and Safety,* London, HMSO.

Ministry of Transport (1965) *Road Safety Legislation 1965-6,* Cmnd. 2859, London, HMSO.

Ministry of Transport (1965a) *Road Accidents 1964,* London, HMSO.

Ministry of Transport (1966) *Transport Policy,* Cmnd. 3057, London, HMSO.

Ministry of Transport (1967) *Road Safety - A Fresh Approach,* London, HMSO.

Ministry of Transport (1969) *Road Accidents 1968,* London, HMSO.

Ministry of Transport (1971) *Road Research 1969,* London, HMSO.

Mogridge, M. (1990) *Travel in Towns: Jams Yesterday, Jam Today and Jam Tomorrow,* London, MacMillan.

Morgan, R. & Smith, D.J. (eds)(1989) *Coming to Terms With Policing,* London, Routledge.

Morris, T. (1989) *Crime and Criminal Justice Since 1945,* Oxford, Blackwell.

Morton-Williams, R. (1962) The Relations Between the Police and the Public; in *Royal Commission on the Police: Appendix IV to the Minutes of Evidence,* London, HMSO.

Moxon, D. & Jones, P. (1984) Public Reactions to Police Behaviour: Some Findings from the British Crime Survey, *Policing, 11,* 49-56.

Muir, A.A. (1963) The Police and Its Public, *Police Journal, 36,* 207-13.

National Audit Office (1988) Report by the Comptroller and Auditor General *Department of Transport, Scottish Development Department and Welsh Office: Road Safety,* London, HMSO.

Newark, M. & Samuels, A. (1970) A Disastrously Complicated Offence, *Med Sci Law, 10,* 59-68.

Nokes, G.D. (1966) Self-Incrimination by the Accused in English Law, *University of British Columbia Law Review, 2,* 316-34.

Noordzij, P.C. & Roszbach, R. (eds)(1987) *Alcohol, Drugs and Traffic Safety,* T86, Amsterdam, Excerpta Medica.

Norman, L.G. (1962) *Road Traffic Accidents*, Geneva, World Health Organization.

Oats, J.F. (1976) *Study of Self-Test Drivers*, Final Report no. DOT-HS-501241, Washington, DC, NHTSA.

O'Brien, J. & Light, R.A. (1993) *Promoting Responsible Retailing: a review of alcohol-Server training in England and Wales*, London, Alcohol Concern.

Office of Health Economics (1981) *Alcohol: reducing the harm,* London, OHE.

Office of Population Censuses and Surveys (1980) *Drinking in England and Wales,* London, HMSO.

Okonkwo, O.C. (1966) *The Police and the Public in Nigeria,* London, Sweet & Maxwell.

Organisation for Economic Cooperation and Development (1978) *New Research on the Role of Alcohol and Drugs in Road Accidents,* Paris, OECD.

Packer, H.L. (1968) *The Limits of the Criminal Sanction*, Stanford, Stanford University Press.

Parry, M.M. (1968) *Aggression on the Road*, London, Tavistock.

Pasternoster, R.L.E. et al. (1983) Perceived Risk and Social Control: Do Sanctions Really Deter? *Law & Society Review, 17,* 457-83.

Paton, W., Cobb, P.G.W. & Dabbs, M.D.G. (1985) *Report on the Performance of the Lion Intoximeter 3000 and the Camic Breath Analyser evidential breath alcohol measuring instruments during the period 16 April 1984 to 15 October 1984,* London, HMSO.

Paul, D.M. (1980) Consultation Paper on Drinking and Driving, *Med Sci Law, 20,* 3, 151-3.

Phillips, L., Ray, S. & Votey, H.L. (1984) Forcasting Highway Casualties: The British Road Safety Act and a Sense of Deja Vu, *Journal of Criminal Justice, 12,* 101-14.

Picton, W.R. (1979) An Evaluation of a Coin Operated Breath Self-Tester, in Johnston, I.R. (ed)(1979) *Seventh International Conference on Alcohol, Drugs and Traffic Safety,* Canberra, Australian Government Publishing Service.

P.J.C. (1958) Patterns of Defence: Drink and Drivers, *The Magistrate, 14,* 12, 3-4.

P.J.H. (1984) Detention in Police Cells, *The Magistrate, 40,* 45.

Plowden, S. & Hillman, M. (1984) *Danger on the Road: The Needless Scourge,* London, PSI.

Plowden, W. (1971) *The Motor Car and Politics*, London, Bodley Head.

Plowden, S. & Pole, K.F.M. (1969) The Driver as the Doctor Sees Him, in Leeming, J. J. (ed) *Road Accidents, Prevent or Punish?,* London, Cassell.

Popkess, A. (1956) The Drunken Driver, *The Police Journal, 29,* 124-30.

Prentice, D. D. (1970) The Road Safety Act 1967, *Current Legal Problems 1970, 23*, London, Stevens.

Prevezers, S. (1981) Driving Offences, *The Magistrate, 37,* 7, 102-5.

Quinn, S. (1984) Lion Alcometer SL2 and Lion Intoximeter 3000, *The Solicitors' Journal, 128,* 356-8.

Raeburn, W. (1960) Assessing The Offender for the Courts: What the Bench Should Know, *BJ Crim, 1,* 102-9.

Raffle, P.A.B. (1986) 'War on Drinking Drivers', *AAA Review*, November/December 1986, p.3-4.

Reiner, R. (1985) *The Politics of the Police*, Brighton, Wheatsheaf.

Reiner, R. (1985a) Review of *Road Users and the Police, BJCrim, 25*, 96-7.

Richardson, K. (1977) *The British Motor Industry 1896-1939*, London, MacMillan.

Riley, D. (1983) *Police Action on Motoring Offences*, Research and Planning Unit Paper 20, London, HMSO.

Riley, D. (1984) Drivers beliefs about alcohol and the law, Research Bulletin No.17, London, Home Office Research & Planning Unit.

Riley, D. (1985) Drinking Drivers: the limits to deterrence, *Howard Journal, 24*, 241-56.

Riley, D. (1991) *Drink Driving: The Effects of Enforcement*, Home Office Research Study No. 121, London, HMSO.

Road Research Laboratory (1960) *Road Accidents: Christmas 1959*, Technical Paper No. 49, London, HMSO.

Road Research Laboratory (1963) *Research on Road Safety*, London, HMSO.

Road Research Laboratory (1964) *Fatal Road Accidents at Christmas 1963*, Technical Paper No. 70, London, HMSO.

Road Research Laboratory (1965) *Research on Road Traffic*, London, HMSO.

Road Research Laboratory (1966) *Alcohol and Road Accidents, A discussion of the Grand Rapids Study*, Report No. 6, Harmondsworth, RRL.

Road Research Laboratory (1970) *Road Research 1969*, London, HMSO.

Robertson, B. (1986) Discretion and the Intoximeter, *Crim LR*, 726-30.

Robertson, N. (1989) *Getting Better: Inside Alcoholics Anonymous*, London, MacMillan.

Robinson, A.E. (1975) Practical Scientific Problems Associated with Drinking and Driving Legislation - England, in Israelstam, S. & Lambert, S. (1975) *Alcohol, Drugs and Traffic Safety*, Toronto, Addiction Research Foundation of Toronto.

Rolph, C. H. (1962) *The Police and The Public*, London, Heinemann.

Roscoe, M. (1988) Drinking Drivers or Driving Drinkers, *Alcohol Concern, 4*, 6, 5-6.

Rose, G.N.G. (1966) Concerning the Measurement of Delinquency, *BJCrim, 6*, 414-21.

RoSPA (1969) *Road Accident Statistics 1967*, London, RoSPA.

RoSPA (1970) *Road Accident Statistics 1968*, London, RoSPA.

RoSPA (1974) *Low Level Fines for Drinking and Driving*, Press Notice, Birmingham, RoSPA.

Ross, H.L. (1960) Traffic Law Violations: a Folk Crime, *Social Problems, 8*, 231-41.

Ross, H.L. (1973) Law, Science, and Accidents: The British Road Safety Act of 1967, *Journal of Legal Studies, 11*, 1, 1-78.

Ross, H.L. (1973a) 'Folk Crime Revisited', *Criminology, 11*, 1, 71-86.

Ross, H.L. (1975) The Scandinavian Myth: The Effectiveness of Drinking and Driving Legislation in Sweden and Norway, *Journal of Legal Studies, 4*, 2, 285-310.

Ross, H.L. (1975a) The Effectiveness of Drinking-and-Driving Laws in Sweden and Great Britain, in Israelstam & Lambert (eds)(1975) *Alcohol, Drugs and Traffic Safety*, Toronto, Addiction Research Foundation of Toronto.

Ross, H.L. (1976) The Neutralization of Severe Penalties: Some Traffic Law Studies, *Law and Society Review, 10*, 403-13.

Ross, H.L. (1977) Deterrence Regained: The Cheshire Constabulary's 'Breathalyser Blitz', *Journal of Legal Studies, 6*, 241-9.

Ross, H.L. (1977a) Deterring the Drinking Driver: A Critique of Blennerhassett, *British Journal of Law & Society, 3*, 255-65.

Ross, H.L. (1978) Scandinavia's Drinking-and-Driving Laws: Do They Work? *Scandinavian Studies in Criminology, 6*, 55-60.

Ross, H.L. (1979) Blood Alcohol Concentrations among Traffic Fatalities in Inner North London: a Research Note, *Med.Sci.Law, 19*, 4, 233-4.

Ross, H.L. (1981) *Deterrence of the Drinking Driver*: An International Survey, Washington D.C., U.S. Department of Transport.

Ross, H.L. (1984) *Deterring the Drinking Driver*, Massachusetts, Lexington.

Ross, H.L. (1984a) Comment, *Law & Policy, 6*, 1, 37-41.

Ross, H.L. (1985) Social Control Through Deterrence: Drinking and Driving Laws, in AAA (ed)(1985) *Deterring the Drinking Driver - Time to Think Again*, London, Action on Alcohol Abuse.

Ross, H.L. (1986) Drunk Driving: What Not to Do, *The Nation,* 13 December, 663-4.

Ross, H.L. (1987) Britain's Christmas Crusade against Drinking Drivers, *Journal of Studies on Alcohol, 48*, 476-82.

Ross, H.L. (1988) British Drink-Driving Policy, *British Journal of Addiction, 83*, 863-5.

Ross, H.L. (1988a) Deterrence-Based Policies in Britain, Canada and Australia, in Laurence, M.D., Snortum, J.R. & Zimring, F.E. (eds)(1988) *Social Control of the Drinking Driver*, Chicago, University of Chicago Press.

Ross, H.L. & Blumenthal, M. (1974) Sanctions for the Drinking Driver: an Experimental Study, *Journal of Legal Studies, 3*, 53-61.

Ross, H.L., Campbell, D. T. & Glass, G. V. (1970) Determining the Social Effects of a Legal Reform: The British "Breathalyser" Crackdown of 1967, *Am Behav Scientist, 13*, 493-509.

Royal College of Psychiatrists (1986) *Alcohol, Our Favourite Drug*, London, Tavistock.

Royal College of Physicians (1991) *Alcohol and the Public Health*, London, Macmillan.

Royal Commission on Motor Cars (1906) *Report,* Cd 3080, London, HMSO.

Royal Commission on the Police (1962) *Final Report*, Cmnd. 1728, London, HMSO.

Ruggles-Brise, E. (1921) *The English Prison System*, Maidstone, H.M. Convict Prison.

Sabey, B.E. (1978) *A Review of Drinking and Drug-Taking in Road Accidents in Great Britain*, TRRL Report SR 441, Crowthorne, England.

Sabey, B.E. (1985) paper presented to Action on Alcohol Abuse Policy Forum Deterring the Drinking Driver - Time to Think Again, 29 May 1985, Bristol.

Sabey, B.E. (1986) Drinking and Driving: Options for the Future, in *Drinking and Driving - 10 Years on from Blennerhassett*, London, Institute of Alcohol Studies.

Sabey, B.E. (1988) *Drinking and Driving - the way forward*, Birmingham, Aquarius.

Sabey, B.E. (1990) Drink-Driving in Britain: The Statistical and Economic Factors, in Barker, A. (ed)(1990) *Report of the Drink-Drive Conference*, Colchester, University of Essex.

Sabey, B.E. & Codling, P. (1975) Alcohol and Road Accidents in Great Britain, in Israelstam, S. & Lambert, S. *Alcohol, Drugs and Traffic Safety*, Proceedings of the Sixth International Conference, Toronto, Addiction Research Foundation of Toronto.

Sabey, B.E., Everest, J.T. & Forsyth, E. (1988) *Roadside Surveys of Drinking and Driving*, Research Report 175, Crowthorne, Transport and Road Research Laboratory.

Sabey, B.E. & Staughton, G.C. (1980) *The Drinking Road User in Great Britain*, TRRL Supplementary Report 616, Crowthorne, Transport and Road Research Laboratory.

Saeed, S. (1982) Drunken Drivers: A New Approach? *Police Journal, 55*, 373-7.

Samuel, G. (1980) The Right Approach? *LQR, 96*, 12-5.

Samuels, A. (1970) Review of *Drink, Drugs and Driving*, *Crim LR*, 1970, 712-3.

Samuels, A. (1972) Sentencing the Motoring Offender, *New Law Journal*, 7 December 1972, 1092.

Samuels, A. (1973) Drunken Driving - All the Known Defences, *New Law Journal*, 1 March 1973, 192-5.

Samuels, A. (1974) Drunken Driving - All the Known Defences, *New Law Journal*, 21 February 1974, 168-9.

Samuels, A. (1974a) Drunken Driving, *The Magistrate, 30*, 170.

Samuels, A. (1975) Drunken Driving - All the Known Defences, *New Law Journal*, 28 August 1975, 838-40.

Samuels, A. (1975a) Drunken Driving: The Sentence, *New Law Journal*, 664.

Samuels, A. (1980) Drunken Driving: Challenging the Blood or Urine Analysis, *Med Sci Law, 20*, 1, 14-6.

Samuels, A. (1980a) Prison for the Motoring Offender, *JPN, 144*, 95-6.

Samuels, A. (1983a) Drunken Driving: Has the Juridical Nature of the Offence Changed? *New Law Journal*, 426-7.

Samuels, A. (1983b) Defences to the New Drunken Driving Law, *New Law Journal*, 435-6.

Samuels, A. (1984) Drunken Driving: Are There Any Valid Defences Still Available? *The Solicitors' Journal, 129*, 8, 124-6.

Samuels, A. (1984a) Suggestions, Guidelines and Starting Points, *The Magistrate, 40*, 7-8.

Samuels, A. (1987) Road Traffic - Viable or Arguable Defences to Drunken Driving, *The Law Society's Gazette*, 659-70.

Saunders, A. (1975) Seven Years Experience of Blood - Alcohol Limits in Britian, in Israelstam, S. & Lambert, S. *Alcohol, Drugs and Traffic Safety*, Proceedings of the Sixth International Conference, Toronto, Addiction Foundation of Toronto.

Saunders, D.E.G. (1964) Intoxication and Motor Vehicles, *Police Journal, 37*, 388-95.
Sayce, J. (1969) Brewery Shares and the Breathalyser, *New Law Journal*, 18 January 1969, 54.
Seago, P. (1969) Offences Under the Road Safety Act 1967, [1969] *Crim LR,* 292-302.
Seago, P. (1970) Driving to Drink, [1970] *Crim LR*, 683-92.
Seago, P. (1970a) The Road Safety Act 1967 and the Courts, *Modern Law Review, 33,* 85-9.
Seago, P. (1973) The Breathalyser Reblown, [1973] *Crim LR,* 153-63.
Shapiro, P. & Votey, H.L. (1984) Deterrence and Subjective Probability of Arrest: Modelling Individual Decisions to Drink and Drive in Sweden, *Law & Society Review, 18*, 4, 584-604.
Shapiro, P. & Votey, H.L. (1986) Moral Compliance, Private Self Interest and Exposure to the Law: The Response of Swedish Drivers to Drunken Driving Controls, in Shapiro, P. & Votey, H.L. (eds) *Econometric Analysis of Crime in Sweden*, Stockholm, The National Council for Crime Prevention Sweden.
Sheppard, D. (1968) *The 1967 Drink and Driving Campaign*, Crowthorne, RRL.
Silvey, J. (1961) The Criminal Law and Public Opinion, *Criminal Law Review*, June, 349-58.
Simpson, J. (1953) Police Problems in Drunken Driving Cases, *Med Leg J, 21*, 49-61.
Simpson, J. (1963) Police Procedure in Relation to the Drinking Driver, in Havard (ed)(1963) *Alcohol and Road Traffic*, London, BMA.
Sixsmith, G. (1970) The Breathalyser Again, *The Magistrate, 26*, 6-7.
Sloss, R.T. (1905) *The Book of the Automobile*, New York.
Smart, R.G. (1987) Changes in alcohol Problems As A Result of Changing Alcohol Consumption: A Natural Experiment, *Drug and Alcohol Dependence, 19*, 91-7.
Smith, D.J. & Gray, J. (1985) *Police and People in London*, Aldershot, Gower.
Smith, J.C. (1963) Alcohol and Road Traffic: The English Law and its Reform, in Havard (ed)(1963) *Alcohol and Road Traffic*, London, BMA.
Snortum, J.R. (1984) Alcohol-Impaired Driving in Norway and Sweden: Another Look at "The Scandinavian Myth", *Law & Society, 6*, 1, 5-37.
Snortum, J.R. (1984a) Rejoinder: On Myths and Morals, *Law & Society, 6*, 1, 5-37.
Snortum, J.R. (1984b) Controlling the Alcohol-Impaired Driver in Scandinavia and the United States: Simple Deterrence and Beyond, *Journal of Criminal Justice, 12*, 131-48.
Snortum, J.R. (1988) Deterrence of Alcohol Impaired Driving: An Effect in Search of a Cause, in Laurence, M.D., Snortum, J.R. & Zimring, F.E. (eds) (1988) *Social Control of the Drinking Driver*, Chicago, University of Chicago Press.
Snortum, J.R. & Berger, D.E. (1986) Drinking and Driving: Detecting the "Dark Figure" of Compliance, *Journal of Criminal Justice, 14*, 475-89.

Snortum, J.R., Hague, R. & Berger, D.E. (1986) Deterring Alcohol-Impaired Driving: A Comparative Analysis of Compliance in Norway and the United States, *Justice Quarterly, 3*, 139-65.

Southgate, P. & Ekblom, P. (1984) *Contacts Between Police and Public: findings from the British Crime Survey*, Home Office Research Study No.77, London, Home Office.

Snow, R.W. & Anderson, B.J. (1987) Drinking Place Selection Factors Among Drink-Drivers, *British Journal of Addictions, 82*, 85-92.

Spencer, J.R. (1983) Motor Cars and the Rule in Rylands v Fletcher: A Chapter of Accidents in the History of Law and Motoring, *Cambridge Law Journal, 42*, 1, 65-84.

Spencer, J.R. (1985) Motor Vehicles as Weapons of Offence, [1985] *Crim LR*, 29-41.

Spencer, J.R. (1987) Some Aspects of Sentencing Policy in Road Traffic Cases, paper presented to IAS conference, 'Drinking and Driving: Controlling the Massacre, London, 15 July 1987.

Spencer, J.R. (1988) Road Traffic Law: A Review of the North Report, *Crim LR*, 707-21.

Steele, D. (1984) *Drinking and Driving, Briefing Paper*, London, AAA.

Steele, D. (1985) Drinking and Driving, *Alcohol Concern*, 1, 6, 9-11.

Steer, D.J. & Carr-Hill, R.A. (1967) The Motoring Offender - Who is He? [1967] *Crim LR*, 215-20

Stein, R. (1966) The Automobile Book, Hamlyn, London.

Stevenson, S. & Bottoms, A. (1990) The Politics of the Police 1955-1964: A Royal Commission in a Decade of Transition, in Morgan, R. (ed)(1990) *Policing and Crime Prevention*, Bristol, Bristol Centre for Criminal Justice.

Strachen, B. (1973) *The Drinking Driver and the Law*, London, Shaw.

Strachen, B. (1976) *The Drinking Driver and the Law*, 2nd ed, London, Shaw.

Strachen, B. (1976a) Drinking and Driving: A Comment on Blennerhassett, *NLJ*, 1225-6.

Strachen, B. (1983) *The Drinking Driver and the Law*, 3rd ed, London, Shaw.

Sumner, C. (1991) *Censure, Politics and Criminal Justice*, Milton Keynes, Open University Press.

Sutton, L.(1986) The Effectiveness of Random Breath Testing: A Comparison Between the State of Tasmania, Australia, and Four States in the Eastern United States, in Noordzij, P.C. & Roszbach, R. (eds) *Alcohol, Drugs and Traffic Safety*, T86, Amsterdam, Excerpta Medica.

Taylor, J. (1986) Policy for Managing the High Risk Offender in *Drinking and Driving - 10 Years on from Blennerhassett*, London, Institute of Alcohol Studies.

Tarry, F. T. (1938) The Search for Safety on the Roads, *The Police Journal*, *XI*, 182-96.

Tether, P. & Godfrey, C. (1990) Drinking and Driving, in Godfrey, C. & Robinson, D. (eds)(1990) *Manipulating Consumption: information, law and voluntary control*, Avebury/Gower, Aldershot.

Tether, P. & Robinson, D. (1986) *Preventing Alcohol Problems: A Guide to Local Action*, London, Tavistock.

Thomas, D.A. (1976) Driving with excess alcohol - when prison appropriate, case note, *Crim LR,* 264-66.

Thomas, T. (1937) The Drunken Motorist, *JPN, 101,* 116.

Transport and Road Research Laboratory (1983) *The Facts About Drinking and Driving,* Crowthorne, Transport and Road Research Laboratory.

Tryhorn, F.G. & Smith, J.C. (1963) Report of the Working Party (IX) on Problems of Presenting Evidence of Chemical Tests in Courts of Law, in Havard (ed)(1963) *Alcohol and Road Traffic,* London, BMA.

Tuck, M. (1981) *Alcoholism and Social Policy: are we on the right lines?* Home Office Research Unit Study No.65, London, HMSO.

Tucker, D. (1990) Drink-Drivers' Pace Rights: A cause for concern, *Crim LR,* 177-80.

Turner, A.J. (1984) Drinking and Driving: A Round-Up of Recent Developments, *JPN, 148,* 675-8; 692-5.

Vayda, A. & Crespi, I. (1981) *Public Acceptability of Highway Safety Countermeasures,* Report no. DOT-HS-6-01466, Washington, DC, NHTSA.

Vernon, H.M. (1937) Alcohol and Motor Accidents, *The British Journal of Inebriety, 34,* 4, 153-65.

Voas, R.B. (1988) Emerging Technologies for Controlling the Drunk Driver, in Laurence, M.D., Snortum, J.R. & Zimring, F.E. (eds)(1988) *Social Control of the Drinking Driver,* Chicago, University of Chicago Press.

University of Indiana (ed)(1966) *Alcohol and Traffic Safety, Proceedings of the Fourth International Conference on Alcohol and Traffic Safety,* Indiana, University of Indiana.

Vingilis, E.R. (1987) Deterrence: A Reconceptualisation for the Alcohol and Traffic Safety Problem, in Noordzij, P.C. & Roszbach, R. (eds) *Alcohol, Drugs and Traffic Safety,* T86, Amsterdam, Excerpta Medica.

Vingilis, E.R., Chung, L. & Adlaf, E.M. (1981) *The Evaluation of a Toronto Drinking Driving Programme Called RIDE (Reduce Impaired Drivers Everywhere),* Substudy No.1216, Toronto, Addictions Research Foundation.

Vingilis, E.R. & De Genova, K. (1984) Youth and the Forbidden Fruit: Experiences with Changes in Legal Drinking Age in North America, *Journal of Criminal Justice, 12,* 161-72.

Vingilis, E.R. & Vingilis, V. (1987) The Importance of Roadside Screening for Impaired Drivers in Canada, *Canadian Journal of Criminology, 29,* 17-34.

Votey, H.L. (1982) Scandinavian Drink Driving Control: Myth or Institution? *Journal of Legal Studies, 11,* 93-116.

Votey, H.L. (1984) The Deterioration of Deterrence Effects of Driving Legislation: Have We Been Giving Wrong Signals to Policymakers?, *Journal of Criminal Justice, 12,* 115-30.

Walker, M. (1983) Self-Reported Crime Studies and the British Crime Survey, *Howard Journal, 22,* 168-76.

Walker, N. (1980) *Punishment, Danger and Stigma,* Oxford, Blackwell.

Walker, N. (1991) *Why Punish?,* Oxford, OUP.

Walker, N. & Hough, M. (eds)(1988) *Public Attitudes to Sentencing: Surveys in Five Countries,* Aldershot, Gower.

Walker, R.J. & Walker, M.G. (1970) *The English Legal System*, London, Butterworths.

Wallis, P.S. (1982) *Transport Act 1981,* London, Fourmat.

Wallis, P.S. (1985) *The Transport Acts 1981 & 1982*, London, Fourmat.

Wallis, P.S. (1988) The North Report: a Triumph for Common Sense, *The Solicitors' Journal, 132,* 26, 946-7.

Walls, H.J. (1958) Urine - Alcohol Tests and "drunk-in-charge" Survey of 312 cases, *BMJ*, 5058, 1442-4.

Walls, H.J. & Brownlie, A.R. (1970) *Drink, Drugs and Driving*, London, Sweet & Maxwell.

Walls, H.J. & Brownlie A.R. (1985) *Drink, Drugs and Driving*, 2nd ed. London, Sweet & Maxwell.

Ward Smith, H. (1960) Drinking and Driving, *Criminal Law Quarterly*, *3*, 65-124.

Watkins, D. (1987) *Drinking and Driving: The Decided Cases*, London, Police Review Publications.

Weeks, C.C. (1931) Alcoholic Indulgence in Relation to Motor Transport, *The British Journal of Inebriety, 28,* 4, 163-82.

Weir, R.B. (1984) Obsessed with Moderation: The Drink Trades and the Drink Question, *British Journal of Addiction*, *79*, 93-107.

Weiss, E.D. (1938) Legislation and Road Accidents, *M.L.R.*, *2*, 139-52.

Wesson, J. (1988) *Alcohol Related Issues Raised by the Road Traffic Law Review Report*, Birmingham, Aquarius.

Whitaker, B. (1964) *The Police*, Harmondsworth, Penguin.

Whitelock, F.A. (1971) *Death on the Road; A Study in Social Violence*, London, Tavistock.

Wilkinson, G.S. (1953) *Road Traffic Prosecutions*, London, Solicitors' Law Stationary Soc.

Wilkinson, G.S. (1956) *Road Traffic Offences* (2nd ed), London, Solicitors' Law Stationary Soc.

Wilkinson, G.S. (1960) *Road Traffic Offences* (3rd ed), London, Solicitors' Law Stationary Soc.

Wilkinson, G.S. (1963) *Road Traffic Offences* (4th ed), London, Oyez.

Wilkinson, G.S. (1965) *Road Traffic Offences* (5th ed), London, Oyez.

Wilkinson, G.S. (1970) *Road Traffic Offences* (6th ed), London, Oyez.

Willett, R.E. & Walsh, J.M. (1983) *Drugs, Driving & Traffic Safety*, Geneva, World Health Organization.

Willett, T.C. (1964) *Criminal on the Road*, London, Tavistock.

Willett, T.C. (1966) The Motoring Offender As A Social Problem, *Medico - Legal Journal*, *34*, 146-57.

Willett, T.C. (1973) *Drivers After Sentence*, London, Heinemann.

Williams, C. (1961) The Criminal Law and Public Opinion. Some Police Reactions, *Criminal Law Review*, June 359-67.

Williams, G.P. & Brake, G.T. (1980) *Drink in Great Britain 1900 to 1979*, London, Edsall.

Wilson, G. (1991) *The Traffic Officer's Companion*, London, Police Review Publishing.

Wilson, G.B. (1940) *Alcohol and the Nation*, London, Nicholson & Watson.

Wilson, O.W. (1940) The Police and the Public, *The Police Journal, 13,* 80-90.

Wilson, R.P. (1938) The Traffic Problem, *The Police Journal, XI,* 426-54.

Winterton, W. (1968) *Breath Taking History,* London, Winterton.

Wood, D. (1986) *Beliefs About Alcohol*, London, Health Education Council.

Wood, J.C. (1979) Review of *Drinking and Driving in Scandinavia, BJCrim, 19,* 191-2.

Wooton, B. (1959) *Social Science and Social Pathology*, London, Allen & Unwin.

World Health Organization (1954) First Report of Expert Committee on Alcohol, *World Health Organization Techn.Rep.Ser.*, 1954, *84,* 14.

World Health Organization (1990) *Health Indicator Database*, Geneva, WHO.

Wright, B.M. (1967) 'Alcohol, The Motorist and the Law', *New Law Journal,* 8/6/67, 631-2; 15/8/67, 659-31.

Young, A.B.F. (1904) *The Complete Motorist*, London.

Zimring, F.E. (1978) Policy Experiments in General Deterrence: 1970-75, in Blumstein, A., Cohen, J. & Nagin, D. (eds)(1978) *Deterrence and Incapacitation: Estimating the Effects of Criminal Sanctions on Crime Rates*, Washington D.C., National Academy of Sciences.

Zimring, F.E. (1988) Law, Society, and the Drinking Driver, in Laurence, M.D., Snortum, J.R. & Zimring, F.E. (eds)(1988) *Social Control of the Drinking Driver*, Chicago, University of Chicago Press.

Index